Praise for Pamela Des Barres

"Pamela Des Barres is the Lewis and Clark of wanton women, who prowled the world anew from sea to shining sea."
   —Professor Virginia Scharff

"Des Barres' quality of writing is yards ahead of the standard first-person memoir."
   —*Music Week*

"One of the most important, revealing and unabashedly honest books about rock ever written."
   —*Boston Phoenix*

"Pamela Des Barres is one of the most important rock historians of our time."
   —Dave Navarro

LET IT BLEED

LET IT BLEED

HOW TO WRITE A ROCKIN' MEMOIR

PAMELA DES BARRES

A TARCHERPERIGEE BOOK

An imprint of Penguin Random House LLC
375 Hudson Street
New York, New York 10014

Most TarcherPerigee books are available at special quantity discounts for bulk
purchase for sales promotions, premiums, fund-raising, and educational needs.
Special books or book excerpts also can be created to fit specific needs.
For details, write: SpecialMarkets@penguinrandomhouse.com.

LIBRARY OF CONGRESS CATALOGING-IN-PUBLICATION DATA

Names: Des Barres, Pamela, author.
Title: Let it bleed: how to write a rockin' memoir / Pamela Des Barres.
Description: New York, New York: TarcherPerigee, 2017.
Identifiers: LCCN 2016058084 (print) | LCCN 2016059194 (ebook) |
ISBN 9780399174209 (paperback) | ISBN 9781524704742
Subjects: LCSH: Autobiography—Authorship. | Biography as a literary form. |
BISAC: REFERENCE / Writing Skills. | LANGUAGE ARTS & DISCIPLINES /
Composition & Creative Writing. | BODY, MIND & SPIRIT / Meditation.
Classification: LCC PE1479.A88 D47 2017 (print) | LCC PE1479.A88 (ebook) |
DDC 808.06/692—dc23
LC record available at https://lccn.loc.gov/2016058084

Printed in the United States of America
1   3   5   7   9   10   8   6   4   2

Book design by Elke Sigal

CONTENTS

PREFACE

When I decided to add teaching to my ongoing life repertoire, I happily discovered I had a built-in audience for my writing workshops—my readers! As I sat nervously in my colorful, cluttered living room the very first night, one by one, the girls arrived at my door, a delightful group of music-loving ladies of all ages with pent-up tales and soulful stories to share. I was as skittish as my first bunch of students, but we soon discovered we had found kindred spirits, and heaved a collective sigh of relief as the words began spewing forth like vivid gemstones. Most of them had read my two autobiographies and felt comfortable with me because I had already opened my heart to them. I had told all, some of it wildly personal, scandalous, and deeply confessional, so they were willing to join me in that sweet freedom of expression.

Perhaps it was naïveté or my penchant for ruthless truth, but I've been told many times that after reading my loquacious life stories my students felt freed up to share their own. "*She* wasn't afraid to make a hee-haw of herself, or reveal insecurities, heart-wrenches and embarrassing guffaws, along with scandalous merriment, so why can't I?" Since I've shared my way, way ups and low, low downs, it has impelled my writers to defy their own trepidation and doubt. And if you are reading this with the aim of writing your own life story, I emphatically encourage you to do the same. No holds Des Barred!

I'm as pleased as a rescued pup that my students wanted to chime in here about the workshops. My Nashville doll, Jessi, continues the fearless act of surrendering to her muse:

As a young girl, I wished for a lifetime of adventures like Miss Pamela Des Barres—the original Muse. Because of her, I wished for and gained a life that I could write passionately about, with an open heart full of wonder, embracing the upsets and challenges with humor and grace, each one fueling a passionate need to learn and grow and then, in due time, to document and describe. Every hug from Miss Pamela feels like an embracing of the divine feminine. She has distilled for me the essence of the muse, inspiring and compassionately holy. From the pages of a courageous paperback, my own muse burst forth into my life with an impassioned plea: Be amused, let life fill you to your fingertips and toes, surrender to it all and then let it spill over onto the pages. Never hold back, not in your life or in your writing . . .

Let it bleed, child, just let it bleed.

JESSI GUNTER, NASHVILLE

I have been teaching for sixteen years now and am always surprised and spellbound by the candor, clarity and tenacity that my writers bring to the table (which is laden with all manner of edible treats, as it's a Writing Party!). My students often surprise themselves as forbidden memories, long tamped down, spring up like an unbidden jack-in-the-box, then burn down to harmless embers when shared. Or shrieks of laughter fill the room when a wild night of madness is remembered, written about and released like a flight of drunken doves.

Come, join our writing party and revel in the razzle-dazzle of your own rowdy escapades. Or come to poke around in your past and make sense of those profoundly painful days and sleepless nights. Come to write it all down and love yourself like you love your favorite song.

My longtime Los Angeles student Nichole eloquently expresses how the classes have helped to pull out her best prose.

> *Words are big. In the right combination, they can make silken nets strong and supple enough to capture sensations and feelings and moments too elusive and intangible and magical and unattainable to keep any other way. I walked through Pamela's door into her jungle room more than six years ago to take her weekly writing class, knowing I was entering the home of someone I admired, someone whose writing struck a chord in me. I will walk out that door tonight, six years later, knowing I am leaving the home of the matriarch of my rock 'n' roll family, someone who calls the best and purest prose out of my insides and onto the page. The moments are too numerous and too precious to catch in this one net of words. I have beauty to last me a lifetime.*
>
> NICHOLE JAYMES, LOS ANGELES

If the same thing happens to you that happens in workshops with me, I can guarantee not only will you get a lot of writing done, you will have a new understanding about what makes you *you*! By the time you've completed the final assignment, the same compassion and acceptance that you have for your special loved ones you will also be showering upon yourself. And ahhhh, that cleansing rain will feel so good.

My favorite song of all time is Dylan's "Like a Rolling Stone." I try to live by one of the many credos put forth in that masterpiece: "You shouldn't let other people get your kicks for you."

Get your own kicks, dolls, and proudly tell your tale.

My Austin writer Kris has certainly scribbled enough in the workshops to tell *her* tale, and I hope to be reading her mischievous memoir soon.

Slide a white-gloved finger across the soul of one of Miz Pamela's writing groups and it comes up covered in honey. If you've started to suspect who you really are or you already know and have stopped apologizing: it's time to write that down.

Bring your open mind. Bring the girl you were at age nine. Bring the liner notes you memorized from your favorite music in junior high. Come ready to describe your details. Don't say you can't write; if you're reading this, you know you could've written it yourself. For almost a decade, I've attended Pamela's sessions and I've written a solid bridge back to the girl I was. It's a back rub for my mind. It's hard and delicious and funny.

Come and write.

KRIS KOVACH, AUSTIN

A back rub for the mind. Oh yeah . . . What a lovely compliment, and perfectly expressed!

INTRODUCTION

I started keeping diaries at the tender age of eight, when I found my first little red leather book under the Christmas tree. Tragically, the neighborhood bully had gleefully told me there was no Santa Claus, so I knew it was my dear mama who had tucked it under our brightly bedecked pine. The small book came with a lock and key, so not only did I feel obligated to write in it every day, I figured my thoughts, ideas and experiences must have some value since they needed safekeeping. Every year I found another diary under the tree and couldn't imagine being without my personal, private confidante. I gushed over teachers, schoolboys, music, James Dean and Elvis and, as I got older, scrawled reams of mush about my crushes and rock idols, heartache, heartbreak, longing and teenage desires—tears blurring the ink.

Luckily my copious treasure trove of diaries (later I called them "journals"—it sounded more important) came in very handy when I decided to tell my tale of free-spirited hippie abandon from the center of the action, made all the more immediate by the breathy diary entries.

When *I'm with the Band: Confessions of a Groupie* was published in 1987, I never dreamed that it would be such a controversial, anarchic smash, that I'd be introduced on NBC's *Today* show as "Queen of the Groupies" and that I would eventually become a spokesperson for my most misunderstood generation and the revolutionary music it produced. For a while there, I was startled by the media ruckus my stories were causing, how riled up people got about the way I lived my life and how I dared to spill my own beans all over the page.

This scary response was quelled by the exact opposite reaction from women who were actually reading the book. Writing my heart out, and letting it bleed, seemed to open theirs. Misunderstood for various reasons, often by their love of music and musicians, they told me they'd found a kindred spirit who spoke up for them, and I was humbled by this totally unexpected bonus! It reminded me of a long-ago time when Dylan spoke my mind for me (and my entire generation) and I knew I wasn't alone.

I went on to write an autobiographical sequel and two more books focusing on musicians and the women who loved them. It's been a long and winding blast, but for the last sixteen years, my most surprising and greatest joy has been teaching my women's memoir—"femoir"—workshops.

I've always been open to creative input, so after my third book, *Rock Bottom*, was published, my lifelong pal Moon Zappa encouraged me to enroll in classes with her favorite writing coach. Halfway through the first session, as I was intently scribbling away, I realized I could be teaching the class myself! Hey, what a groovy idea! I had written two of my own well-received memoirs, so why not?

It took me a few months to screw up the courage to call myself a Teacher, before finally announcing my first very own eight-week writing workshop in Los Angeles. I have been called many things: fan, groupie, girlfriend, wife, mother, actress, singer, performance artist, writer, journalist, producer, even best-selling author, but Teacher? It definitely took ovaries (since I do not possess a pair of balls) to make that highfalutin claim.

I have always had a great fear, like most of us do, of public speaking. For me, standing alone addressing a circle of students seemed a whole lot scarier than hanging out on a sofa with Oprah, or sitting in the hot seat across from Larry King. Oddly enough, I can usually handle conversational one-on-one chitchat, answering questions. Yet now here I was, seemingly ready to impart teacherly wisdom to a group of wide-eyed strangers. Very deep breath.

As my career as a writer/former groupie slowly grew, I got invites to speak at colleges and clubs, bookstores and festivals, and every time I had to step onstage, I worried myself rotten for days about screwing it all up. Stuttering. Stammering. Sweating. I even imagined running off the stage and out the door, never to return. To overcome my nerves, I fell back on a technique that has served me well and has gotten me though many such arduous episodes. I wound up simply acting "as if." I embraced the three Cs of composure—to be calm, cool and collected. As I shared in *I'm with the Band*, I often had to practice acting "as if"—this particular experience took place at the Fairmont Hotel with the Stones after the agony of Altamont: "I arrived and sat around with the group as they rehashed the sequence of events that led up to this odd death right in front of their eyes. Mick kept saying he felt like it was his fault and maybe he would quit rock and roll forever. Everyone was extremely high. I felt like some inadequate female fly on the wall, stuck in the middle of No Laughing Matter." However, I did act "as if" I belonged in that room, and began massaging Mick's shoulders to stop myself from fainting. Yes, acting "as if," and ignoring those pesky heart palpitations and the desire to flee the coop, has actually helped me to stay put when I've felt completely out of my element.

And now here I was, seemingly ready to impart teacherly wisdom to a group of wide-eyed strangers. Very deep breath.

As it turned out, they were strangers only until after the first assignment. And holding forth in class has helped me lose the dastardly fear of spouting off in public. Nervousness has turned to excitement. My heart still palpitates when I step onto a stage; but now it pounds with gusto, not foreboding.

Although my first eight-week workshop was all women, in the beginning I invited men to join the class as well. Only a few came, and I soon discovered that the women weren't as likely to let 'er rip when guys were around. I made the decision that most of my workshops would be For

Women Only, and despite a little ribbing from the fellas, it's worked out splendidly. Of course, that doesn't mean this book won't assist men in writing their memoirs, as long as they are ready, willing and stable enough to blow their own cover.

I've found that most people want to write about what they know best—themselves. Nobody's life is boring. I believe that completely and it's become my mantra in class. I truly believe that every one of us has led a fascinating life full of curiosities, intrigue, discovery, danger and delight, most certainly worth telling—you just need to figure out how to tell it! And when you tell it with verve and tenacity, and perhaps a bit of recklessness, not only will you discover your own "whys," your readers will have their own "aha!" moments. Through the years I've developed a whole slew of twelve-minute assignments geared to help my dolls recall, remember, relive and reveal their magical memories, their transgressions and temptations, their sleepless nights and brilliant afternoons, their loves and losses, fears and regrets, secrets, sins and sorrows. It's been an incredibly cathartic experience for my students. Surprise. Relief. Realization. Self-acceptance. Fury and forgiveness. Joy!

My femoir classes are like a living diary, where women can safely expound, express, rant and rave, reevaluate and relax into their true selves with respect and appreciation for who they are. And they quickly discover that the madness, sadness and badness they've been through can make quite a compelling tale!

I had no idea when I began this long, enchanting trip that I would fall in love with every woman who sat down in front of me with a tentative smile or eager rage, along with an open notebook or laptop, ready to tell it like it was. Like it is. Like they hope it will be. The hundreds of dolls all over the country who have graced me with their presence and willingness to share their exploits tell me that the workshops have changed their lives for the better, altered their ideas about themselves, helped them to understand who they are down deep inside. The classes have made them feel fearless, free-spirited and ready to rock! They are more spontaneous, assertive and willing to try something new and different—and they truly do fall in love with themselves. Sometimes for the very first time.

No experience is too small or large to wound a human heart—from a childhood memory of pulling the wings off a butterfly to the grown-up hell of going to jail for a DUI—and everything in between; our failures become our demons (which is really just the blaming, shaming ego). It is only through facing those pesky devils that we free ourselves from their stranglehold. I'm often thrilled when I give a seemingly simple assignment—to write about a time a student made a mistake, for instance, or to describe an uncomfortable childhood experience—at how visceral, fresh and unique these stories are. The most cathartic ones are written fearlessly, when my girls strip their hearts bare to reveal painful and protected spots without honey-coating the truth. Honest self-assessment makes them truly free from the sting of long-held self-judgments. They are no longer held captive by the past, and the guilt-tripping disappears. Reflection can actually change, if not the outcome, then the attitude about particular heart-rending events. And it's so often the case that brave writing begets brave living. I've seen my girls squarely face their formidable memories time and again in their writing, sometimes through a single sudden revelation, sometimes through continual sharing of a specific troubling experience that gets a little less daunting each time. When certain events are brought into the light and seen with new awareness, the writer discovers that her perception of the event was actually faulty. In the pieces I've included to illustrate this, you'll see how different two women's tales are, yet how neither is afraid to examine herself honestly, and maybe, just maybe, find a smidgen of humor in the most harrowing places.

I believe *all* women have a wild streak, a rebellious, rip-roaring inner voice, and can find out who they really are by recalling and recapturing the events and relationships that have shaped their unique lives. They discover that the good, the bad and the bummers helped to create the fabulous women they've become. Writing about our life experiences is a form of therapy (we often call it "groupie therapy" in class!), and as I have often witnessed—it can actually be a cleansing revelation.

My goal is to bring a little of the same magic to those of you who can't make it into my living room. I am elated and honored to offer my readers the same opportunity to experience their own creative, emotional and spiritual breakthroughs within these pages.

It took a bit of trial and error, but this is how I came up with my teaching approach. After a few early workshop timekeeping trials, I discovered that a twelve-minute time frame is just long enough and just short enough to keep the howling wolf-ego cowering in her cave for a quick blast of nonstop writing. Yep, nonstop writing. No editing, scribbling out or starting over. No judging, censoring or searching for just the right word. The right words will come if you let go and let it flow onto the page or screen. By bypassing your inner critic, your heart will have its say and your truth will come to light in unexpected and wondrous ways. Trust me, there will be plenty of time for rereading and polishing your prose later. The first step in creating your femoir is to allow your true essence to spill herself onto the page.

When you allow yourself a mere twelve minutes to get your memories onto the page, it's not such a massive commitment, is it? When you decide on a prompt you find in the book, simply turn on an alarm, turn off your brain and trust your heart.

In class, I spring the writing assignment on my dolls, set my iPhone timer, then disappear into another room while my students type, scribble and jot—but not before I soak up a few drops of those creative heart wheels spinning through space and time. If I peek into the room and see a pen hovering over the paper or hands perched above the keypad for too long, I cut loose with, "Stop thinking!" (Miss P's Rule Number One.)

When the timer rings and the writing winds down, each student reads her work aloud to the class. Again, no self-judging, qualifying or criticism allowed during the reading process either. No matter how flawed they imagine their writing might be, there are always gems to be found in every selection—the telling detail, perfect turn of phrase, intriguing image, heartfelt wording or revealing remembrance that makes the whole room gasp with emotion or get a case of the giggles. I encourage you to look for the diamonds in each of the seemingly rough pieces you write.

The variety of memories triggered by any one prompt is always astonishing. Everyone's lives are *so* different and yet as each selection is read aloud, there is something that touches all of us at a soul level. To share what happens in class with you, I've included assignments from many of my students that streamed out during these twelve-minute bursts, much of it very personal. I'm honored that they've given me permission to share their work. This way, throughout the book you'll be meeting several of my dolls personally by reading their stories, along with a few of mine (written during class just for the fun of it!). You'll see that despite how different my writers' tales are, they're not afraid to examine themselves honestly, and can often find a smidgen of humor in the most harrowing situations.

I'm hoping your memories will be triggered by theirs and you'll feel an instant comfort level, knowing you're not alone. I want you to feel you're a part of this kindred group of like-minded women, sitting between people like Nichole and Jessi.

One of my L.A. students, Kathleen Morgan, a sassy Southern belle who lost her home in Hurricane Katrina, expressed herself exquisitely in twelve minutes about how the workshops enhanced her creativity:

> *My blood became wine in those classes. I was able to use both humor and surrealism to characterize and transform pain. To use absurdity and sarcasm to accept and understand my past. Being able to make people laugh about events I'd always considered tragic allowed me to see how humor, honesty, forgiveness, and compassion superseded the*

tragedy I held inside. The writing freed me from my sins and trans-
gressions. From my own sense of otherness. From feeling bad that my
favorite word was "fuck." No longer were those hidden sources of
shame, but now funny and entertaining stories of survival, my out-
sider views of the world, and my own unique translation of the
human condition. Nobody judged me for it. In fact, they laughed
their fucking asses off. I became a writing junkie.

As a dear cousin of mine, who was also a brilliant musician, used
to tell me, "When you are being creative, you are closer to the creator."
I don't think he meant God in the traditional sense, but that whatever
created us meant for us to be creative. Creativity puts you in the
moment and takes you out of time. Sometimes I was scared, some-
times I was tired, but once I put those words on paper, I was closer to
the creator.

Everything a person writes is a memoir in one way or another. So
whether it is about having wild sex with Axl Rose on your mom's yellow
Naugahyde couch or about trailer trash gamblers in love, it's all you.

Join the family, become a doll. Share your voice and get closer to
the creator. You won't regret it. Ever.

It took awhile for Kathleen to reveal that her cousin had been a dear
friend of mine way back in my heyday, Chris Ethridge of the Flying Burrito
Brothers. It is indeed a small world, and we are all connected in some way.
Chris cowrote one of my favorite songs, "She," with Gram Parsons, so it's
not surprising that his creativity made him feel closer to his creator.

So free your muse (amuse your muse!), shake off any fears and discover
what lies within your precious, precocious heart. Write it down, read it
aloud, untangle your personal history and appreciate your life experiences
in an illuminating new way. Think of this book as your safe space to dive
head (and heart) first into your uniquely personal pot of platinum!

I

Dare to Write

Besides my bursting-at-the-seams diaries and school compositions, my first foray into creative writing began in earnest when, along with my Beatle birds, I began conjuring up weekly chapters about our romances with John, Paul, George and Ringo. Oh, how I wish I had those impassioned blue-lined missives I scribbled for Kathy, Linda and Stevie as I lay in my twin bed (always under many watchful photos of the long-lashed, bedroom-eyed Paul McC, of course), inventing tales about how the Quiet Beatle proposed to Kathy in a song, while gently playing his guitar, or how John tearfully left his wife, Cynthia, because my bubbly Reseda neighbor, Linda Oaks, had melted his gruff, ironic heart.

Yes, I could enthrall my Beatle buddies with the written word, but having seen Patty Duke accept the Academy Award for her stunning portrayal of Helen Keller in *The Miracle Worker*, I had decided at age twelve to become an actress. This declaration led to a long and mostly fruitless pursuit of Glamorous Hollywood Fame. As I slogged through commercial interviews and embarrassing theatrical auditions, helped along by a series of B-minus or C-plus acting agents, I never stopped babbling into my trusty diary.

At Cleveland High I was an English devotee and pled allegiance to a tough-minded creative-writing teacher, Mr. Constantine Thomas, who most everyone else despised due to his scathing attention to detail. I enjoyed it so much, I planned on taking some college writing courses after graduation, but—oops!—the Sunset Strip got in the way. From my sophomore year on, Cleveland High became an afterthought as the Byrds, Buffalo Springfield, Captain Beefheart and long-haired Hollywood weirdos became my main focus. On graduation day, Mr. Thomas looked me up and down in my white ruffled dolly bird dress, lace stockings and red patent flats, and sadly shook his head. This one had gotten away from him. Still, when I asked him to sign my yearbook, he screamed at me in a ferocious hand, "Dare to write!!!!"

Mr. Thomas didn't know that I had already begun writing tortuous teenage poetry, teeming with indignation and self-discovery, railing against authority and rampant with clichés. I suddenly felt an overwhelming need to *express myself.* Some of the poems were wild with love for an unattainable rock star, some described the ethereal beauty of Laurel Canyon, "God's Golden Backyard," and some pitted the new *Us* against the old *Them.*

All the Evidence
June 1966

Evening has started abruptly
The circus has come to town
"These teenagers are invading the city!
They're turning it upside down!"

The owners of the restaurants
Are ranting and raving about
Trying to clear the hippies away
And let their customers out

The police drive into the parking lots
And climb out of their cars
They stomp and storm and carry on
And start a few minor wars

The older people driving by
Turn to gawk and stare
"My God, Harold, what is *that*?
You can't really tell with that hair!"

Then there are others who try to pretend
That they belong with you and I
But they scratch their crew-cuts, fix the crease in their pants
They'll never make it but they try

They call us insane, and try to figure us out
For loving, being loved and having fun
For letting our hair grow, dressing the way we please
Yet they come, hypocrites each one

To say "non-conformist" isn't quite true
We come to love each other and try . . .
To become better people, inside instead of out
To learn the truth instead of living a lie

I carried my book of verses everywhere I went and when struck by that
lofty desire to pronounce, I pulled out my pen and oh, what a relief it was!
I was daring to write whatever heaviosity came oozing out of my heart.

At Wil Wright's Ice Cream Parlor
on Sunset Blvd.
October 1967

Alone—searching
Quite unaware of what it is I'm seeking
Asking the same question
To each passing answer
But not one turns to greet me
Perhaps I am not really here
Perhaps I *am* the answer to every unanswered question
In conclusion I've discovered
Answers come not at all
Or in great abundance
Either I thirst
Or I drown
Why is there a "w" in Answer anyway?

In the late '80s, poetry readings were de rigueur in L.A., and after many of my hipster cohorts expressed their distressed couplets, I'd open to a page of solemn sincerity I'd written long before about David Crosby's magical elf-infested cabin, or the mysterious majesty of Mick Jagger's slippery unavailability, and soon the groovers would stop wincing and laugh heartily at my dippy bygone prose.

Dear Mr. Jagger
December 1969

You took me under
Your wild wings

Of untamed freedom
And let me experience life's joys
Through your eyes
Peering into your secret world
of abandon
and I found myself
Entirely free
Open to all of you

At least the part
That you gave me

And what part was that? Hmmm? These poems still crack people up whenever I pull out my shredded ledger and take them back to a place and time when revolution thrummed in the air, incense burned, music changed lives and flowers wilted in our long, wavy locks.

II

Butt in the Chair

Despite my early forays into dopey moonstruck poetics, during one of the many creative writing workshops I attended in the '80s I realized I might actually be a writer. I sat in a schoolroom in the San Fernando Valley, along with a dozen other determined souls, at Everywoman's Village, following instructions from the hippieish gray-haired teacher to "write about a memorable incident in your past." I wrote intently about my teenage obsession with the Rolling Stones, and Mick Jagger in particular, giggling at my own antics as my goofy memories poured out onto the page. I found I was looking back at this particular "memorable incident" with a humorous understanding that surprised me.

The following week, the teacher took me aside and said she'd enjoyed my writing and had shown my work to her agent husband, who suggested I continue this "exploration." That same week I was interviewed by Stephen Davis for his breakthrough book, *Hammer of the Gods*, about Led Zeppelin, and after our hours-long exchange, he said, "You should write your own book." Hmmmmm.

It was a pretty unusual idea for that time. Nowadays on Amazon you can scroll through tales about a drunk, a stripper, a teacher, a prisoner, a fashionista, a brawler, a bouncer, a preacher, a panhandler, an alcoholic, a mom, a minstrel and a bipolar hypochondriac! But back then—a couple decades ago—only celebrities told their tales and got into print. I was actually one of the first "unknowns" to come out with a memoir.

I knew I had lived wildly and well, and imagined that one day I'd pore through my dusty diaries and jam-packed journals and tell my tale, but it seemed the universe was announcing that *now* might be a good time to begin. My five-year-old boy, Nick, had just started first grade and was right down the street from our leafy Laurel Canyon pad, ensconced at the Wonderland Avenue school, so several hours a day had suddenly freed up. I had no excuse (and oh boy, are those easy to come up with!) so I dragged out my little red typewriter—and spent several moments looking at it intently.

I discovered pretty quickly that being your own taskmaster is tough, and I conjured up many tasks that just *had* to get handled immediately. Suddenly the plants were screaming for water, the refrigerator had to be scoured, my roots needed dying the vivid red I favor. But eventually I faced that first hurdle: *sitting down*. Butt in the chair. Yes, just making the decision to sit in front of your notebook, computer or, in my case in '84, the typewriter, is step number one. By performing that seemingly simple, yet bravura act, you are setting your intention to *write*, and it's the most important decision you'll be making in this profoundly passionate process. Over and over again. Hopefully daily. So get used to it.

I didn't set out to write a best seller. In fact, no one ever knows when deciding to write a book if a single person will ever crack it open, or Kindle-scroll through the pageless pages. The main reason for writing your tale is to reveal yourself to yourself; all the rest is savory gravy. It soon becomes a rousing trip down your very own ragtag memory lane, and an ongoing one-on-one therapy session with your very own soul. *(Did I really do that? Did I actually say that?)* As I wrote, certain memories stood out sharply in 3-D Technicolor, easily making the cut because I realized they created who I became. I relived the good, the bad, the comical and the glorious.

I'd like to say that the first publisher my agent sent the manuscript to leapt out of his seat to give me a deal. Nope. It was sent out to over a dozen publishing houses that kindly but firmly rejected my story. And in the case of memoir, they were actually rejecting *me*, which doesn't feel so hot, dolls. But I persisted. And kept writing the darn thing. After *Hammer of the Gods* by Stephen Davis hit the *New York Times* best-seller list, William Morrow, one of the rejecters, did a flip-flop, and the very cool James Landis signed me to a deal. I saved my rejection letters and when *Band* hit number 6, I sent a copy of the book and the best-seller list to Random House, along with its rejection letter, which read, "This will never be a book. Maybe an article in *Rolling Stone.*" Ha-ha-*ha*!

I also sent my old pal Gene Simmons of Kiss a copy as a way to thank him, because he'd suggested I change the subtitle from *Memoir of a Groupie* to *Confessions of a Groupie*. Gene has dilated dollar signs for pupils and always knows the power of the perfect word.

When I started writing there were basically no "How to Write a Memoir" books crowding the shelves. I sure wish I'd met the Now version of my teacherly self back then. And had access to all the assignments I've given my students through the years! It would have made the long process of reliving, remembering, uncovering, revealing and rediscovering so much easier. Instead, I unpacked my trusty, dusty diaries, long sequestered away in a vintage trunk, and pored through them, pulling out moments, experiences and memories, calling up places, people, feelings and fears, dipping in and out of my own history like plunging into the great Pacific Ocean. Once you begin to write your life, it's astounding what comes back to you. I could actually smell the wreaths of roses entwined in my hair at love-ins, feel the ouchy pangs of teen love for each crazy musician I gave my heart to. I could see the light beaming down on Jimmy Page as he tore up the stage, glancing at me atop his amp, my heart palpitating. I relived my very first gig with the GTOs at the Whisky a Go Go, feather boas flying, Mr. Zappa at the helm with his baton.

I wrote both of my memoirs chronologically, except for that first horny Jagger assignment at Every Woman's Village, but that isn't always necessary. Go through this book and choose whatever prompt strikes your fancy and write! In class my students use their twelve minutes to complete each assignment, with my two-minute warning so they can start wrapping it up, and we are always amazed at the amount of writing that gets done in that seemingly short period of time. The clock actually seems to stop ticking. I just love listening to the tap-tap-tap of the keyboards and the scribbly scratching of pens and pencils as souls, hearts and minds hum with creative energy.

I don't have many rules in my workshops. I dole out a lot of encouragement but very little criticism. There are plenty of books and classes you can find that teach grammar and punctuation, what not to do, what not to say, poking and picking apart each sentence until the flair is gone. Do it this way or that way. Miss P says, *Just do it, damn it!*

CHAPTER TWO

I

Out, Damned Spot! Out, I Say!

I have only six rules, and if you stick to them, I promise your writing will surprise and startle you. I want to start a blaze in the hearts of my dolls— my Femoir Fatales!

MISS PAMELA'S SIX UNRULY RULES

1. *Don't think!* (The most important!)
2. Don't second-guess what you've just written or reread every sentence.
3. Don't cross out or erase.
4. Don't censor or judge yourself.
5. Don't lift your pen off the paper or your fingers from the keyboard.
6. Don't hold back!

Actually I do have a seventh rule, and that is to never qualify your writing after the exercise is completed. Don't ever read it and say, "This sucks." "I'm not a writer." "I didn't do it right." Blah blah blah. Not even to yourself. Especially not to yourself.

Merriam-Webster's Collegiate Dictionary defines *inspiration* thusly: "a

LET IT BLEED

divine influence or action on a person believed to qualify him or her to receive and communicate sacred revelation." Indeed. Inspiration is always there, a breath away, ready to be received.

I have asked many of my brilliant musician friends how they write a song, and without fail they say it "comes through them," or some version of that sentiment. (In other words, No Thinking!) Sometimes they have no idea where it comes from, or they feel it was somehow "channeled" when they got out of the way.

> *There's an element to songwriting that I can't explain, that comes from somewhere else. I can't explain that dividing line between nothing and something that happens within a song, where you have absolutely nothing, and then suddenly you have something. It's like the origin of the universe.*
> NICK CAVE

The late Indian mystic Osho says basically the same thing in Zenspeak:

> *[Creativity] is allowing something to happen through you . . . It is not a doing, it is an allowing. It is becoming a hollow bamboo, just a hollow bamboo.*
> OSHO, *Creativity: Unleashing the Forces Within*

Cave and Osho are describing the act of being egoless. (Actually a nonact!) If you remove the ego from the equation, your true self can shine through unfettered and, corny as it might sound, your soul is free to do the writing. Without that jabbering blabbermouth dictating what you should or shouldn't write ("You can't mention that! So-and-so will be horrified!" "Are you sure you want to use *that* word?"), the truth shimmers out onto the page, undaunted and defiantly revealed.

When you actually write for twelve minutes without lifting your fingers from the page or keyboard, there's no time to think, question, worry or procrastinate. And if you're not thrilled with the first go-round, use a few of the other topics, then come back to the first one and start all over again! And you will be amazed at all the details you'll recall. For your first couple of writing weeks, try to commit to three assignments a day, and you might as well be sitting in my comfy cozy pad and writing with me and my dolls.

II

You Do Have Something to Say

As you take that first step and begin to write, I'm here to tell you that you aren't *supposed* to know exactly what to write yet or have a clear idea about the theme of your memoir, or even which moments will ultimately make the cut. Many of my dolls didn't know or believe they had material worthy of a memoir until weeks or months or even years after starting class. But encouraged by myself and their pen-sisters, they realized that they'd been crafting the story of their life all along. And you can too.

A memoir isn't scary or insurmountable, just as life itself isn't scary or insurmountable when broken into a few moments at a time. By completing the brief twelve-minute assignments throughout this book, you will be writing your memoir. And you'll soon find that one topic leads to another, to another, and another. Each piece you write will bring a different hidden memory to the forefront for you to explore, review and expand on. As the stories pour forth, suddenly you have empathy for the little girl you once were. The teenage bloomer figuring herself out. The heartbroken woman who believes love will never find her again.

If later you decide to take the assignments further, that's when additional reflecting and editing comes in. Then you can ask yourself, "What did I learn from that?" But my students are often pleased at how little editing is needed when the heart is wide open and the nitpicking, censoring ego has been pushed aside. (If that soul shamer shows up, I call on my inner Lady Macbeth and yell, "Out, damned spot! out, I say!" Or I imagine the Supremes and me as Diana Ross in the center, holding my hand out like a human stop sign, and sing aloud, "Stop! In the name of love!")

If you feel the need to write, it's proof you have something to say. The tone and sound of your voice will be created as you work. Don't worry about the mood or message of your memoir before you begin. The prompts will help you put everything on the table so you can examine your stories, and the themes will just suddenly appear.

Also as you go through the book, challenge yourself by choosing a writing prompt you might consider either supremely mundane or, on the opposite end of the spectrum, insurmountable. Some of the best writing in my classes comes from situations when students initially feel they have nothing to say about the given prompt and therefore nothing to prove—but when they leap in anyway, they end up doing their most daring and imaginative writing. They follow the snippet of memory to the pounding heart of it, and let it unravel into something beautiful.

What you know makes your story unique in all the world. And only you can tell it.

III

Jot Things Down

As you start working on the assignments, I suggest you also begin journaling. Why? It helps writing come more naturally, which is a good confidence builder and will also help you to discover your true voice.

Jotting in a notebook is handy-dandy; a blog is divine; using the Notes app on your iPhone works. But you don't have to go the traditional route. How about dishy letters to a friend or a nonjudgmental family member? It can help you find your voice. Do you speak the same way to everyone? Start listening to the way you talk to the different people in your life. You can even imagine a hero or heroine reading your words. I wrote my rambling thoughts to Marlon Brando for several months and found a whole new freedom in my voice! (I never sent these letters, but I *did* leave longing messages on his phone machine, the very first of its kind I'd ever come across, with his very own oh-so-recognizable mumbled greeting on the other end of the line.)

As I mentioned earlier, my first diary was a little beauty tucked under my ninth Christmas tree, and I felt obliged to scribble my daily deeds into it, such as:

"January 1, 1957: It's a new year. I watched the Rose Parade, a lot of pretty flotes. I made a doll party for Twinkle. She's 2. I made Play-Doh cupcakes, they were cute. My best friends are Rose Marie, Harvelee, Michele and Bonita. We watched *Lucy* and *Honeymooners*. And listened to Elvis Presly on the records for three hours and danced outside a lot, dear diary. The end."

As a teen, when life got much more interesting and the little daily space provided couldn't possibly hold my compelling jottings, I graduated

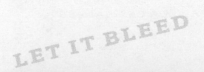

to hefty black art books with unlined pages, into which, along with my imperative ideas, I glued in all manner of important artifacts. I carried one in my purse at all times and if I left it at home, I felt all discombobulated. I'd have to find a piece of paper somewhere, scribble down Keith Moon's exact words and secure it in my journal as soon as possible. You fortunate modern dolls can just tell Siri to take dictation!

Perusing one of my fat, stuffed journals recently, I came across a little map that Gram Parsons drew for me, along with the phone number at the most recent "Burrito Manor" he shared with my first love, Chris Hillman, in Nichols Canyon. Wow. I studied Gram's loopy handwriting and the long-ago address where I first met my precious goddaughter, Polly Parsons, over forty years ago. And just like that I was able to add a new location to my "Rock Tour" of Hollywood and Laurel Canyon, the directions channeled directly from cosmic heaven by my beloved G.P.

When I got married and became a rock-and-roll housewife and mom of a rambunctious toddler, the journal entries dwindled, but I still found ways to get some writing in. Along with taking a few college courses, I wrote my three longhand stream-of-consciousness "morning pages" as suggested in the book *The Artist's Way* by Julia Cameron. I found sleepyhead blathering a wonderful way to capture my thoughts before the vampire ego had a chance to charge in and block me. So along with the assignments in this book, begin jotting down your feelings—what's pissing you off, what's cheering you up, whatever burbles out of your waking-up brain—and get used to writing something, anything, every single day.

Even if you never plan to publish a memoir, having a collection of richly written remembrances will add so much color, sweetness and joy to your experience. It could also be a gift for children and loved ones, forever cherished. And remember, nothing is too boring to write about. You'll be stunned at the flights of fancy you embark on, even when a prompt in this book appears to be a simple one. Wizardry and hidden wisdom can be found in seemingly mundane situations. Emily Dickinson, a hero of mine, was a housebound recluse and she wrote some of the most simply profound poetry imaginable! Even though she lived mostly as a recluse, she was an avid reader, and her beloved books allowed her to visit many worlds within her cabin walls.

A Book

There is no frigate like a book
To take us lands away,
Nor any coursers like a page
Of prancing poetry.
This traverse may the poorest take
Without oppress of toll;
How frugal is the chariot
That bears a human soul!

—EMILY DICKINSON

If you *are* interested in getting your memoir published, you too can invite readers into your unique history, taking them lands away while they sit quietly holding your life in their hands. Besides adding to your heart's coffers, you may uplift someone on a similar path or offer a way out of a difficult situation or sorrowful mind-set. Your reader may discover something about herself she might have never found out any other way. When *I'm with the Band* was published, I was bowled over by the letters I received from women all over the world who related to my feelings. Here's part of a lovely e-mail from Paige Davies-Baah in London:

I have been suffering with severe anxiety and depression for months, so completely hopeless and uninspired, that my plans to start a post-school life have been scuppered. I've watched my friends lead exciting new lives at university as they pitied me for fantasizing about the ridiculous career path I have chosen (film acting) and obsessing over members of various unreachable bands; so you can imagine the hilarity and relief I felt reading your book and my own thought processes and dreams mirroring those of a successful woman—I just didn't feel so pathetic anymore.

For the first time in a long time, I don't feel like my far-fetched hopes are futile, that my sometimes heart-breaking love for these bands and their music is juvenile or that I am in any way lesser than my peers for this. You have enlightened me to a mind-set that nurtures these dreams and doesn't dash or mock them, and I hope to conquer these mind demons and start the process of living again, and for that, I thank you, Miss Pamela.

How sweet is that? She even brings up those loathsome "mind demons" that I've mentioned a few times. And for those of you not familiar with Brit lingo, her plans being "scuppered" means that they've gone by the wayside.

The letters used to arrive in the mail, many with photos featuring my dolls alongside fave rockers, and now I have a few thousand e-mails safely ensconced in my MacBook Air. I am humbled and joyous that the nutty situations I made it through have somehow helped my fans to take their own great big scary chances.

Another benefit that comes with writing life stories is how composing your memories can make you more attentive and intentional in the way you *live* your life—finding the whimsical, the bizarre, the poetic and the profound in all that you do. Anything can be an allegory, an adventure or a small enticing part of the big picture. Nothing is too insignificant to be turned into beauty, like straw spun into gold on the magic spindle of a laptop computer!

IV

No One Can Tell It but You

I'm an only child and, even though we'd always been close and I'd confided in her to a great extent, I was concerned that my dear mama would be horrified to read about my extensive drug use. Acid, marijuana and cocaine! Oh my! What would my various famous rock-and-roll lovers feel about me revealing what went on between us under the sheets? What would my darling son, Nick, think of his mom's high jinks when he got old enough to read it? And what about the rest of the world? Would I be seen as a loose and lecherous wild woman? Would I even be believed? The word "groupie" had become a negative slur over the years. Did I dare use it in the subtitle of *I'm with the Band*? What if no one cared at all and the manuscript sat in my desk drawer until I drew my last breath? And scariest of all, what if the right words never came calling?

After pondering each possible scenario, I broke all the self-stymieing rules I'd conjured up and gave the heave-ho to the fears I'd worried about. If I caused a commotion, so be it. I had a story to tell. And no one could tell it but me. You have a story to tell too. And no one can tell it but you, baby! Nobody but you!

Remember, as you're writing, don't imagine what someone else might think, and certainly don't start condemning your thoughts and deeds, and don't overthink. Time yourself for a dozen precious minutes, pick up the pen or put your fingers on the keypad and pounce. Writing is a brave and courageous act, especially when you're telling on yourself. So get out of your own way and let it all come tumbling out in any way it wants to.

LET IT BLEED

NINE RULES FOR BREAKING THE RULES

1. Don't even think about grammar and punctuation.

2. Don't stop your flow to read over what you've written until the twelve minutes are up.

3. Don't ask for anyone's opinion while you're writing.

4. Don't try to make potential readers like you.

5. Don't worry about upsetting or pissing anyone off. It's *your* story. Tell it.

6. Don't start at the beginning if you don't want to.

7. Don't try to write like anyone else. It won't work anyway.

8. Don't skew your story in any direction, and don't add an opinion. Just tell the story. You can reflect and revise later.

9. Don't leave anything out. Be reckless. Don't color in the lines. Don't even use the proper colors. Cut loose and roar.

CHAPTER THREE

I

Read! Read! Read!

*Read, read, read. Read everything—trash, classics, good
and bad, and see how they do it. Just like a carpenter who
works as an apprentice and studies the master. Read!
You'll absorb it.*

—WILLIAM FAULKNER

Whenever I start another eight-week class in L.A. or a two-evening workshop somewhere around the globe, I ask that the students bring in a short, scrumptious piece of writing by someone they admire to read aloud. When they reveal why the author and the particular paragraph resonates with them, it tells me a lot about that person and the kind of writing they're interested in creating. If they read from a book by David Sedaris or Amy Poehler, I know their funny bone is on alert, ready to chortle and crack wise. If they open a tome by Yogananda, it's obvious they're ready to focus on what's humming within their soul. Several of my dolls have brought in Patti Smith's books; she certainly seems to touch a nerve, with passages such as this sagacious pronouncement from *Just Kids*:

"The artist seeks contact with his intuitive sense of the gods, but in

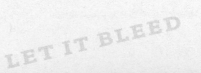

order to create his work, he cannot stay in this seductive and incorporeal realm. He must return to the material world in order to do his work. It's the artist's responsibility to balance mystical communication and the labor of creation."

All my books are available on Kindle, and I recently gave in and got one of those magical little devices. Since I travel so much and have been dragging pounds of pages everywhere I go, the modern age finally came calling. I now have my fave authors, Walt Whitman, Jack Kerouac, Henry Miller, Anaïs Nin and F. Scott Fitzgerald, literally ensconced in my velvet pocket. I recorded all my books for Audible as well, and now listen to reams of audiobooks thirty thousand feet up in the sky, traversing the country, meeting up with my creative companions. My son, Nick, tells me I have finally stepped into the twenty-first century, and yes, I do appreciate the convenience of my doohickeys, but actually turning the page of a book will always be sexy to me.

One of my incredibly prolific heroes is the great horror-meister Stephen King, who agrees that to be a writer, you must turn those pages. In *On Writing: A Memoir of the Craft*, he writes:

"If you want to be a writer, you must do two things above all others: read a lot and write a lot. There's no way around these two things that I'm aware of, no shortcut."

I have been a readaholic since I can remember, and I regularly have several books going at once, stacks of them in every room, spines slowly cracking, holding my place. I began reading at age five and my adoring, attentive mom started magazine subscriptions to *Highlights* and *Jack & Jill* and signed me up to children's book clubs, and I danced for joy when the mailman brought those treasured Trips around the World to my door. Wonder Books! Little Golden Books! Illustrated Junior Classics! Not to mention Walt Disney's gloriously colorful Whitman books. As I got lost in those fascinating stories, the faraway people and places (and Disney characters—I'm still a fiend for the Mouse) became real-live movies behind my eyes. My imagination soared and I was no longer tucked into my chenille-covered twin bed in Reseda, California, but flying around Neverland or traipsing through the jungle with Jane. I also devoured comic books, spending my forty-cent-a-week allowance on Little Lulu (hysterical), Archie and his pals (Betty and Veronica taught me how to talk to boys) and Katy Keene with her extravagant wardrobe, itty-bitty waistline and haughty demeanor.

The first "real" book I read was *Angel Unaware* by Dale Evans Rogers, a slim volume about her and cowboy Roy's daughter, Robin, who was born with Down syndrome. This touching tale is written in Robin's voice; she speaks to us from heaven after passing away at age two and a half.

"Yes, there was music," she tells us. "I even heard happy songs that they couldn't hear. They just saw my sickness, and they felt sorry for me. But I knew *why* I was sick, and because I was sick I could do things for them; and as they say Down There, that was 'music to my ears.' It was quite an experience, Father. When you sent me on that earthly mission, I never dreamed what it would be like, or how much we could do, in two short years. We did a lot."

Angel Unaware was a huge success, selling in the millions, and is still in print today. I was probably ten or eleven when Robin's story kept me up long after my parents were asleep. I'd gaze up at my glow-in-the-dark stars on the ceiling, questioning our creator, and pondering the sorrows that life and death could bring.

II

Always, Always Break the Rules

There are always a bunch of books covering my bed: a couple of novels (I get easily lost in Alice Hoffman's chimerical take on reality, Anne Tyler's elegance and Edna Ferber's straightforwardness); some poetry (*Leaves of Grass*, over and over again; Anne Sexton's despairing, ecstatic mind trip); a memoir (one of my faves is Tennessee Williams's *Memoirs* a spiritual tome or two by Eckhart Tolle or Byron Katie; and of course a classic—one I've read several times, such as *Tropic of Cancer* by Henry Miller, *East of Eden* by Steinbeck, *Dharma Bums* by Kerouac, Anaïs Nin and Virginia Woolf's endless outpourings (*A Writer's Diary*!) or the perpetual *Great Gatsby* by the eternally tortured F. Scott.

Whether I'm reading a book for pleasure, discovery or enlightenment, I find that all of them are full of writing lessons. Of course, we can read just for fun, or for pure enjoyment or to escape for a little while, but to read as a writer, you must keep a discerning eye out for those startling aha! moments when an author reveals wondrous new ways to use the language. Through another writer's bravery we learn how to express ourselves in a new way. How to use a word in a different context. How to make dialogue sing and shout.

I have several copies of *Gatsby* and often pass them around in workshops so my dolls can swoon over his delicate, unnerving descriptions. He helped me realize that we are not limited to what has been said before. Or *how* it's been said.

> *That was it. I'd never understood before. It was full of money—that was the inexhaustible charm that rose and fell in it, the jingle of it, the cymbals' song of it.*

I remember when I first read Fitzgerald's quote that Daisy's voice sounded like "money." I reeled. He seemed to be breaking a tried-and-true rule, and I felt suddenly freed up and unconstrained. That single description opened new vistas and made me want to dance down the untraveled road, a vast, empty space waiting to be filled with my words. "We know our limits," Fitzgerald whispered to me from the beyond, "and there are none."

It felt like I was mentally yanking off an old-fashioned fifties girdle when I discovered Kerouac's disregard for punctuation and grammar. When I first read *On the Road*, it was a literary bra-burning moment for me. Hoorah! Despite all the stern instructions in Strunk and White's *Elements of Style,* or the more modern take in *Eats, Shoots & Leaves* by Lynne Truss, we are not really limited by commas, periods or paragraphs anymore. But keep in mind that before flouting convention, Kerouac made sure to learn all those damnable grammatical rules, and *then* threw them out his car window and took his foot off the brake. (If you need a quick grammar brushup, I suggest taking a look at my pal "Weird" Al Yankovic's witty, charming "Word Crimes" on YouTube.) Personally, the wrong use of the apostrophe makes me want to yank(ovic!) out strands of my flaming red hair. (No Dog's Allowed. CD's and DVD's For Sale! Ack!)

Ahhhh, I have long adored and admired creative rule breakers and am always on the lookout for the next literary rebel rouser. And Kerouac's (often made-up) words made me feel like I wasn't all alone, like someone out there understood the impossible madhouse swirling in my marrow. "I like too many things and get all confused and hungup running from one thing to another till I drop," he says in *On the Road*. "This is the night, what it does to you. I had nothing to offer anybody except my own confusion." Whenever I feel stuck in my writing, I open to any page in any one of Kerouac's books, and the fierce freedom of expression that flies off the page shatters my prissy fears to smithereens. Kerouac even left us a lavish list of writing tips, complete with brand-new words and the usual recklessness regarding punctuation. All of his advice is spot on, of course,

LET IT BLEED

but, ahhh, number 6: "Be crazy dumbsaint of the mind." Indeed, ignore the mindbleat and let it swirl, swell, ooze, and flow baby. And number 29: "You are a genius all the time." Yes, if you believe you are.

III

The Gush, Throb
and Flood of the Moment

The secret of it all, is to write in the gush, the throb, the flood, of the moment—to put things down without deliberation—without worrying about their style—without waiting for a fit time or place. I always worked that way. I took the first scrap of paper, the first doorstep, the first desk, and wrote—wrote, wrote. By writing at the instant the very heartbeat of life is caught.

—WALT WHITMAN

With my proud groupie soul (I must have been born with it), I've always had a plethora of heroes. Following Walt's sage advice, I carried my diaries around with me so I could write at the instant my heartbeat blammed along with Keith Moon's drums, or as the tears slopped onto the pages over Zeppelin's plane lifting off the tarmac at LAX. Walt Whitman's lifework, *Leaves of Grass*, was basically his diary, an impassioned discourse and blatant plea that his readers see life as gloriously as he did. Every single page has me in his divine embrace; I can actually see the twinkle in his eye. I call him Saint Walt (or my Walter ego! Ha!), a man ahead of his time in terms of accepting and adoring the holiness of the flesh, and how the soul can reside very comfortably there.

I had read Walt Whitman in school, of course, without truly understanding his sensual, spiritual nature. It took a golden-eyed rock god and genius soul man, Terence Trent D'Arby (now called Sananda Maitreya), to hip me to the immortal madness of the bearded fellow long ago banned in Boston—our Great American Poet. In *Sex, God & Rock and Roll*, the memoir I am currently writing on my stupefying spiritual life, I describe my first visit with TTD this way:

I had a mound of errands to run that day so I fit the visit neatly into the schedule, pretending he was just number 5 on a list that included cat food and dry cleaning. I wish I could say I was feeling mellow. I had done tons of spiritual work after all, and knew that we were all One. What was there to be all heart-thrummy about? As John Lennon once said "I am you and you are me . . ." But I was almost gasping for breath when I knocked on the front door of Mr. Soul's secluded canyon pad. After a few seconds too long, he opened the door wearing a long glittering caftan and ushered me into his den of hushed expectancy—greeting me like he was reclusive royalty receiving a much-honored guest. After he showed me around—the frothy, overgrown grounds, the state-of-the-art recording studio, the sweeping staircase, a quick peek into his tousled, perfumed bedroom—tea was served. It was some kind of minty herbal, and the aroma swirled around and about as we sat on the long brocade couch covered in lavishly embroidered velvet pillows. After a few silent sips, he tossed back his shoulder-length braids, picked up a worn and creased book, opening to a passage.

"This is the female form;
A divine nimbus exhales from it from head to foot;
It attracts with fierce undeniable attraction!
I am drawn by its breath as if I were no more than a
    helpless vapor—all falls aside but myself and it;

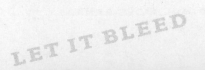

Books, art, religion, time, the visible and solid earth, the
　　atmosphere and the clouds, and what was expected of
　　heaven or fear'd of hell, are now consumed.
Mad filaments, ungovernable shoots play out of it—the
　　response likewise ungovernable;
You are the gates of the body, and you are the gates of the soul.
The female contains all qualities, and tempers them—she is
　　in her place, and moves with perfect balance;
She is all things duly veil'd—she is both passive and active;
She is to conceive daughters as well as sons, and sons as well
　　as daughters.
As I see my soul reflected in nature;
As I see through a mist, one with inexpressible
　　completeness and beauty,
See the bent head, and arms folded over the breast—the
　　female I see."

After an endless span, he set aside the book—Walt Whitman's *Leaves of Grass*—and looked at me, into my eyes, into some part of me that remembered who I was, who I had been, who I would always be, and time stopped. My soul took a forever photograph, as his flecked golden eyes burned into mine. The moment breathed. Inhale. Exhale. I was aware of birds chirping outside. Wind rustled the leaves on the trees. Car horns honked somewhere far away. It was all music. I had just been made love to by Walt Whitman through the honey-sweet mouth of my favorite living singer.

I was so inspired I couldn't wait to write about it. Please don't let your precious moments slip by without capturing them in your butterfly net of winsome words.

I've discovered that with all great art there is no separation between the artist and the witness to the art. Whenever I stand in front of a Van Gogh, my open heart, whirlpooling along with his paintbrush, confirms this. And once, leaning against the stage at a Jimi Hendrix gig, the notes spilled from his guitar in a brand-new way. I could see them sparking colors through the dark air; my solar plexus opened wide and it felt like a thousand new possibilities were being born inside me. Whitman understood this little secret too. When I read this passage for the first time, I could feel my heart beating inside Saint Walt's chest:

When you read these, I that was visible am become invisible. Now is it you, compact, visible, realizing my poems, seeking me.
Fancying how happy you were if I could be with you and become your comrade. Be it as if I were with you. (Be not too certain but I am now with you.)

IV

Turning Inside Out

Another celebrated rule breaker is the brutally explicit Henry Miller. It seemed he could see the brightest light and the deepest darkness in all he surveyed, and the reader teeters on the switchblade right along with him. After a literary adviser suggested to him, "Write as you talk. Write as you live. Write as you feel and think," Miller cranked out *Tropic of Cancer*, one of the most banned books in the history of American literature. I use this passage in my workshops to provoke my writers to go beyond the typical mind-set. His description of birth itself, a seemingly basic experience, is anything but.

"Deep in the blood the pull of paradise. The beyond. It must have all started with the navel. They cut the umbilical cord, give you a slap in the ass, and presto! You're out in the world, adrift. You look at the stars and

27

LET IT BLEED

then you look at your navel. You grow eyes everywhere—in the armpits, between the lips, in the roots of your hair, on the soles of your feet. What is distant becomes near, what is near becomes distant. Inner-outer, a constant flux, a shedding of skins, a turning inside out."

One of our earliest memoirists is the wildly prolific Anaïs Nin, a valiant liberal who had a long, tempestuous relationship with Henry Miller. She chronicled their romance in *The Diary of Anaïs Nin* (first released in 1966), which she began writing at age eleven, in 1914. The pair also wrote copious letters to each other, now gathered in the book *A Literate Passion: Letters of Anaïs Nin and Henry Miller, 1932–1953.*

An excerpt from Nin to Miller

Before, as soon as I came home from all sorts of places I would sit down and write in my journal. Now I want to write you, talk with you . . . I love when you say all that happens is good, it is good. I say all that happens is wonderful. For me it is all symphonic, and I am so aroused by living—god, Henry, in you alone I have found the same swelling of enthusiasm, the same quick rising of the blood, the fullness . . . Before, I almost used to think there was something wrong. Everybody else seemed to have the brakes on . . . I never feel the brakes. I overflow. And when I feel your excitement about life flaring, next to mine, then it makes me dizzy.

It seems Ms. Nin had no use for brakes in her writing either. There are now several published volumes of Nin's diaries, along with *A Literate Passion* the lovers left for us to devour. As I mentioned before, a liberating way to tell your story is to relate it to someone you love.

In the bravura *Henry Miller On Writing*, Miller insists that we go for our own jugular, adding the caveat that one must be willing to "bear the consequences, which a pure act always involves." He stresses over and over again that to truly create you must be totally *yourself.*

Every day we slaughter our finest impulses. That is why we get a heart-ache when we read those lines written by the hand of a master and recognize them as our own, as the tender shoots which we stifled because we lacked the faith to believe in our own powers, our own criterion of truth and beauty. Every man, when he gets quiet, when he becomes desperately honest with himself, is capable of uttering profound truths. We all derive from the same source. There is no mystery about the origin of things. We are all part of creation, all kings, all poets, all musicians; we have only to open up, only to discover what is already there.

V

Tricks of the Trade

"Writing is seduction," says Stephen King, and so is reading! As writers, we read to pick up the tricks and tools that make vivid writing spring off the pages. Here are some key tools to keep an eye out for and learn to weave into your own work.

Simile and Metaphor

I've always been titillated by a little S&M. Ah yes, a tantalizing simile or metaphor is unfailingly seductive as I'm tearing through a book I just can't put down. Sometimes I have to read the sentence over a couple of times to marvel at the witty wordplay and striking imagery. As you go through the exercises in this book, I hope you will enjoy and employ these spectacular little tools. The use of metaphor and simile can perk up your prose and help your reader visualize the scenes, sounds and ideas you're trying to express.

I'm sure thrilled when I'm hit with a simile that twangs in my head like a Duane Eddy guitar lick!

In *I'm with the Band*, I describe the first glimpse I got of Miss Mercy, using a metaphor and a simile in this passage.

> *Conversation ceased and we were staring at a plump version of Theda Bara, wrapped in layers and layers of torn rags, an exotic bag girl with black raccoon eye makeup that dusted down both cheeks and looked like she'd twisted two hunks of coal round and round on her eyelids. Her lipstick was a red seeping slash and both earlobes had been split down the middle by too many dangerous earrings dangling too far down.*

Her "black raccoon eye makeup . . . *looked like*" makes this a simile. "Her lipstick *was* a red seeping slash" makes this a metaphor.

The main thing to remember about metaphors and similes is that the metaphor makes the subject equivalent to the thing it's being compared to. It generally can be spotted when the subject is connected to the descriptor by "is" or "was."

The simile qualifies the comparison, letting the reader know that one thing is simply "like" another thing, not equal to it. If you see the word "like" in a description, it's a pretty sure bet you've spotted a simile. Or sometimes a simile will show up after "as": "She was as still and cold *as* a mannequin on ice."

"The embroidered dragon climbing up his leg *is* a living, breathing creature" is a metaphor.

Here are a few humdingers by Brandy Batz, a grade-school teacher in my L.A. class.

> "Dan and I *were two books sitting side by side on a shelf in the Kurt Vonnegut library.*" (metaphor)

"On the Disneyland monorail *I was a silver missile of time encapsulated in an alternate Mickey reality.*" (metaphor)

"*My face turned all red like a blister in the sun*, but not the good kind like in the Violent Femmes song." (simile)

"Blue eyes have always been my jam. For me *they are pools of sexy that I want to fully dive in.*" (metaphor)

My fave rave book of the moment, Emma Cline's *The Girls* is rampant with staggeringly creative similes and metaphors. These four are all on the first two pages!

"These long-haired girls seemed to glide above all that was happening around them, tragic and separate. Like royalty in exile." (simile)

"She was flanked by a skinny redhead and an older girl dressed with the same shabby afterthought." (metaphor)

"All their cheap rings like a second set of knuckles." (simile)

"Sleek and thoughtless as sharks breaching the water." (simile)

Alliteration

I so adore alliteration that I've been aptly accused of overusing this amusing device. (Ha!) Stemming from the Latin word *latira*, it literally means "letters of the alphabet." It's a stylin' device in which a number of words beginning with the same sound (not necessarily the same letter) occur close

together in a series. Such as: "Jagger jumps jaggedly across the gym like a gyrating juggernaut." Pretty crummy writing, but you get the picture!

Here's a decidedly more desirable example from *Conclusive Evidence*, by another fave of mine, Vladimir Nabokov:

*A **m**oist young **m**oon hung above the **m**ist of a neighboring **m**eadow.*

And of course, the very last line of *The Great Gatsby*, a subtle gem from the pen of F. Scott:

*So we **b**eat on, **b**oats against the current, **b**orne **b**ack ceaselessly into the past.*

As you dip into your favorite books, start to read like a writer. Keep an eye (or two) open for authors' similes, metaphors and witty wordplay. If you pay close attention, these literary gambits will start to come naturally to you as well.

Clichés

Avoid them like the plague! Ha-ha! The reason most clichés hang around our vernacular for so long is because they're the easiest (and therefore laziest) way to get a point across or to describe something without anyone having to think too hard. Overused phrases such as "You can't teach an old dog new tricks" and "Money is the root of all evil" usually state a truth but also betray a lack of original thought. I admit to being a fan of the musical competition shows, but nine times out of ten (a cliché!) the performers announce that winning "would mean the world" to them. What does that even mean? It's a passive platitude used instead of creating a dynamic new way to describe something, or reveal how you're actually feeling.

For decades, one of my heroes has been the insanely prolific Stephen

King. He captures the foibles, fears and fantasies of humanity, makes it all so real, then salts and peppers it with wicked clowns and little kids with ungodly powers. You rarely find a cliché in a King book. He can also write wildly well about wicked women! Here's a chill-inducing description of Annie Wilkes I love from *Misery*:

> *She smiled, a pulling of the lips that was grotesquely puppetlike, and slipped to his side in her silent white nurse's shoes. Her fingers touched his hair. He flinched. He tried not to but couldn't help it. Her dead-alive smile widened.*

Hopefully you've enjoyed this little spate of reading like a writer, because, whether you believe it yet or not, you *are* one!

Paying close attention to picturesque touches, and avoiding the dreaded cliché, can make your writing more imaginative, visual, more lively and more *you*!

CHAPTER FOUR

I

Engaging Your Senses

When you feel the muse biting your ass, and are truly ready to knuckle down and buckle up (it's going to be a bumpy ride!), I suggest you begin by contemplating the central themes of your life. Depending on how long you've been dancing on sweet Mother Earth, it may seem like a hair-raising enterprise to mull over the vastness of all you've seen and done. "How will I remember it all?" you might wonder. "And how the heck can I possibly put my entire life into words?"

Here is a good first step: since it seems to be a list-driven world nowadays, and checking off each completed task feels so darn good, I suggest starting off with a simple *list*. What do you consider to be the Highlights and Lowlights of your life—the standout events—the milestones, miracles, realizations, predicaments and people that cannot be left out of your memoir? The experiences that made you who you are today? List making is an easy way to begin, a calming, mindful process to start the proverbial ball rolling in the right direction. Don't even think about being *writerly* at this point. If you find lists inspiring, then consider this like your writing to-do list and let it serve as a blueprint that, along with the topics and suggestions presented in this book, will help you fill in the blanks and jog your memory in all kinds of mercurial, wayward directions.

Even though it's loaded with the most vivid, visceral and vital scenes that have formed your present-day persona, at this point your all-important tally may still read like a laundry list—"The day I left home," "My trip to the UK," "My first kiss"—and that's perfectly fine! I'm sure you're wondering how on Mama Earth you'll be able to bring these scenes, feelings and situations sharply to life so the reader can understand why they're meaningful to you.

This is where we learn about the divine ability to paint lucid pictures with our words. The authors that I am enraptured by have finely tuned their talent—using their five senses as their own personal palette.

You may not realize why you are compelled to stay up way past bedtime to keep reading a certain book, why you're so captivated and feel like you're right in the middle of the action. Oftentimes you're enveloped by the words because the author has engaged all his or her senses—describing what's happening in the scene with an apropos combo of sight, hearing, smell, taste, touch. Done effectively, these descriptions stimulate *the reader's* senses, thereby pulling you into the story. "Writing to the senses" creates a tactile experience; a complete sense-o-round for the reader.

Let's see how it works to give a simple life experience some zest. The first paragraph below tells exactly what happened to me but is written with little attention to detail. Before I wrote the second version, I closed my eyes for a moment and recalled the scene, then chose my words so that I was "writing to the senses."

1. I wound up in the hotel pool with Noel Redding after their Shrine Auditorium gig. He plays bass in the Jimi Hendrix Experience. The band was so good. They were staying in a really nice hotel. It was late at night and pretty dark. He was drinking, but I didn't feel like it. I was nervous and tried to swim away from him, but Noel stopped me and told me I was just his type. Then he gave me a long kiss, so I decided to stay awhile.

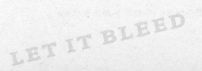

2. Noel Redding invited me over after I saw him play stellar
   bass with the Jimi Hendrix Experience at the Shrine
   Auditorium downtown. I was amazed at how he'd perfectly
   kept up with Jimi's insane guitar licks and felt his deep
   rumbling bass down deep inside me the whole time like a
   throb. It was an elegant hotel in a fancy neighborhood, lush
   and balmy with ruffling palm trees making shirring sounds
   as we frolicked in the massive sky blue pool. We were all by
   ourselves way past midnight, but I could still see his
   dimples in the moonlight. I was sure he could hear my
   noisy heartbeats so I pretended to swim away, but he swept
   me up in his skinny pale arms and I chill-bumped with
   shivery anticipation. In his swoony British accent he said,
   "You're just my type," then took a swig of cognac and
   breathed it all over me before kissing me hard. It burned.
   I'd never tasted cognac before. And I wasn't really going to
   leave anyway.

Ah, that took me back . . .

All of the description in the second paragraph helps you see, feel, taste,
touch and smell, right? These are the kinds of details that will bring your
memories to life on the page, plunging your readers right into your scenes
as if they were there with you, living the experience themselves.

Sooooo . . . before you embark on this rip-roaring writing spree, now's
the perfect time to hone your delicious sense of sight, touch, taste, hearing
and smell.

Take five days for this exercise and besides sharpening up your writing,
it will enhance your life in surprising ways. Bring your eyes, fingertips,
tongue, ears and nose into all that you do. Take nothing for granted. Even
the great scientists say the universe is pure energy, and if you allow yourself
to be open instead of blocking the flow, the vibrance of the world comes

fully into view. Since it usually happens unconsciously, why not start paying close attention to it all?

Nabokov said, "Caress the divine details," and I think he meant that we should Be Here Now and experience each moment fully, especially if we intend to recall it in our writing. The secret is to Pay Attention. The philosopher J. Krishnamurti taught me that as I sat in front of him many times under massive oak trees in Ojai. His frustration was palpable as he searched our eyes and pleaded in his lilting Indian accent, "The observer *is* the observed. Please, are you paying attention?"

"Stop, look and listen, baby, that's my philosophy," Elvis wails in "Rubberneckin'"—so let's commit to being like the King this week and be aware. Be awake. No blinkers allowed.

Day one. With your first breath, begin your day by taking in everything you see. Let your eyes linger a moment longer on the faces of your loved ones, the way the invisible breeze ruffles the trees; study the lacy, intricate pattern on a leaf of kale, or the sparkles of the water gushing from the faucet, the beauty of a gleaming piece of fruit, the way your dog's ears perk up when you call his name, and even the scary blaring headlines or a ragged homeless person on the side of the road. Try not to pass judgment on anything you observe, just take it all in with your glorious gift of sight. At the end of the day before you go to bed, make a list of the things you truly saw and describe them as vividly as you can. Set your timer for twelve minutes and write what you saw.

Day two. Pay close attention to everything you touch: the nubby texture of the fabric on your couch, the feel of the steering wheel under your hands, the sleek fur of your cat, the sun's heat on your skin, the wind tossing your hair, the deliciousness of a kiss or comfort of being enclosed in an embrace. If possible goop your hands up in clay or cookie dough, or rub coconut oil all up and down your arms, and enjoy that delightful sensation of touch. Trail your fingers along a chain-link fence; sink into a warm bubble bath. Write about how it all feels on your skin. Again, set your trusty timer and write for twelve minutes about what you touched.

37

LET IT BLEED

Day three. Experience as much tasting as you can stand! Bring your taste buds to life in as many ways as possible. Don't worry about dieting for this one day and indulge in your favorite taste treats. Savor the salty cashews, swirl chocolate or honey around in your mouth, lick an ice-cold Popsicle, crunch into a crisp apple, delight in a cup of mint tea. Gargle with tingly Listerine, then enjoy the distinct taste of your lover's lips! Whatever you put into your mouth today, experience it completely. Twelve minutes on what your taste buds experienced.

Day four. Listen avidly to every sound that enters your eardrums from the moment you wake up. Is it really silent? Is someone running a lawn mower? Is a TV on in another room? The sound of water running, the scratch of the toothbrush, the sizzle of eggs frying, the bark, the meow, the purr, the laughter. The rev of the engine, the din of traffic, the chatter of coworkers. Listen to as much music as you can today. Switch channels on the car radio, let Spotify or Pandora play all day, and pay attention to every hum, twang, growl, lick, chord, yawp and yowl. Before you sleep, write for twelve minutes about all the incredible sounds you heard today.

Day five. Inhale, inhale, inhale! Breathe deeply all day long and thrill at the various scents all around you that you usually take for granted. The aroma of coffee brewing, muffins baking, the scent of your dishwashing liquid, laundry detergent, body lotions, hair spray. Take a moment to sniff flowers blooming in the yard, cut open a lemon, light your favorite perfumed candle, press your nose into your cat's fur and breathe in the singular essence of feline. Notice the bad smells too. The garbage that needs taking out. The cat box that needs changing. Take time to inhale the subtle nuanced odor of each room you step into today, and if you have a chance to take a stroll in the glory of nature, truly experience each and every peppery, spicy, ambrosial fragrance that surrounds you. Twelve minutes on what you smelled today.

Day six. Today you will discover that all your senses are heightened, so enjoy this newfound awareness and utilize your intensified senses to the fullest. Keenly observe, take any opportunity to see, touch, taste, smell and listen. Hopefully day six falls during the weekend so you can spend an entire day exploring your eye-popping, tactile, fragrant, melodic, savory/ sweet world. But if it's a weekday, don't worry. Wherever you are or whatever you're doing—at work or puttering around your 'hood, cram as much touchy-feely, looky-loo Being-Here-Nowness as you can into this day of renewal—and rejoice!

II

The Youness of You

Day seven. Let's write about what makes you *you*!

But where to start?

A memoir, unlike an autobiography, can begin anywhere. What transitional moment in your life will reveal the most about who you really are? What watershed incident altered you forever or set you on a brand-new course? An experience that took you over the rainbow or put you under a spell. Your starting place speaks volumes about how your story will play out, and it should intrigue your readers, keep them reading and hold them captive until the end.

Where you begin should also invoke the theme and tone of your memoir and subtly let readers imagine the path you'll be taking them on. The way you use words, your style and pacing, plus the boffo story you choose as your opener, will give readers a taste of the rollicking ride you're about to take them on.

Of course, you're not stuck with this first intro. In fact, as you dredge up more memories, the perfect one may click into place at any time. You can start your memoir anywhere in your life when you were grabbed by the

heart; shaken and stirred by something or someone. A moment when there was no turning back. One instant you were one person, and the next a brand-new one. A time you'd been dazzled. Horrified. Broken. Renewed. Reborn. Transformed. Undone.

All shook up, in my case.

We now hopefully have the 20/20 to look back and realize when that transformative moment took place. For me it was at the Reseda Theater when I was eleven years old. And of course, it involved a rock god.

I get shivers whenever I see those old black-and-white films of Elvis getting shorn for Uncle Sam. When he rubs his hand over the stubs of his former blue-black mane, I get a twinge in my temples. In the glorious year of 1960, I was at the Reseda Theater with my parents, and I saw the famous army footage before the onslaught of Psycho. *I don't know which was more horrifying. I hung on to my daddy's neck and inhaled the comforting familiarity of his drugstore aftershave and peeked through my fingers as Norman Bates did his dirty work, and the army barber did his. I tried to believe that Elvis was doing his duty as an AMERICAN, but even at eleven years old, I realized his raunch had been considerably diminished. I tacked my five-and-dime calendar onto the dining-room wall and drew big X's as each day passed, knowing he would let his hair grow long when he came home from Germany. Being an adored only child, my mom let me keep the eyesore on the wall for two years. I was always allowed to carry out my fantasies to the tingling end, and I somehow survived several bouts of temporary omnipotence.*

The opening paragraph from *I'm with the Band* says a lot about Pam Miller from Reseda, California.

Here are ten more examples to show how these authors chose to invite the reader into their lives. The opening paragraph sets up each memoir perfectly and is tantalizing enough to make you want to keep turning the pages.

Just like in her saucy TV series, *Girls*, Lena Dunham begins her nervy memoir *Not That Kind of Girl* by blatantly telling on herself:

> *When I was nine, I wrote a vow of celibacy on a piece of paper and ate it. I promised myself, in orange Magic Marker, that I would remain a virgin until I graduated from high school. This seemed important because I knew my mother had waited until the summer before college and also because Angela Chase seemed pretty messed up by her experience at that flophouse where high school kids went to copulate. If my relationship to liver pâté was any indication—and I had recently eaten so much that I barfed—then my willpower left much to be desired. I would need something stronger than resolve to prevent me from having intercourse too early in life, so I wrote the vow up and asked my mother to sign the document. She refused. "You just don't know what life will bring, and I don't want you feeling guilty," she said.*

Jeepers! Nine is pretty young to be thinking about celibacy! I was jumping rope and playing hopscotch. From the first line, Ms. Dunham treats the reader as her confidante, as if the two of you were chitchatting in the privacy of her bedroom, spilling girlhood secrets.

Viv Albertine, founder of the seminal female band the Slits, titled the opening chapter of *Clothes, Clothes, Clothes. Music, Music, Music. Boys, Boys, Boys.* "Masturbation":

> *Never did it. Never wanted to do it. There was no reason not to, no oppression, I wasn't told it was wrong and I don't think it's wrong. I just didn't think of it at all. I didn't naturally want to do it, so I didn't know it existed. By the time my hormones kicked in, at about thirteen years old, I was being felt-up by boys and that was enough for me. Bit by bit the*

experimentation went further until I first had sex with my regular boy-friend when I was fifteen. We were together for three years and are still friends now, which I think is nice. In all the time since my first sexual experience I haven't masturbated, although I did try once after being nagged by friends when I complained I was lonely. But to me, masturbating when lonely is like drinking alcohol when you're sad: it exacerbates the pain. It's not that I don't touch my breasts (they're much nicer now I've put on a little weight) or touch between my legs or smell my fingers, I do all that, I like doing that, tucked up all warm and cosy in bed at night. But it never leads to masturbation. Can't be bothered.

By beginning with such a private admission, Viv manages to reel us in to make sure we get the rest of the scoop!

As I mentioned earlier, you no longer have to be "somebody" to entice people with your memoir. Many noncelebrities have had smashing success with their memoirs by sharing common (or uncommon) experiences, such as this riveting chronicle of teenage alcoholism—*Smashed: Story of a Drunken Girlhood* by Koren Zailckas:

I can't remember the trauma of my first period, or the year (was it sixth grade or seventh?), but I know that I told my mother about it in the front yard, where she was watering the hydrangea tree with a green rubber hose. The memory of the first time I drove the family Ford has been reduced to a vacant parking lot. My first sex has the solid darkness of its windowless room.

But like most women, I remember my first drink in tender minutiae.

What a last line grabber! For the entire paragraph Koren intrigues the reader, making us wonder why her memory is so strangely foggy, and then whammo - the demon alcohol is at it again!

The Bald Mermaid by Sheila Bridges tells the candid story of an interior designer who loses her hair due to alopecia. The way she describes the color of her skin is certainly original!

Like the songstress Billie Holiday I was born in Philadelphia on the seventh day of the month. Just like her, I eventually made my way to Harlem many years later, though under very different circumstances.

My newborn skin was the color of cauliflower, my hair the shade of ginger, and I had blue eyes. I wouldn't find out till much later in life that being born black and blonde would pose its own unique set of challenges. But within my first few hours I caused controversy as a doctor tried to pry me from my mother's arms, insisting that a mistake had been made, that she had been given the wrong baby.

Invoking legendary songstress Billie Holiday in the first sentence makes us curious to continue on, right? And the idea of being the "wrong baby" sets up the story in an intriguing way.

Lucky by Alice Sebold is a heartrending account of a rape victim and the remarkable coming-to-terms aftermath.

This is what I remember. My lips were cut. I bit down on them when he grabbed me from behind and covered my mouth. He said these words: "I'll kill you if you scream." I remained motionless. "Do you understand? If you scream you're dead." I nodded my head. My arms were pinned to my sides by his right arm wrapped around me and my mouth was covered with his left.

He released his hand from my mouth.

I screamed. Quickly. Abruptly.

The struggle began.

43

LET IT BLEED

"If you scream, you're dead." But Alice screamed anyway, which tells us right away that we're in for a perilous ride with an indomitable, unforgettable heroine.

The two openers below are pivotal accounts by two very different musicians describing the instant they realized their marriage was kaput.

Jennifer Lopez is beloved around the world for being so relatable despite her stardom. The straightforward language she uses to open *True Love* draws us right in, as she exposes the sad truth behind her seemingly magical life.

> *I remember the exact moment when everything changed. I was in the desert outside Los Angeles, getting ready for a photo shoot.*
>
> *It was a beautiful day in July 2011, and Marc and I had just celebrated our seventh wedding anniversary. Anybody looking from the outside in would have thought my life was going great: I had a husband and two beautiful children, and my career was flying high. I was on* American Idol, *the number-one show on the planet, and my new single "On the Floor" had gone to number one all over the world. To top it off,* People *magazine had named me their very first Most Beautiful Woman in the World, a few months earlier. How could life get any better?*
>
> *What people didn't know was that life really* wasn't *that good. My relationship was falling apart, and I was terrified.*

We know from the very opening paragraphs that Sonic Youth's bassist Kim Gordon is going to reveal the harsh reality of being female in a punk-rock male world. She begins *Girl in a Band* by taking us onstage with her for the final gig she played with her husband/fellow bandmate.

> *When we came out onstage for our last show, the night was all about the boys. Outwardly, everyone looked more or less the same as they had for the last thirty years. Inside was a different story.*

*Thurston double-slapped our bass guitarist Mark Ibold on the
shoulder and loped across the stage, followed by Lee Ranaldo, our guitarist, and then Steve Shelley, our drummer. I found that gesture so
phony, so childish, such a fantasy. Thurston has many acquaintances,
but with the few male friends he had he never spoke of anything personal, and he's never been the shoulder-slapping type. It was a gesture
that called out,* I'm back. I'm free. I'm solo.

*I was the last one to come on, making sure to mark off some dis-
tance between Thurston and me. I was exhausted and watchful.
Steve took his place behind his drum set like a dad behind a desk. The
rest of us armed ourselves with our instruments like a battalion, an
army that just wanted the bombardment to end.*

Kim begins her memoir at the harrowing peak of an auspicious occasion. You can certainly feel the fractious tension between the bandmates,
which makes you want to know how it all began and how it turned into war.

In *Can I Say: Living Large, Cheating Death, and Drums, Drums, Drums,*
Travis Barker, the drummer for Blink-182, opens cute:

*Animal. He was pure primitive orange insanity, and he was my hero.
He would go buck wild, play an awesome drum solo, and then eat his
cymbals. The first time I saw Animal on* The Muppet Show, *I wanted
to eat my cymbals. I wanted to be a drummer. I was four years old.*

By announcing straight off that his drum hero is a Muppet, Travis invites us into his musical world with quirky charm and humor.

And of course, Keith Richards makes sure to riff on the disobedience
and danger of the Rolling Stones in the first paragraph of his memoir, *Life.*

*In which I am pulled over by police officers in Arkansas during our
1975 US tour and a standoff ensues.*

45

Why did we stop at the 4-Dice Restaurant in Fordyce, Arkansas, for lunch on Independence Day weekend? On any day? Despite everything I knew from ten years of driving through the Bible Belt. Tiny town of Fordyce. Rolling Stones on the police menu across the United States. Every copper wanted to bust us by any means available, to get promoted and patriotically rid America of these little fairy Englishmen. It was 1975, a time of brutality and confrontation. Open season on the Stones had been declared since our last tour, the tour of '72, known as the STP. The State Department had noted riots (true), civil disobedience (also true), illicit sex (whatever that is), and violence across the United States. All the fault of us, mere minstrels. We had been inciting youth to rebellion, we were corrupting America, and they had ruled never to let us travel in the United States again. It had become, in the time of Nixon, a serious political matter. He had personally deployed his dogs and dirty tricks against John Lennon, who he thought might cost him an election. We, in turn, they told our lawyer officially, were the most dangerous rock-and-roll band in the world.

Keith invokes all that the Rolling Stones stand for in his opening paragraph. Sex, rebellion, corruption, and most of all—danger.

Dandelion: Memoir of a Free Spirit by Catherine James is a very special memoir to me. Not because she's been one of my dearest friends for decades, or because I helped edit this incredible story of abuse and triumph, but because Catherine had the courage to share her history, which in turn has helped many women deal with their horrific experiences in a way they hadn't imagined possible.

The first time I saw my father as a woman was at the grand old restaurant Musso & Frank Grill on Hollywood Boulevard. He had called me the week before asking if we could meet for lunch, as he had something important he wanted to discuss. It sounded serious, but he didn't want to speak about it on the telephone. I had my suspicions as to what the conversation might be about, but nothing could have prepared me for that notable afternoon.

I arrived at noon, and Musso's was buzzing with its regular upscale crowd and a battalion of aging Italian waiters who were as stiff as the white table linens.

My heart sank when I saw a frightful-looking character coyly flagging a paisley handkerchief in my direction. I thought, "Dear God, don't let this be my father."

I often read the opening page of Dandelion in my classes when we're working on *Where to Begin Your Memoir*. I'm sure you can see why. From the first stunning line to the last, we're hooked.

III

C'mon, Everybody, Away We Go!

I know that starting anything new can be terrifying, and choosing just the right words to convey what's inside your heart must seem like a formidable task. But you're holding this book in your hands right now for a reason. You've decided to ignore the jabberwocky in your head, pull on your sexiest big-girl undies and *write*!

Whenever I give this assignment in my workshops—Where would your memoir begin?—it's phenomenal what spills out.

Here is a spirited twelve-minute response from one of my Austin writers who didn't stop to think, but jumped in with the first scenario that sprang to mind.

*One insomnia-filled late-night MTV marathon came to later save
my life. My household didn't even get cable until I was almost out of
high school. We had only gotten a telephone the year before. They
were luxuries and there'd been no space or place for luxuries in that
house. There I was, teenaged me, with undiagnosed and untreated
depression, surfing through the channels when I got to MTV and four
guys in all their long-haired, grunge-covered glory. An angel with a
voice like a raspy mountain man, blond dreadlocks, eyes bright and
blue as the sky was bellowing out, "Won't you come and save meeeee!"
Those words spoke to my soul. I had to know more. What kind of
name was Alice in Chains anyway? I became obsessed, but it was a
hidden obsession, away from prying eyes and questioning glances. I
was Black, after all, and Black people don't listen to that kind of
music. In my angst-filled rebellion I had gravitated to hip-hop. It was
vulgar and angry, just like me. But those four beautiful faces and
their filthy guitars never left my memory. Years of heartache, disap-
pointment and sadness turned to acceptance and righteous indignation, so I returned to the love of those sludgy melodies, and there I
have remained. Constantly feeling the need to "affirm my blackness"
gave way to the blackness being only one part of the complicated, con-
voluted mess that is me. I no longer felt the need to hide the love for
my rock-and-roll soul mates. The people surrounding me that de-
manded my silence were exiled. I was the phoenix rising from the
smoke, ashes and ruin. Rock music became the soundtrack to my triumphs, and not just my defeats.*

YOLANDA VICKERS, AUSTIN

You can certainly see the turn Yolanda's life took when she released
the idea that she was pigeonholed due to her race. This is an excellent
lead-in to show how her life shifted from that stunning realization.

So, as Peter Pan says hundreds of times a day at my home away from home, Disneyland, "Come on, everybody! Away we gooooooo!" It's your turn now. Time to zip the imaginary lip of that self-censoring know-it-all, forget about Aunt Fanny's sour expression, close your eyes and breathe deeply for a few seconds. Pick up your pen or open your laptop and *know* that the first thing that pops into your head may be the perfect opening into the unique world of you!

Here is your very first writing prompt!

WHERE WILL YOUR MEMOIR BEGIN?

Time yourself. Twelve minutes. Go.

Brava! You have just begun your thrilling climb up the Mount Chimborazo of memoir writing! (Yes, Mount Everest is considered the highest, but this mighty rival in Ecuador is the highest mountain above the earth's center—and besides, referring to Mount Everest is a cliché. Right?)

LET IT BLEED

CHAPTER FIVE

I

The Meaning of Within

Fortunately I had my very own diaries, my very own words, laden with ec-
stasies and sorrows, dates, times and places to remind me of who I was then,
and who I still was in '85 when I began my first memoir. If you have some
previously written reflections, great! Those long-ago angsty passionate passages will help you recall, relive and write. But even if you've never scribbled
a single sentence about yourself, it's all there inside you, waiting to be revealed and revered. All those crazy goings-on made you who you are
today—this spunky chick ready to write it all down! And of course you have
your handy-dandy *list* for inspiration and guidance! Hang on to it!

I have found in my writing workshops that certain prompts enable my
girls to discover huge revelatory truths about who they are today, which, of
course, makes it easier to dig deeper about who they were, what they've been
through, what's been hidden, what's been holding them back, and what
might be ahead. Most of the assignments are geared toward the creation of
a completed memoir, but there are a lot of outlets these days to get your work
noticed. Each prompt will stand on its own and can be used as an inspiration
for blogs, short-form essays, inclusion in anthologies, self-reflection, insight,
realization or just plain fun! All of the "getting to know you" assignments
I've included were written by my students in the twelve minutes allotted in
class. Many of them hadn't written anything since their school days. Others

had written only poetry or songs, blogs or business letters. It doesn't matter what you have or haven't done in the past. All we have is *now*.

"Turn off your mind, relax and float downstream," the Beatles said in "Tomorrow Never Knows." "Lay down all thoughts, surrender to the void." You may very well see the meaning of within as you begin to trust your very own voice.

In each of my evening workshops, we do three different writing prompts, with short breaks in between for reading the stories aloud. I suggest you start by doing three of these prompts each day for two weeks yourself. It may not feel like it at first, but the pages will pile up, more and more tales of passion and pain will be jogged loose and you will actually be writing your memoir! Be sure to time yourself!

First off, let's consider exactly where all this wonderful writing is going to take place. While some people feel perked up and content in the bustle of their favorite coffee shop, if you're like most of us, a quiet room with no distractions is an excellent place to compose.

Even better would be to create a safe space with a door you can close behind you. I'm a mellow hippie at heart, so I might "smudge" the area with a little burning sage for a fresh start, then light up a yummy scented candle and hang a few pictures of creative heroes to gaze down at me (like Beatle Paul did as I wrote my breathy first stories).

I just looooove feeling connected to my heroes, and I print out a lot of my fave quotes from authors and post them all around my work space. You can also bookmark pages of inspiring quips from poets, musicians, masters and wordsmiths to tweak your imagination. Or put all of your snazzy modern devices to stellar use. One app I peruse daily is Inspiration and Motivational Quotes by Steven Boynes. Get your burst of insight from people as varied as Winston Churchill—"Your greatest fears are created by your imagination. Don't give in to them."—and Leonardo da Vinci—"Obstacles cannot crush me. Every obstacle yields to stern resolve. He who is fixed to a star does not change his mind."

Although it's ideal to start your creation in a peaceful, scented room, sometimes it's just not possible, so don't let that deter you. I began writing my first book in a makeshift office in a cluttered corner of my dining room. With my son's video games blasting, and my hubby's music turned up loud, I sat down and settled into a focused realm of resolve and pounded those keys. My usual writing refuge is my little home office where I'm surrounded by copious vintage collectibles such as romantic silhouettes from the thirties, smiling ceramic animals, images of heroes—Elvis, James Dean, Walt Whitman, Mary Magdalene, and all manner of bible quotes reminding me that *anything* is possible: "If we ask anything according to His will, He heareth us." (1 John 5:14) With my wackadoodle schedule, I write whenever and wherever I can grab an hour or two. I need to be comfortable and cozy, with nothing pinching or poking, so the first thing I do before I sit down is to yank off my damnable bra! (A man must have designed those beastly mammary-straitjackets.) When my kitties, Lulu and Kokoro decide to accompany me, their purring gently hums in my head and the words stroll out onto the page. And I drink a lot of coffee! Depending on what I'm working on, I sometimes prefer quietude and check into a local motel where the walls are bare, sound is rare, and no one knows my name! If your home situation is too tumultuous, look for a different place where you can sit alone and concentrate—the beauty of a park, the corner booth at your favorite café or even the quiet isolation of your vehicle! Park under a friendly tree, slide the seat back and have at it. I have written many pages within the comfort zone of my Scion XB.

As you continue the process and get more confident with your writing, eventually the muse will strike you anywhere, anytime, so get prepared for her visits!

No matter where I set myself up, before I dig in to my session, I take several deep breaths to quiet my ramshackle mind, and sometimes even repeat a mantra, before settling down to write. It's always something different. Any phrase that inspires you is hunky-dory, such as, "The creative muse flows through me now" or "My heart and mind are open and ready to rock!" Just allowing your mind to spend a couple of silent moments away from its ever-present back talk can open a direct passageway to your sweet and trusting spirit. (Recently I signed up for Oprah's online streaming meditations with Deepak Chopra, and he offers a splendid new mantra daily.)

II

Revving Up

A good way to jump-start the flow is to write a brief description of yourself in two hundred words or less. Call it a rapid review of your life; add it to your list, and fill in the blanks later. If you're typing in a computer program, you can see the word count at the bottom of the page. (Most typewritten pages run 250 words.) If you're writing by hand, you'll probably fill a couple of pages.

SO . . . WHO ARE YOU, IN TWO HUNDRED WORDS?

Here's one of those quickies by one of my Portland writers. Trisha made sure to cram in her most crucial life moments, the memorable situations and realizations that created who she is right now.

A Bicentennial baby, born right before the hum of a thousand air conditioners ushered in the summer. A little girl, dividing my time between my family's game room and backyard swimming pool, all the while trying to fold up into myself and become as tiny as possible. Music quickly became the only language I understood. A switch had been flipped, and there was no turning back. Realizing I didn't have to wait for music to come to me, all bets were off. Spending my teens and

twenties at shows and on the road, an endless and glorious parade of
nightclubs, highways, rest stops and hotels. Some memorable, others lost.

Halfway through my thirties, struggling to strike a balance between
the rock-and-roll chaos I so desperately loved and the tranquil domes-
ticity of everyday life: the comforts of good food, animals at my feet and
the sound of records scratching through the speakers of my turntable. But
I know something is still lurking around the corner to make me wild-
eyed and anxious, to whisper in my ear and pull me away. Music is my
savior and it will destroy me, and I wouldn't have it any other way.

TRISHA HEY, PORTLAND, OREGON

As I am such a music-loving soul, I understand that switch being
flipped, the saving grace Trisha describes, along with the fearsome flash-
backs certain songs can trigger. Depending on what I'm working on, I
often have my faves playing as I tip-tap along the keyboard, allowing the
sounds to free my mind from distracting invasion. The Doors' "Light My
Fire" can always make me feel woozily stoned, especially the long, soaring
keyboard solo, and I have been known to crank up Jack White's version of
"I'm Shakin'" if I need to power through a tough assignment. I'm shakin',
I'm tremblin', I'm Bo Diddley too, Jack.

If music helps to arouse your creativity, blast it, especially if it accelerates
your memories and gets your motor running! By the end of the first two weeks,
you'll be all geared up and the momentum will keep you chugging along.

How about all those car references? Ah! A memory has been triggered!
Or should I say, revved up?

She was a 1959 white Chevy convertible. Huge sexy fins. Lots of
chrome. Sky blue leather interior. A gift for my upcoming sweet sixteenth
birthday, September 9, 1964. Not brand new but hotter and dreamier
than the newest Impala model, I was certain of that. The fins were def-
initely slantier and wider, like a knowing smile. She was low-slung and

floaty, purring like a two-ton cat as I slid out my Jamieson Avenue driveway and onto the street for the first time. My parents were away for the weekend and I didn't have my license yet, but could not bear to wait a second longer to nestle in behind the wheel. She was mine, after all, or would be in a few days. I cruised the familiar Valley streets, but now I owned them. I was teaching myself to drive and nobody knew where I was and no one could stop me. The freedom was the kind of exhilaration I didn't know existed. I turned on the radio and found a station playing the Rolling Stones, and turned it up loud. Here comes your nineteenth nervous breakdown. Here it comes. Here it comes. Here I come. I pulled up next to some cute boys on their bicycles, and they nodded in appreciation. As I revved the engine, tossed my hair and put the pedal to the metal, I knew my Chevy's cherry red backlights were grinning and those boys on their bikes would never forget me.

I hope that little rant triggered your own vehicular memories. Just for a kick, why don't you . . .

DESCRIBE YOUR FIRST CAR. HOW DID YOU GET IT? WHERE DID YOU DRIVE ON YOUR FIRST ADVENTURE?

Let's continue with assignments that will help conjure up who the heck is holding this book and ready to write her memoir.

WHAT THREE ADJECTIVES WOULD YOU USE TO DESCRIBE YOURSELF? ELABORATE ON EACH.

The poem below, written by my L.A. student Susyn Reading in those twelve allotted minutes, sums up her greatest strength in four stanzas. A former hippie maven in her midfifties, Susyn once brought to class the makings for a "flaming groovy." We all watched avidly as she poured a little booze into a large Sparkletts water bottle and tossed in a match. Boom! Poof! Blammo! Very colorful display!

WHAT IS YOUR GREATEST STRENGTH?

It isn't my intelligence
Though some might think it so
I still have so much more to learn
So very far to go

It isn't my persistence
How I power through my fears
That's only me resisting change
And settling through the years

It isn't in my Loved Ones
Though we're getting closer now
They all believe that I am strong
That makes it so, somehow

My greatest strength is symbolized
By my toe tattoo, you see
My strength is in this partnership
I've agreed upon with me

    SUSYN READING, LOS ANGELES

Susyn's "toe ring" was done in varying shades of black, gray and white, and it gleams like a silver circle around her toe. She says it's a symbol of her commitment to love, honor and cherish herself!

Applause!

We all need a break, right? Wow, I just recalled that old McDonald's slogan "You deserve a break today." (Excellent advice; cruddy food.) I suggest you write several versions of this prompt, just to let off steam. I think Valerie speaks for a lot of women in this one:

SOMETIMES I JUST NEED A BREAK FROM . . .

In my weakest moments, I find myself overanalyzing. Overthinking every facet of my existence and just being overly critical of myself in general. Sometimes I just need a break from me. I relate, perhaps far too much, to the Pink song "Don't Let Me Get Me":

"I am my own worst enemy . . . it's bad when you annoy yourself."

The lyrics speak to me. At ear-splitting decibels. I can hear it so loud in my head, I'm sure I am going off the rails on a crazy train. (But that's a whole other song . . .) It is in these moments of cerebral chaos that I retreat. To my two steadfast companions. My journal, where the only noise is the faint scrawl of my pencil across paper. I am free to spill my thoughts and feelings without fear of reproach or judgment. I can say anything, I can purge my inner havoc and embrace my own shortcomings.

Or I retreat to music, where the internal noise is drowned out by the soundtrack to my chaos. The velvety lilt of Karen Carpenter or the power scream of Rob Halford. The gravel swoon of Rod Stewart or the chill-inducing Ann Wilson. Like the warmth of finely aged whiskey washing over me, I am able to relax. To forget the craziness of life. I can step off of the carousel that spins in my mind, if only temporarily.

In these moments when I allow my life to spin like an out-of-control carnival ride, I strive to find refuge, to find comfort and sanity. I spin until I feel sick to my stomach, my head dizzy and begging to slow down. The wheels underneath me going much faster than my soul can tolerate, and I just need to stop . . .

"Cuz I'm a hazard to myself . . ." (Lyric by Pink.)

VALERIE JENSEN, LAS VEGAS

57

Valerie's stirring description of cerebral chaos being quelled by the faint scrawl of her pencil screams as loud as Pink's lyrics.

III

Touched by Beauty

Nichole Jaymes has been coming to my L.A. workshops for almost seven years, so you will find several of her class assignments in these pages. Her idea here about being plugged into something reminds me of how I feel when I gaze upon Van Gogh's living paintings or read Whitman, even down to his idea of beauty being orgasmic.

DESCRIBE THE FEELING YOU GET FROM YOUR FAVORITE FORM OF ART.

I cannot narrow down to one form of art. All works of art affect the depths of me. They make me feel ancient and ethereal all at once. I feel connected to the pulsing blood of this world but also above and beyond it. My favorite art is why I know God is real. A mentor of mine once repeated a piece of wisdom his father had given him: "We create because we were created."

I would wither and die without art. My body might survive, but I don't even know if that much is true. Art exists to plug us in to something. When I feel absolutely alone in my thoughts and emotions, certain that nobody on the planet understands what's raging in my brain and soul, I throw on a Jackson Browne record and I feel less solitary because this twenty-three-year-old kid with beautiful hair sang about this feeling forty years ago. When I kneel on the ground sighing with agony reading Heathcliff's tortured cry, "I cannot live without my life! I cannot live without my soul!" I understand that, nearly two hundred years ago, a twenty-something spinster on a bleak English moor spilled more heart and pain, visceral emotion and deathless torture out of her ink pen and onto a blank page than I will ever have the power to understand.

And so it is in every form of art. Life, as the philosopher said, is nasty, brutish and short. But humans strive for heaven. And so we take whatever horrible, limited, inept materials we are given—experiences, emotions, pains, physical flaws, diseases, urges, physical functions—and we render them exquisitely into these polished bits of orgasmic beauty.

NICHOLE JAYMES, LOS ANGELES

I was touched by this piece by Nichole because I have long believed that art is a living thing: the soul of the artist coming alive within the observer, the listener or the reader, which wakes our own sleepy muse.

We will revisit these themes in later chapters, but let's move along with a few more prompts about who you believe you are today. Perhaps you'll discover that some of your most knotty, baffling problems will be solved as you go through these assignments. By the time you've gone through this book, you may discover you are someone else entirely!

DO YOU HAVE A CREATIVE OUTLET THAT GIVES YOU JOY?

DO YOU COLLECT ANYTHING?

DO YOU PLAY OR HAVE YOU EVER PLAYED A MUSICAL INSTRUMENT?

DO YOU CONSIDER YOURSELF TO BE A FUNNY PERSON?

DO YOU HAVE A GOOD SENSE OF HUMOR?

WHAT MAKES YOU LAUGH?

DESCRIBE WHAT TRIGGERED YOUR HEARTIEST LAUGH EVER.

I'm going to have to embarrass myself, and fess up, but since I still crack up whenever I think of this particular incident, here goes:

I have never been one who shares the bathroom and what goes on in there with my significant others. Certain everyday bodily functions are just not romantic and I like to keep romance wildly alive for as long as possible. My boyfriend at the time, Mike, was spending the weekend with me in my cozy dark bedroom, and we were snoozing away contentedly early in the predawn morning. Unfortunately I was dreaming that I was in my cozy bed alone, and released a powerful, long, noisy blast of wind. Ooooops. In my sleepy haze I reached my hand over to the other side of the bed, and uh-oh, Mike was definitely there next to me. I held my breath for a moment. Had that unmistakable blast jarred him from his usual deep slumber? Please no. Slowly he rolled over. "And top of the morning to you!" he exclaimed. Oh dear. Oh my. How could he come up with such a spectacular one-liner from a dead sleep, I wondered, before apologizing and trying to explain that I'd been all alone in my dreams. As I blathered on and on, he started laughing and couldn't stop. Soon my exhortations turned to hysteria and we laughed so hard for so long that tears streamed down our faces. We became unhinged. Apoplectic. We roared for at least thirty minutes, and howled about it many times that day. Maybe you had to have been there to grasp the humor, but I'm really glad you weren't! And top of the morning to you!

PAMELA DES BARRES

IV

Fess Up to Your Flaws

When I am on the road teaching, I hold all my classes at the home of one of my students and, of course, comp her workshop for opening her heart and hearth to such a diverse group of women. I adore all my hostesses and so appreciate their generosity. Linda hosts my Chicago workshops at her two-story, hundred-year-old home in Wicker Park. She has a handsome, creative spouse and a talented musician son, both of whom help me haul my gigantic packed suitcases up the grand old stairs when I come to stay. Besides being beautifully written, Linda's piece is chock-full of self-awareness and great advice!

WHAT ARE MY ATTRIBUTES AND/OR GIFTS AND HOW DO THEY AFFECT MY LIFE AND THE LIVES OF OTHERS?

I am an infinitely patient person who understands how to listen. These attributes make me a good friend, have probably helped me be a stronger mother and have had a lot to do with the duration of my marriage. I can sit and wait while others spew their anger and listen carefully for what's really motivating the spew. Many times it is not what the spewer originally thought and by the time we are done talking, due to me listening and choosing my words carefully, the anger is gone and a new door to sanity is opened.

During the countless moments of uncertainty that dog any mother as she tries to do what's right for her kid, I decided to take my cues from my son. While this sounds like a chapter heading from a What to Expect *book, it is easier said than done. You have to truly squelch all your instincts toward correcting, steering, pushing—all the things mothers do that drive their children away—and decide to pay attention and actually listen. You have to exercise the kind of patience that keeps you glued to the kitchen chair as you listen to your one-year-old make his way down the stairs by himself for the first time. And you have to do that over and over again, listening patiently to discover the person who is unfolding, rather than taking the new cloth into your hands and trying to fashion the person you imagined him to be.*

As a wife, well, the examples are endless. Marriage is a constant state of compromise, but if you don't listen honestly, then you miss out on the whole person you are married to. Filling in the blanks with an idea of who he should be or an image of how your life together should look not only cheats you, but your partner, as well.

As a child my parents lived a lie and I was taught to sit quietly, not ask questions, and be a good girl. What I actually did was listen to everything, patiently gathering clues about what the hell was really going on. I often think I was born with my ear to the ground, waiting for the other shoe to drop. Sometimes, these strengths, like any others, can become weaknesses. Sometimes, I remain silent when I should speak up. I hesitate before acting and I lose. Whenever that happens, I tell myself to be patient, you'll get another chance, and to always, always listen for what others might not hear.

LINDA BECKSTROM, CHICAGO

Don't be afraid to write about something that's awkward or embarrassing. Shine a light on your perceived flaws. While writing the *whats*, you may figure out the *whys*. Leigh has been coming to my New York workshops on a train from Philadelphia for several years, and she is quiet and shy. But she comes and she writes. This courageous, confessional piece is an exquisite description of social anxiety.

DESCRIBE A TIME YOU FELT OVERWHELMED.

Fists clenched so tight you imagine if you were holding little lumps of coal, they would turn into sparkly diamonds. Feeling the blood in your veins beginning to heat up, then boil, threatening to blow like a manic pressure-cooker. Exhausted. Spent. Mind-circling frenzy. Gyroscopic swirls. Let's just hope we don't lose our lunch here. Hold on, pull up, grab the reins or there will be a crash. Can't think. Can't process. No progress. Back against the wall, beginning to fall. Too much to handle. Not strong enough to figure it out, work it out. Not going to make it to that finish line today. Calgon, take me away! Can there just be an end to this day? Flailing about. Put a hook in me and fish me out.

LEIGH BUCK, NEW YORK

DESCRIBE A TIME YOU FELT COMPLETELY ALONE.

When my Austin doll Kris began coming to workshops years ago, she was skeptical and uncertain, even though she had been keeping journals from the age of seven and had even been published a couple of times.

"I had to be shoved into that first session with you," she recalls, laughing. "I was walking down South Congress and saw a poster advertising the first Miz P writers' coven in Austin. In retrospect, I suspect the venue, a hip and happening hair salon, was the real hurdle for me. I was a frizzy, freckled Yankee girl from the projects and I felt maybe there'd be no place for me in some upscale Steel Magnolia biddy salon full of hot-rod honeys and expensive-smelling alternagirls. So incredibly glad I was wrong."

Alternagirls! Despite her misgivings, Kris hung in and took my Unruly Rules to heart. I've had to lay into her a couple of times for disobeying Rule Number Seven (No Qualifying). Before reading aloud the twelve-minute piece below, she said, "This sucks," and as you'll discover, she was wrong.

DESCRIBE A PAINFUL ANNIVERSARY.

It came in the fall and was all over by early summer.

A play in three acts most commonly called trimesters.

At a perennial campout with the kids, there were a lot of things I should've noticed. I was distracted, a little dizzy. I could barely lift my head while I listened to John and the kids finish packing our gear to leave. I had to nap, and I awoke suddenly, thickheaded and heavy, a bonnet string of drool already cooling on the side of my head. I knew right then as I crawled to my feet that I was pregnant and just as instantly knew that I wasn't going to do this. In the end my soul's scorecard might read: "she had one girl, one miscarriage, one boy and one she threw back." The abortion itself was early and "easy." It came the day after my oldest turned eleven. There was no question that I'd not be driving one more kid around Texas in a twelve-year-old Toyota with no AC in a town where I was struggling to start a career. No way, by any standard, that the blue vinyl pee-and-goldfish-cracker-stained ugly-ass third-hand car seat could accommodate one more listless, sticky kiddo whose mama couldn't give him the time he was born deserving. That day the next June when a baby would've matriculated into my arms, I would've taken off work if I'd been thinking. Normally due dates are just ballpark but not for a kid who didn't get picked to play. I work on a maternity unit. So I whispered endearments as I handed newborns over to their mamas and helped them to the breast all day. My brain was far away, though, tumbling through colors as scary as the boat ride scene in Willie Wonka *and as freeing as the fragile hot air balloon Dorothy lifts away on.*

KRIS KOVACH, AUSTIN

This piece is loaded with hot-button emotion and sublimely described, beginning with metaphor ("a play in three acts most commonly called trimesters") and ending with a simile ("as freeing as the fragile hot air balloon Dorothy lifts away on"). With such spot-on sensory description you can immediately see the "blue vinyl pee-and-goldfish-cracker-stained ugly-ass third-hand car seat," right? The poignancy expressed about her due date, from the scorecard to the ballpark, is simply heart shattering.

V

Nobody's Perfect!

Imagining how others see you can actually alter how you see yourself, usually for the best! I know it might be hard at first to extol your own virtues. So how about trying a few prompts by using another person's voice to extol your darn virtues? Imagine a best friend sizing you up. Seeing the best in you. It may free you up a bit to be more objective about yourself as you continue with the prompts. You can also do this assignment imagining how an acquaintance or even someone you've just met might view you.

Mary Grace is a spitfire college girl in New York. She relished this assignment and chose someone who must know her quite well.

DESCRIBE YOURSELF IN SOMEONE ELSE'S VOICE.

Oh, my God, I can't even handle Mary Grace. You have to meet her; she's like a Greek love child of Bettie Page and Courtney Love. When I first met her, she looked at me and was, like, "I love your Wednesday Addams dress, I can never find one myself." And I just knew: this bitch is fabulous.

And the best part about her is she's real. I wish I could ship her out to L.A., because I'm lacking people who are honest and genuine. Mary Grace is a hot mess, but she'll readily admit to it. We'll be rolling on the floor screaming to Hole, drunk on absinthe, and I know if she was late to work the next day she'd be, like, "Sorry I'm late, I was up all night screaming to Hole, drunk on absinthe."

She's my sister. Out of all the motherfuckers from Philly, she was the only one I could bring to my house, with my crazy screaming Is-raeli mother. Mary Grace just stays calm, has a lollipop and sits along for the ride. I don't think anyone would be able to handle it.

Dude, she really needs to come to L.A., but I get that she has to get her degree, so I'll wait it out till then. That bitch could rule the world, and she knows it, so I guess for now I'll take the West, she'll take the East, we'll meet in the middle to conquer all the lesser states.

You know you've found someone special when you'd be comfortable taking over the planet with them. And that's who Mary Grace is. She's a supervillain with a heart of gold, and I can't imagine life without her.

MARY GRACE GARIS, NEW YORK
(*in the voice of illustrator/designer/friend*, DANIELLA BATSHEVA)

It's a treat to imagine how our loved ones view us in a brighter light than we shine on ourselves. Usually it's easier for us to write about our irksome quirks, foibles or failings. We all have 'em!

DESCRIBE AN IDIOSYNCRASY.

I suppose people would call me obsessive-compulsive, but I've never been able to endure a label stuck to my shoe like a piece of somebody's old gum. Yes, I have to look under the bed at least three times before

I leave the house. I rarely admit this, and it's why I live alone, but I check the burners on the stove on an hourly basis. I make sure every surface I come in contact with is spick-and-span. My hands are chapped and inflamed, but I'm afraid rubber gloves will hold in the germs, or maybe get mildewed. I know how textbook it sounds, but you can never be too careful or too clean.

My family home (if you can call it that) was always dirty growing up. I could hear the rats skittering around inside the walls like the fingernails of a ghost when I tried to sleep at night. And it was infested with various types of insects that wriggled around in the sink drains, in the crevices, under the baseboards. The maggots even made our garbage move like a miniature ballet was going on amid the eggshells, rotting chicken bones and coffee grounds. It made me queasy and sick to my stomach, to the point of having to hold in the vomit, so I promised myself that my house would sparkle and shine.

If anyone visits they have to remove their shoes, of course, and I don't understand how anyone could wear shoes in the house. All that invisible gunk pulsating on their soles could wind up in their food, for godsakes!

I know there's medication for my type of disorder, but I don't really want to change. I believe cleanliness is next to godliness even though I don't believe in God.

CARINA GRANT, ATLANTA

Whoa! Quite an unabashed shot of self-awareness from Carina. And a few crackerjack similes to boot! I feel so good that the women in my workshops feel comfortable enough to share their gremlins, even though the image of a maggot ballet is almost too picturesque for me! Ewwwww. Needless to say, Carina got noticed and appreciated in our Atlanta workshop. She's now hard at work on *Why Can't You See Me?*, a book she hopes will shake up and wake up the self-involved strangers beside us.

LET IT BLEED

DESCRIBE A TIME YOU CHICKENED OUT.

WHAT WAS THE BIGGEST CHANCE YOU EVER TOOK?

WHAT'S THE WORST THING YOU'VE EVER DONE?

As Alice in Wonderland observes, "if you drink from a bottle marked 'poison,' it is almost certain to disagree with you, sooner or later."

WRITE ABOUT A TIME YOU DRANK THE POISON (DID SOMETHING YOU KNEW WAS BAD FOR YOU).

Leashya cannily likened the poison to a toxic relationship. We've all been there.

There he was with a tag that read, "Drink me." And there I was with enough self-loathing and guilt to say, "Bottoms up." I cried on my wedding day. I found a small sliver of relief in reminding myself that I was living in Nevada, where dissolving a marriage is as quick and easy as legalized prostitution. I held my nose and swallowed. "I do." I wretched. I swallowed more. It was my penance for crimes unspeakable. My guilt tasted far more bitter than his poison . . . at first.

I stayed until the toxins numbed my limbs, took my voice and rendered me nearly lifeless. And then I stopped. Just before it was all too late. Not another drop. Time to Detox—Detach—Divorce. Since then I'm never without my skull-and-crossbones warning labels to slap on any potentially deadly potion.

LEASHYA FITZPATRICK MUNYON, AUSTIN, TEXAS

Bambi Conway is one of my L.A. writers and has been coming to class for seven years. She played bass in an all-doll rockin' band, the Pandoras, in the '80s, and no matter what she writes about, it is always tinged with twisted humor. I wish you could hear her read! She should be a comedian! Don't ever be afraid to bonk your own funny bone!

WHAT IS ONE RULE YOU WILL NEVER BREAK?

I love to break rules, but I hate to hurt people. Especially children. So I will never be a child molester. Child molesting is worse than murder! So maybe I should pick something else because that is something obviously none of us will do.

I will also never rob anyone. I will not go to the bank or 7-Eleven with a fake or real gun and hold them up. The worst thing I did at 7-Eleven was steal a beer at three a.m. when I was drunk in my early twenties. Then we prank-called the guy who worked at 7-Eleven because he caught us before we got away with the beer.

I will never be a peeping Tom or whatever the name they have for a woman who peeps. Not that I am not curious enough to see whatever is going on, but I am afraid of getting caught. I am also not going to be a flasher. Once a guy flashed me when I was a little kid. He drove up and flashed me and my friend and we first thought it was a little baby pig. The last time I was flashed I laughed quite a bit and the flasher guy seemed disappointed. Also I'm not going to "Show my tits" no matter how much they chant at the bar. I'm just too old and too self-conscious to do that. One time I streaked during the '70s during the streaking phase but it was with friends at the beach at night. So that doesn't really count. And mutually skinny dipping at a private pool isn't flashing either.

I am not going to rape anyone either. Your boyfriend saying "Rape me" doesn't count as real rape. I am making a joke about rape, which is against the rules, but those are the rules I like to break.

69

I'm not going to commit arson, unless it was truly an accident, which I don't think technically counts as arson. I would be very remorseful if I did burn your house down.

BAMBI CONWAY, LOS ANGELES

Procrastination can make you miserable, so if you've been putting off your writing, boss yourself around a little! (But don't beat yourself up!) If you're feeling stuck, take a walk, read or listen to an audiobook for a while, meditate or write a letter to a friend to get the flow going. If you *have* been doing three of these prompts daily for two weeks, look what you've accomplished! Keep it up! It'll make you feel so goooood!

Writing your life is indeed cathartic therapy, but have you asked yourself *why* you want to write a memoir? For healing? To inspire others? To share lessons learned? To set the record straight? Hopefully to give back, and not to *get* back at anyone. That might create a big fat boomerang, right back atcha! You don't need to embellish the truth either. I was careful not to tell anybody's truth but my own, and I recommend not trying to figure someone out on the page, what their motives might have been, or speculate about what they were thinking. Do we ever really know what's going on in someone's cluttered mind? Just the facts, ma'am! Hopefully you are writing to uplift and make peace with yourself, and to make people happy that they came across your book!

If you're having any doubts about your process at this point, here's what Stephen King, in *On Writing*, says about the purpose of it:

> *Writing isn't about making money, getting famous, getting dates, getting laid, or making friends. In the end, it's about enriching the lives of those who will read your work, and enriching your own life, as well. It's about getting up, getting well, and getting over. Getting happy, okay? Getting happy.*

Hopefully your writing *is* getting you happy. Even if you don't find that you're happy writing, I guarantee you will be happy you've *written*. But whether you're feeling up or down or even *fed* up or *let* down about the writing process, it is vital to ask yourself the all-important "why." Hence this merry little prompt!

WHAT DO YOU HOPE TO ACCOMPLISH BY WRITING YOUR MEMOIR?

LET IT BLEED

CHAPTER SIX

I

Childhood Living

Now that your writing is humming right along, let's get a little more chronological. (Remember I mentioned that's how I wrote my own memoirs.) At this point, it makes sense to reexperience your life in sequential order, so one memory will easily lead to another. Feel yourself go way back, and let whatever pops to mind about your childhood, family and growing up pour out onto the page. See, feel, taste, touch and hear. You will find that each phase of life or self-discovery is revealing in its own quirky way. There's a lesson in everything we've experienced, and the "Ah! I get it!" moments will astound you, and compassionate understanding often follows.

So let's begin at your very beginning. This single prompt inspired two recollections of pleasant first memories from the tender age of four, but that isn't always the case. Go with whatever comes up for you.

WHAT IS YOUR EARLIEST MEMORY?

I'm walking down a hallway into a bedroom. I look up at my mom and she has excitement in her face, as if she's waiting for my assessment of the situation.

"Is this our house, Mama?" I ask her, inquisitive four-year-old that I am. It is a legitimate question, as we had lived all over the

place at that point. Grandma's place had been "our" place up until that moment. My mother had left the man I knew as my father. "Separation" and "divorce" were not words I knew or understood. My mother was a stay-at-home mom with little job training and little formal education. She could not get a job, a car or even a place of her own.

The expectancy and excitement on her face was the expression of defying the odds; a recurring theme in our lives, I would later come to learn. "Yes," she answered. "This is our house now."

I mulled this over (in my far too smart for a four-year-old mind). It was a single-wide trailer with two bedrooms, and an ever-increasing number of occupants, but to me it seemed like a palace. I took off my tiny Tom and Jerry sandals (mine and my brother's favorite cartoon) and placed them under the bed.

I was later informed by my mother that this simple action made her truly hopeful for the first time. She felt that as long as she had a place for her baby to put her shoes at night, maybe everything would be alright after all.

I remember this so vividly that the memory still visits me in my dreams these many years later. Walking into that bedroom and placing my shoes under the bed signified a turning point. No more moving around, no more staying with relatives and their kids, who were sometimes mean to me and my brother. We were home. Finally. We were home.

YOLANDA VICKERS, AUSTIN

Can't you just picture those tiny Tom and Jerry shoes under the bed? Images like this can play the reader's heartstrings like a Stratocaster.

Monica was the same age as Yolanda when a certain dreamy rock god helped her settle into preschool.

I was four years old. First day of day care. I cried each day my mom dropped me off. I'd never been around other little kids and didn't know what to do. I wanted to be with Mom, at home, where we'd play Elvis records. My mom was a huge Elvis fan and once broke an ankle hurtling over concert seats trying to get close to him. I was born with his voice all around me.

La Petite Academy had a huge playground. All the teachers tried to push me outside to socialize, but I wouldn't go. They tried to bribe me with candy. I said no. Kool-Aid. No. Toys. No. Nothing worked. Even when the kids came in to watch cartoons, I wouldn't participate. After a week or two of my drama, they told my mom that I was unable to socialize with other children and they didn't have the staff to keep me separated. Mom needed to find a way to get me into the mix.

My first significant memory was when my mother walked with me to the playground and pointed at the big brown apartment complex behind the fence. "See that one? On the second level? Elvis lives there."

That was all it took. I was outside playing, showing all the kids the King's abode. Soon I was even discussing music with them: "Do you like Elvis or Elton better?" The Elton kids were eventually banned to the other side of the playground by Yours Truly. But I made lots of friends and, to this day, my best friends are Elvis fans. I believed Elvis lived in that run-down old apartment building for years. It's still there if you want to drop by: Thirty-First and Sheridan in Tulsa, Oklahoma. Maybe that's where Elvis has been hiding all these years.

MONICA WOOTEN, NEW YORK

Oftentimes our first flash from the past involves some kind of trauma and writing it down can feel strangely purifying. My earliest memory is so sorrowful I still view the scene mostly from above. Since I've often had this vision of tiny little me and an insurmountable staircase, here goes:

I couldn't have been more than a bit over two years old, but I can still see the scene like an omnipotent observer looking down at this little toddler in a pressed cotton dress, her ashy, straight blond hair in barrettes, standing plaintively at the bottom of a tall staircase, looking up at her beautiful parents, arguing loudly at the top of the stairs. I had never experienced this scary feeling before, and was confused. Why were they mad at each other? Or were they mad at me? What had I done? It was total fear and shock and my first feeling of being unsafe. That anything could happen if my adored mama and daddy could speak to each other in this way. They didn't notice me but I can see this scenario like an old-time movie that's on constant replay. I couldn't have been standing there long because my dear aunt Bert snatched me up and whisked me off, probably never realizing that the image of my parents' heated squabbling would stay with me forever.

Decades later, after my daddy's death, my mother revealed that he had just found out she was romantically involved with his sister's husband and they had fallen in love. After that argument he dashed down those same stairs and burst out the door, heading for his sister's house, where he almost beat his brother-in-law to death.

PAMELA DES BARRES

The following exercise takes my students in all kinds of directions. From a description of their birth to a secret their grandmother kept to tales of how their parents met.

WHERE ARE YOU FROM?

I fell from the sky and landed exactly where I was supposed to—right after the honeymoon and the first mortgage and right before my dad's next job and my sister.

LET IT BLEED

I came from the lady with the big hair, who thought that a pitcher of martinis was a good way to move the labor along, and the guy with the big ears, who was a military policeman in the Tropic Thunder division in Korea. The army discovered pretty quickly that he liked to be the bosser, not the bossee, and decided to make the most of it. He came from the poor Irish immigrant who would hand over fifteen cents to his wife every Friday and drink the rest. The big-hair lady came from the Polish orphan girl who was adopted by a couple who could not have children, but then miraculously had eight and now had a babysitter. She would later marry the German butcher who escaped the war and then one by one brought his brothers, sisters, cousins, nieces and nephews over to their home before he accidentally cut off his leg.

I came home in a big car with no airbags, seat belts or car seat to a home with no smoke detector or kid-proof corners, where I played with keys and ate food off the floor.

KARI MCGLINNEN, CHICAGO

The same prompt inspired Nichole's twelve-minute poetic missive below. She's barely thirty. You can do it too.

> I am from the yellow house beneath the yellow sun
> From the California cradle of the Bay—you know the one
> I'm from the sun kissed mid-cent-mod of homes tucked in
>   those hills,
> I've never been inside them, but I know I'm from them still.
>
> I'm from the sound of Neil and Joni coming through
>   the wall,
> When my mom looked out from her backyard and they
>   were who she saw

I'm teardrops flowing from the eyes my auntie clenched
    so tight
While Moody Blues sang "White Satin" in her headphones
    all night

I'm spores beneath a green fern frond in Mount Hood's
    primal air;
I'm leprechauns amidst the mosses I was sure were there.
I'm scent of pine and sound of stream and raven, wolf,
    and bird,
I'm brick and river, burlap bags, I'm coffee and I'm dirt

I'm backs of cars and highway nights, the boom box on my chest
I'm anxious, nervous hopes of parents hoping this is best
I'm truck stop diners, no bedtimes, I'm biscuits, stars, and gas
I'm every golden flower I see as our tired wheels go past

I'm all my father's failings and I'm all my mother's fears
I am those things ingrained in me from years and years
    and years
I am the long dark hair my best friend wore the day we met
I'm still her purring kitten toy; I'm Popsicles we'd get

I'm upstate and I'm downstate; I'm the Sagamore hotel
I am the biting six-month cold, the frozen burning hell
I am the twisted miniblind that's hanging in the tree
At the site where once I stood so high, that tower, too, was me

I am this room, I am this stool, the ceiling and the floor
I'm everyone who's cried in here, who's breathed in
    here before

I'll always be the wallpaper, absorbing all this jazz
Before I was all this, it had been me, it always has.

NICHOLE JAYMES, LOS ANGELES

**RECALL A HAPPY MEMORABLE EARLY CHILDHOOD MOMENT.
KEEP IT UP. WRITE SEVERAL OF THESE.**

*I am a little girl, maybe three, standing in sunlight, the light tickling
my legs, the toastie—my silky soft blanket—in my hand, sucking my
thumb, that good feeling. With the toastie I tickle my face—I am
naked in the warm sun outside my house. It is lovely. I am warm and
happy. The world is at peace. I am loved. I feel good.*

*Dancing for my dad: I am in a white nightgown edged with
purple. It is graceful and I swirl. The whole family is watching as I
dance for them. It is just a little bit sexual. Maybe it is sensual. I am
young, but no longer a toddler.*

*Going to St. Peter's in Rome: I remember the gold everywhere:
gold on the walls, gold on the chairs, scrolls of gold. All I could think
about was how the Church spent all this money on gold for themselves
and how the poor people must have been suffering. The injustice of it
galled me. It still does. I wrote a poem about it. I was nine.*

*And I remember being very small. Maybe four. My mother is
standing at the sink. She is much taller than me, and I pull at her
apron strings—somehow, saying, "Mommy! Mommy! Pay attention
to me!" But she is too busy washing dishes.*

CAMILLA SALY, NEW YORK

Camilla's piece is so tactile—warm sunlight, thumb sucking, the silky
blanket, the sensual dance, too much gold at St. Peter's—you can almost
touch her words.

II

We Are Family

Let's continue to explore your childhood by looking at the people, places and activities that made the most impact throughout your young life. Imagine your family growing up, starting with your mom and dad (or whoever your parental figures were). Close your eyes and picture what they looked like when you were very small. How they dressed. How they spoke. What it was like to sit down at the dinner table. This section will help you to understand how the scenarios and situations you experienced growing up shaped who you became. It's time to find out where the history of you began.

WERE YOU RAISED WITH BOTH PARENTS? HOW DID THIS AFFECT YOU?

DO YOU KNOW HOW YOUR PARENTS MET?

DID YOUR PARENTS TELL YOU THEY LOVED YOU? HOW DID THEY SHOW THEIR LOVE?

HOW WERE YOU DISCIPLINED?

HOW WERE YOU TOLD ABOUT THE FACTS OF LIFE?

At eighteen, Beca is my youngest student. She's preparing for college, and this piece is from her second set of workshops in the tiny town of Fairmount, Indiana.

"Saying good night to my parents shouldn't be a chore," I thought as I walked into their room. My siblings were asleep, or pretending to be. You could never sleep once the yelling started. I reminded myself that down deep and individually, my parents had redeeming qualities, and the fact that my mom had cheated on my dad or that my dad had trapped my mom in a loveless marriage with a child (yours truly) would not change those qualities. So I opened the door and walked into the middle of a game of word tennis. The loud Portuguese bounced to and fro, making the room vibrate, especially when an extra ball was thrown in and they'd both shout at once. I didn't know the language, but I understood the tone like I'd been born speaking it. No one would win this game, so I walked over to my mom, laid my head in her lap, and her hands went to work on my hair, brushing through a knot that always seemed to exist. This loving motion was oddly placed in such a scene. The eye of the storm was me, but no one seemed to take notice as the harsh words were exchanged. In my head I began to shout at my mom for breaking my dad. I yelled at my dad for trapping my mom. There would be no winner that night or any other, so I didn't feel bad for the silent words I hurled. They were cruel, they were hurtful, and they were never to be said. "What did you want, sweetheart?" My mom's voice raised several octaves as if the higher her voice got, the less the situation would hurt. "Oh, nothing. I'm just about to sleep," I lied through a smile, hugged each of them, then got in bed and cried to Joan Baez until I was finally in the safety of my dreams.

BECA STOCKMAN, FAIRMOUNT, INDIANA

The description of the argument between Beca's parents being played as a game, insults being lobbed back and forth like a ball, made me understand why she felt she *was* the eye of the storm, caught in the middle of the hurricane of words.

Imagining yourself at different ages might change the point of view you have about your folks. It's fascinating what insights you can gain from slipping into your own childhood mind.

WRITE ABOUT YOUR PARENTS (OR THE PEOPLE WHO RAISED YOU) IN THE VOICE OF YOURSELF AT TEN YEARS OLD.

IF YOU HAVE SIBLINGS, HOW DID YOU GET ALONG GROWING UP?

I met my goddaughter, Polly Parsons, when she was not quite a year and a half old. At that time, her mother was a delicate, feisty flower, a loving mom who slowly lost herself when Gram Parsons left her behind and then died for real. She would never be able to get him back, and her spirit shattered.

Polly and her younger sister were neglected and ignored, so at age seven, Polly became her sister's caretaker. She had never written creatively before coming to my workshops, but Polly surprised herself and all of her writing companions with her evocative, dreamlike descriptions.

Drawn to her glow, the wooden planks creak under my soles as I pad through the dark, dank wetness of the night. The moths flicker around the lantern's fire as I stop at my mother's bedroom. The smell of red wine seeps down the faded wallpaper flowers, holding years of stories. I peek inside and see her silhouette through her muslin gown. I am accustomed to the fact that my mother glows in the moonlight.

My tiny sister glows as well. When I come to her room, I slowly slide my hand to the doorknob. I am welcomed by the smell of

warm milk and a faint waft of lilac. Gently I step forward and touch the buttery caress of her skin. Her lips in the dim light are the color of dark blood and pinpricks. The pale blue of her veins shines through the alabaster transparency of her child's skin, not yet slapped. Or taught a lesson. A child myself, I bend down to save her and vow in that moment to survive so I can protect her. To implant her in the muscle tissue of my heart and to never let her go.

POLLY PARSONS, AUSTIN

ARE YOU CLOSE WITH YOUR SIBLINGS NOW?

IF YOU GREW UP AS AN ONLY CHILD, HOW DID IT DIFFER FROM YOUR FRIENDS' UPBRINGING?

DID YOU KNOW YOUR GRANDPARENTS? AUNTS AND UNCLES? DESCRIBE A SPECIAL MEMORY WITH EACH.

III

My Hometown

We've looked at the people. Let's look at the places. If you can, take a trip back to your old neighborhood. When I was working on *Band*, I drove around Reseda, stopping in front of my old house on Jamieson Avenue. The chain-link fence my dad put up decades earlier was rusty and sagging, but still stood. The mini palm tree my mom planted now towered high above the house. When I knocked on my old front door, the people were kind enough to let me step briefly inside my long-lost bedroom, and I was flooded with a myriad of tangled emotions.

DESCRIBE YOUR CHILDHOOD BEDROOM(S).

DESCRIBE THE NEIGHBORHOOD (OR MOST MEMORABLE ONE) YOU GREW UP IN.

DID YOU MOVE AROUND A LOT, OR WERE YOU RAISED IN ONE HOME? HOW DID THAT AFFECT YOU?

One of my few homes away from home is the tiny town of Fairmount, Indiana. I've been spending several weeks a year in the small town of 2,500 where James Dean was born, raised and buried. (Yes, I take my lifelong idol-worship seriously!) In fact, much of this book was written as I sat in front of my computer, watching snowflakes cover the trees through the picture window of the perfectly fifties house I rented to "get away from it all."

I had long dreamed of making the pilgrimage to the Indiana flatlands, and on my first trip to Fairmount, I was welcomed like a long-lost sister by Dave Loehr, who runs the James Dean Gallery, and his partner, Lenny Prussack. In fact, I have my own little room upstairs, and stay at the gallery during all the annual Dean events. Lenny is my dance partner every September at the Dean Fest, and we rock it out to Elvis, Dion and Bill Haley and the Comets. We even came in first place a couple of times!

When I held my first writing class at the gallery, my Brothers-in-Dean wanted to participate, so, ever since, I have invited men to that particular workshop.

Recently, a stern-looking fellow in his midsixties turned up at the door amid a howling storm, and even though he claimed he'd never written anything before, he proceeded to blow our minds with his sparse, elegiac

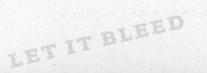

83

LET IT BLEED

description of a place he knows so well. Notice how he uses all five senses as he takes us on this tour. The last line is a stunner.

I would not feel lost in my hometown if I were suddenly blind. Fairmount is in Indiana and fits on a grid that is quite predictable and flat. The curbs here and there are not too high after years of layers of asphalt that make it all very safe to travel. The smells of the trees, cars, cat feces and burning trash would guide me because I see what I smell before I see it for real. The sounds of the wind in the trees would tell me where I was because I've been there many times and have heard those monsters before. I could follow the train tracks from North to South and stop at Playacres Park, remembering the old ruins and the woods that have long been gone.

A glass furnace exploded and green glass was embedded in the concrete chunks. We imagined that the glass was jewels. No eyes really needed now; it's gone anyway and so are we.

D. E. HIPSKIND, FAIRMOUNT, INDIANA

DESCRIBE YOUR HOMETOWN.

DO YOU STILL LIVE IN THE CITY WHERE YOU GREW UP? IF NOT, HOW DID YOU CHOOSE WHERE TO LIVE NOW?

WAS YOUR FAMILY FINANCIALLY COMFORTABLE GROWING UP OR WERE THERE DIFFICULT TIMES?

WAS THERE ANOTHER CULTURE IN YOUR HOUSE GROWING UP?

WHAT WAS DINNERTIME LIKE IN YOUR HOUSEHOLD?

Nadine has been coming to my L.A. workshops for several years and whenever I give an assignment about childhood, she reads her pieces in her little kid voice, and we are always charmed and delighted by her uncanny recall of details and emotions. We are also immediately sucked in because she writes as if her stories are taking place *now*. She studied acting with Lee Strasberg for years and his "sense memory" exercises have served her well with her writing also!

I never know if dinner is going to be good or awful. But on Sunday night, Farmer John's show Polka Parade with Dick Sinclair *comes on. The first song is "There Is a Tavern in the Town" and those men in the little Peter Pan hats and shorts are so cute. The lucky people on the show get to polka. The ladies have big puffy sleeves and really full skirts. The men twirl and twirl them with their arms out to hold on to.*

I always make sure I have on one of my fullest dress-up skirts when it's Polka Parade night. One that's excellent for twirling has black velvet on top with a full taffeta skirt on the bottom. As soon as the polka starts, I just can't help it, I have to jump right up and polka all around the room. I know some of the words so I can sing along too. I just get so excited when I polka. I really could polka all day long. I wish I really could.

Sometimes when I jump up in the middle of eating I might spill my milk a little bit, but I don't mean to; I just have to stomp and kick to the music just right and twirl like the ladies on TV. It makes me happy, it really does.

But then my mommy gets annoyed and tells me to sit down and finish my dinner, then I can polka.

But my daddy gets even more annoyed, and I must have spilled a lot, because he says, "I'm gonna give you such a poach in tuchas if you don't sit down right now, little girl!" He grabs my arm and pulls me down in the chair so hard I know he is serious. When my parents speak in Yiddish they are extra mad! He says if I get up again ever during dinner I'm going to be in t-r-o-u-b-l-e.

LET IT BLEED

It's going to be very hard to sit still, but I know if I dance too much polka after I eat I get a tummy ache on the side. Oh well, I can still watch the program, and sometimes we get to eat Farmer John's hot dogs when the show is on. My mommy boils them in a pot so they don't really taste the same, but it's a lot better than liver.

NADINE BASS, SANTA MONICA

DID YOUR FAMILY TAKE TRIPS WHEN YOU WERE A KID?

DESCRIBE A SHOPPING TRIP WITH ONE OF YOUR PARENTS.

WERE YOU RAISED WITH ANY FAMILY TRADITIONS?

HOW WERE THE HOLIDAYS AND BIRTHDAYS CELEBRATED AT YOUR HOUSE?

DESCRIBE A FAVORITE CHILDHOOD HOLIDAY AND BIRTHDAY.

DESCRIBE THE WORST HOLIDAY OR BIRTHDAY MEMORY.

HOW DO YOU USUALLY CELEBRATE YOUR BIRTHDAY NOW?

WHAT HOLIDAYS DO YOU CELEBRATE NOW?

WHAT IS YOUR FAVORITE HOLIDAY? LEAST FAVORITE HOLIDAY?

WHAT WERE YOUR CHILDHOOD CHORES?

DESCRIBE A MEMORABLE FAMILY EVENT.

He was remarkable in his Panama hat, all six feet three, dressed in white. My father's high school buddy stood at our front door. He and his shadow took up the entire porch. "C'mon," he said. "You've got to come to my house, I have a surprise."

My parents politely refused, still wearing frowns from their last argument. He opened the screen door and reached our living room in one easy step. He plopped down on our couch, crossing his daddy long legs. "I'm not leaving until you come."

Was he drunk? I watched my parents fidget through their thoughts. They couldn't go, they said. Dad had to fill out inventory reports. Mom had dinner dishes waiting in the sink.

"I'll wait," he said. And tipped his hat down over his eyes.

Heaved sighs. Mom took off her apron, Dad grabbed his keys. The tall man herded us all out of the house and into our own car, where we followed him to his house a few miles away. My brother and I braced ourselves in silence, listening to our parents bicker in the front seat.

"What nerve he has!"

"A real nutcase!"

"What will his wife think of us all barging in like this just after dinner! It's insane! Why didn't you put your foot down?"

"Because you always complain we never go anywhere. You always complain . . ."

Backpedaling through the argument they'd had all morning and the night before and the night before that. But the crazy man in the Panama hat couldn't possibly know that. Could he? They were going to get divorced. It was just a matter of time.

His smile stretched to all corners of his face as he hurried us up the walk to his house. "Get ready! You've got to do it! Promise me you'll do it!"

"Do what?" my parents asked, thinking he'd gone mad. He ushered us into the living room where his wife and two kids waited.

In the middle of the room, a bamboo stick hung horizontal between two notched bamboo poles.

"The limbo!" he shouted. "Do the limbo!"

He turned up the record player and a chorus of deep voices and bongos filled the room. He sang along. "Bend down backward, like this." His gangly figure bent halfway back. "How low can you go?!" Then he swung his arms and scooted under the stick like an inside-out upside-down spider. He pulled me over to the stick. "Your turn."

I shyly bent a little backward, but at the last minute, ducked forward and scooted under it. My brother flung out his arms and legs in silly gestures as he rolled under it.

"No, no, only your feet can touch the ground." He turned to my parents. "How low can you go?"

I clenched inside. My brother folded his arms around his stomach. They wouldn't do it. They didn't play games. Not like this. Didn't their old friend know this about them? He acted like he expected them to bend and stretch and bounce to the beat of the bongos. My parents! I felt sorry for him. Embarrassed. My jaw tightened. I had to save him from this hopeless charade.

I began shoving my brother toward the stick, tickling and pinching him, knowing he would pinch me back and cause a scene that would give my parents an excuse for not doing the limbo. An acceptable explanation for their tight lips and steely eyes. My father walked over to us. Would he spank us here? But then . . . he bent down backward. I watched wide-eyed as he squiggled his small, wiry body under the stick, snapping his fingers with each beat of the bongos. And la-la singing! I shot a glance at my mom. Bubbles of laughter floated from her throat. A glimmer of light stood in her eyes. Then . . . she hiked up her skirt and bent backward, shifting her hips this way, and her

bosom that way, until she too was under the stick. Shimmying up, she
skipped over to my father's side.

My jaw relaxed. My brother's arms dropped to his sides. We stood
there watching our parents, both of them smiling and looking at each
other with the sweetness of pineapples on their lips.

CHERA THOMPSON, NEW YORK

The reason this piece works so well is that this incident was completely
out of character for this family. In just twelve minutes of writing we can feel
the teeming dysfunction and the discomfort gradually building, so when
the tension breaks in such a seemingly silly way, it's a fantastic surprise!

Write up several memorable family events yourself, and see what these
recollections churn up.

IN OUR FAMILY, WE NEVER TALKED ABOUT . . .

Love, sex, romance, passion, inebriation.

We never talked about these things, but I'd ask my mom privately
at various stages of growth until I started experiencing glimmers, at
which point inebriation silenced my tongue. And as far as sex goes, it
means first base plus tongue, right? Or is that second base?

There was no discussion of how my parents got together, how their
parents got together or how anyone who knew them met each other.
I was around all these random older unsexy people who read news-
papers in the morning in their PJs. They'd go out to eat a lot and go
on trips, but there was nothing that seemed to hold them together
except their addresses. There was lots of fighting and hollering, and I
knew I was never going to live with anyone for this reason.

My parents seemed to get together only because they were both al-
ready forty in the late '50s when there was something terribly wrong

89

if you weren't married. They thought they were too old to have kids, so when I arrived, the above subjects not mentioned didn't apply.

My mom told me that inebriation leads to addiction, sex causes unwanted children and disgrace for all involved, love is for friendship, romance and passion are fleeting and nothing to base your life on. Oh yes, and never ask out a boy; if he likes you, he'll call you.

NADINE BASS, LOS ANGELES

Luckily Nadine's subtle sense of humor shines through her traumatic teenage tales, turning her seemingly hopeless family life into a tragicomedy. She didn't come out unscathed, but by writing it all down, she's been able to stitch up some of those old wounds.

DID YOU BELONG TO ANY CLUBS OR ORGANIZATIONS, SUCH AS THE GIRL SCOUTS?

HOW DID YOU MEET YOUR BEST CHILDHOOD FRIEND?

WHAT IS A CHILDHOOD SECRET YOU KEPT?

DESCRIBE A CHILDHOOD TRAUMA THAT STILL REVERBERATES TODAY.

I met Roberta in the sixth grade and our friendship ended junior year. Back then the years seemed so long. When I ended our friendship little did I know how much I'd wish we'd stayed friends, despite her (and my) betrayals. Because friends are rare and time goes fast. But back then time seemed so slow and my standards were so high. The first time I saw Roberta at school she was laughing at something a cute boy said, and in her rich laugh I heard who I wanted to be. She wore straight-leg corduroy jeans and they fit her perfectly. She had a silver trench coat and long gold hair that waved down her back in movie-star animation. Sixth grade glamour! She had a mole on her cheek, a mark that some stoner boys would ridicule. Foxy stoner boys were so cruel, so sexy, Marlboro Reds sticking out of jean jackets as they mocked and made out with you, their bicycles and skateboards abandoned behind the gym. In sixth grade making out and getting high was still a grade away, and Roberta was roller-skating on Friday nights and eating ice cream at the parlor on Sundays. Blood on the walls after sex with a man twice her age came later, a laughing story told to virginal me with careless pride. I loved spending the night at Roberta's. Her parents were divorced like mine, but, unlike me, she was an only child so we had her apartment to ourselves, and our moms worked nights. She had a better stereo, and I loved the palette of her mom's style and uncluttered spaciousness. Everything was orange and creamy with wood accents, and polished wood floors under our bare feet. Roberta wanted to lose fifteen pounds. I wanted to lose fifty. Her flat tummy, long legs and small breasts appealed to me in their neat proportions. In seventh grade when she made the transition from roller girl to stoner girl, she started wearing dark denim bell-bottom jeans. They looked so good on her! I wished I could fit into them. I also wished I could fit in with her daring, sexual friends. Tanned and leisurely, they spent summer days painting their toenails red and getting high. Roberta left me for her wild friends, but we both knew I'd always be there when she came back. And I was. I learned all the words to Led Zeppelin songs in her absence. When we got back together I was Robert and she was Jimmy as we played air guitar and air microphone in sublime concert with their records. But at seventeen, I'd had enough. Enough of her laughing at the jokes her wild friends made at my expense, enough of the men

who chose her over me, enough of her accusing me of stealing her
clothes and money (which was true, but how could she think that of
me?). She came by to get those bell-bottom blue jeans, which I could
finally fit into thanks to a food plan and a floor plan (I had to lie on
the floor to get them on). "But what did I do?" she asked over the
phone when she got home. "You know," I replied. Roberta was be-
fuddled, as if being carried away by water, and there was an island
of silence. "No, I don't!" she said finally, her voice sounding so young
and far away. I was certain as I stayed ashore, then we said good-bye,
borne ceaselessly into the future without each other.

LUCRETIA TYE JASMINE, LOS ANGELES

Lucretia's piece took me back to the days when I felt "lesser than" many of my prettier, more popular peers, and the anguish it caused. And I love how she closes the story by taking apart the famous last line of *The Great Gatsby*: "So we beat on, boats against the current, borne back ceaselessly into the past." Referencing Fitzgerald's most memorable line in such a perceptive way adds an irrefutable dash of finality.

IV

School Days

WHAT SCARED YOU THE MOST AS A CHILD?

It's remarkable how ancient memories still bubble up when you commit to putting pen to paper (or fingers to keyboard), finally ready to relive your scariest moments and get the truth onto the page. It took me decades to get over this potboiler scenario.

My life had been exquisitely free from fears until my ninth summer. I had been a happy camper most of the time, doted on and shielded from harm by my attentive mother and big handsome daddy. But a conversation between my gabby aunt Edna and my mom ended that peaceful serene certainty in one swell foop.

It had been a long summery day of playing in my aunt Edna's overgrown yard in North Hollywood. Tiara Street, to be exact. One house just like the next. Even though it was only a few miles from my Reseda home, it always felt like a faraway place where I could make up scenarios that just couldn't happen in my own backyard. My chest hurt from what my mom said was "playing too hard," but was actually from breathing the tarnished toxic Valley air, so I collapsed on her lap and quickly fell halfway asleep. But my ears perked up when Aunt Edna started regaling my mom with a shocking tale about her day as the janitor at a local grade school.

During recess while all the kiddies were out on the yard frolicking, a man across the street came careening out of his front door, brandishing a shotgun. Right in front of the children, he held the gun to his head and pulled the trigger.

At this point in the story my mom whispered, "I don't want Pam to hear this," but Edna waved it off—"Awww, she's sound asleep, Margaret"—and went on to describe in colorful detail how the top of this fellow's head sailed through the air, landing atop the chain-link fence that encircled the playground, dripping blood and brains, as the rest of him collapsed in a heap on the sidewalk. And that's not all. Apparently a large black crow fluttered over and perched on the man's shiny pate as it wobbled precariously on the fence. And what had made this poor man turn the top of his head into a fleshy Frisbee?

"Oh, we found out later he had brain cancer. He was in agony and couldn't stand the pain for another minute."

Brain cancer. Cancer. My eyes were closed but I'd taken in every word, and trembled inside. What was cancer? Could children get it? Could it get me? The next day when I asked my mom if children could get this dreaded disease, I knew she silently cursed my chatty aunt. But always honest with me, my mama told me the big bad truth. It was rare, but yes, children could get cancer. And so, the Big C was my under-the-bed, hiding-in-the-closet boogey-monster for decades to come. The fear lingered like sticky smoke until I got it. And even though we wrestled and I beat it, I can still see the florid image of that long-ago fellow's shiny head spinning and twirling through the air as if I were still a ponytailed eight-year-old, pretending to be asleep on my mama's lap.

PAMELA DES BARRES

RECALL A LIFE-ALTERING MOMENT FROM YOUR CHILDHOOD.

HOW DID YOU GET YOUR FIRST PET?

ARE YOU A DOG OR A CAT PERSON? OR HAVE YOU HAD BIRDS? HAMSTERS? SNAKES? FISH?

DO YOU REMEMBER THE LOSS OF YOUR FIRST (OR ANOTHER) PET?

HOW DID YOU LEARN TO SWIM?

WHO TAUGHT YOU TO RIDE A BIKE?

DID YOU PLAY SPORTS GROWING UP?

HOW DID YOU FARE IN GYM CLASS AT SCHOOL? WERE YOU A TEAM LEADER, AN AVERAGE PLAYER OR CHOSEN LAST?

WHAT WAS YOUR FAVORITE SUBJECT AT SCHOOL? YOUR FAVORITE TEACHER?

WOULD YOU SAY YOU WERE STEREOTYPICAL IN SCHOOL (A BRAIN, A CLOWN, MOST POPULAR, A CHEERLEADER, A NERD, ETC.)? WHAT DID THAT MEAN IN YOUR SCHOOL?

DID YOU EVER CAUSE A RUCKUS AT YOUR SCHOOL?

I was a punk-ass little kid and put myself on a high horse others did not see. I was the Queen of my World, and no one could convince me otherwise.

"Bang. Bang. Clap!" was the noise on repeat in school detention. "We will, we will . . ." Bang. Bang. Clap! "Rock you!" Bang. Bang. Clap! "Rock you!" I started the chant of Queen's "We Are the Champions" in the middle of detention. I often created weird moments like this to piss the teachers off. She probably thought we were becoming Children of the Corn. The other students spontaneously joined in, and we sang out like the rules did not exist at that moment. The whole secluded classroom broke out in an uproar of rebellious passion during those few seconds of chanted words and tabletop beats. The abyss of punishing silence was broken. My best friend and I felt so proud as officials came to escort us out of the room. We had big grins on our faces. Hyped up by the energy of the commotion, we were two teenagers poking sticks at authority.

TORY HARGROVE, AUSTIN

Tory is my youngest student in Austin, and she's been through more tough times than should be allowed, but her resilience was on display in detention that day. She continues to poke sticks at authority, but now she gets away with it.

WERE YOU PICKED ON OR BULLIED AS A CHILD OR WERE YOU THE BULLY?

My titties never grew. They were little mounds that I watched like a hen kept watch over her eggs, waiting, waiting, waiting for them to hatch into delicious globes of luscious womanly power. My mom had a bouncy pair, so I must just be a late bloomer, I thought. Waiting. When I entered Northridge Junior High I was mortified to discover that most of my classmates were already bursting out of their bras. It was 1961, basically the fifties, and brassieres were pointed rockets, teasing the boys, sending them into horny spirals of desire as they followed behind the giggles and swishing skirts. Pam Miller was not being followed even though her skirts swished and her forced laughter filled the air. What to do? How would I ever entrance Frankie DiBiase or Phil "Caveman" Carlito? I knew about bra stuffing, but imagined the crumpled tissues feeling hard when hugged, or moving around in the hollow cups, creating disfiguring shapes, or making papery sounds when I danced. They might even disintegrate during gym class and cause even worse embarrassment than being almost titless. After trying the aforementioned Kleenex, and a pair of cotton hankies, I finally settled on a couple of my mom's silky scarves, winding them round and round into soft fluffs of fraudulence, thrusting myself in front of the mirror hopefully, just so.

When I showed up at school the next day with instant boobs, the girls with actual décolletage were not amused and started bumping into me on purpose, yelling "Falsie!" The worst offender actually punched my chest whenever we passed in the halls. Ouch! Underneath the scarves my burgeoning nubs throbbed. I was low-down and demoralized but didn't disembowel my bra until the wickedest bleached-blonde at Northridge Junior High waited for me, as I walked home from school. I tried to squirm by, but she knocked me down, straddled my belly, pounded on my chest several times, then reached inside my blouse and yanked out the silky scarves. "Aha! I knew it!" she pronounced, holding them triumphantly aloft, streaming in the breeze.

I suffered with small-tit-itis until I became a flower child, proudly threw away my padded bras and let my freak flag fly higher than my mom's scarves that fateful day on Jamieson Avenue.

PAMELA DES BARRES

Barbara was a bully. She pounded my little nubs. So was Carol. I wonder where they are today. It is so hard (impossible, actually) to know, while you're being bullied and abused, that one day you'll be a best-selling author or the president of the United States. We all go through hell. Write it down.

DESCRIBE AN EARLY ACCOMPLISHMENT THAT MADE YOU PROUD.

WHAT DID YOU DREAM ABOUT BEING WHEN YOU GREW UP, AND HOW DID IT TURN OUT?

I dreamed about being a writer since I was twelve or thirteen and started out by working for my junior high newspaper in Franklin Lakes, New Jersey, after I was given a tan Smith-Corona electric typewriter for Christmas 1972. My father always said it was the best gift my family ever got me since it helped pave my way in a journalism career at an early age. Anytime that I see that model of electric typewriter on a TV show or movie set in the 1970s, I giggle. If I recall

LET IT BLEED

correctly, I stuck smiley face stickers on mine as well as Rickie Tickie Stickies—these super-large dark and light pink daisy stickers that they sold at Spencer's Gifts.

As a junior high reporter, I covered the cheerleading squad, the fencing team and after-school activity listings circa 1973–1974 . . . this was before late 1974, when I asked my grandfather (who knew the owner of the Paterson, New Jersey, Evening News) to hook me up with the features editor. I got to interview bands I loved but was not paid. Circa 1974–1978, I interviewed a bunch of odds-and-ends artists including Patti Smith (who noticed via my monogrammed canvas tote bag that I had the same initials as her literary idol, Arthur Rimbaud), Frank Zappa (who came to the room door of the decaying Carter Hotel in Times Square with his pants unzipped), Mink DeVille (who was managed by my mother's best friend's sleazy bearded son who looked like Jerry Garcia) and more.

I eventually moved on to regional entertainment publications like the Aquarian, *a rock paper based out of Montclair, New Jersey—and then the college paper of the University of Missouri.*

Did my dream of becoming a writer pan out to be as glamorous as I thought it would be? I would say half yes and half no. It's a hell of a hard way to make a living, even though I have a lot of fun. Unfortunately, I feel that ageism has crept into the business of writing about entertainment, so I have had to branch out to other topics—some a little more mundane than I'd like.

ANNE RASO, NEW YORK

Anne is one of my New York writers and has only missed one class in seven years (she was on a writing assignment). She actually made her early dreams come true, even though it ain't easy these days. Anne has some very colorful memories, and it all started with that Smith-Corona covered in Rickie Tickie Stickies.

V

Parental Units

Delving into family history can churn up all kinds of childhood traumas, awkward admissions and dramatic discoveries. After you write up a few of these topics, in which you recall events from your point of view, imagine your parents as individuals and not just your mom and dad—people whose emotions, desires and disappointments were colored by your view as their child or a hormonally charged teen. After my dear mama passed, I found some notes tucked away that she'd written to herself, wishing she'd followed her secret desire to write. Since she had never expressed this deep wish, and seemed fairly content in her housewife and mother roles, I was saddened and a little shaken up. I thought I knew my mother well. If I'd known she had stifled this creative itch, I would have dragged her to one of the many creative writing classes I attended through the decades.

IMAGINE WHAT YOUR MOTHER'S SECRET DESIRE MIGHT HAVE BEEN.

WRITE A DIARY ENTRY IN THE VOICE OF YOUR MOTHER AT THE AGE YOU ARE NOW ABOUT HOW SHE SPENT HER DAY.

WRITE IN YOUR MOTHER'S VOICE REGARDING A SITUATION THAT YOU'VE ONLY HEARD ABOUT OR WITNESSED FROM YOUR YOUTHFUL (OFTEN NARCISSISTIC) PERSPECTIVE.

WAS YOUR FATHER (OR FATHER FIGURE) A CONTENTED MAN? DID HE ACHIEVE HIS GOALS OR WAS HE FRUSTRATED?

I definitely got my darling daddy's adventurous soul. He also came with a crooked sense of humor, a hearty laugh and pent-up dreams that he tried very hard to make come true, even though it meant hardship for me and my mostly patient mom. He'd been a navy man in WWII, and barely survived the sinking of his ship, but he never discussed the brutal agony of that three-year experience. Men from his generation didn't even realize they could let their (old) guard down and reveal the emotions that churned and burned within. Where did all the pent-up torment, fear and tenderness hide inside his six-foot frame? The only time I saw him weep was when his beloved mother died, miles away in the hills of Kentucky. I can still see his bowed head, and shaking shoulders, and hear the wrenching held-in grief as it struggled to get release.

Oren Coy Miller was a modern pirate, a swashbuckling, Caddy-driving, poker-playing, hard-drinking scalawag from the South who saw his fortune gleaming across the border, down Mexico way. Not content with his five-year-old Fleetwood, his tract house in the Valley or his beer-bottling job at Budweiser, he saw real gold sparkling aplenty in them thar hills of Mazatlán. He went off to seek his fortune as an emboldened middle-aged man, leaving his little family in Reseda to fend for themselves, and returned two years later, in total despair and almost broken. It had been so close, but the needed funds to get the gold out of the mine never materialized. Daddy went back to work in the brewery, and eventually rallied, but once in a while I'd see him gazing at a little bottle of gold chips like it held the future he'd never live to see.

I wrote a song for him that didn't make it onto the GTOs album, Permanent Damage. *Here's the chorus:*

Daddy's got gold fever
Temperature 105
He needs his gold fever
It's what keeps him alive

PAMELA DES BARRES

WRITE IN THE VOICE OF YOUR FATHER. HOW DID HE SEE YOU AT AGE THIRTEEN?

WHAT WERE YOUR PARENTS' DREAMS FOR YOU?

DOES YOUR FAMILY HAVE ANY SKELETONS LURKING IN THE CLOSET? DO YOU?

DESCRIBE THE WORST ARGUMENT YOU EVER HAD WITH YOUR FATHER. YOUR MOTHER.

I argued with my parents in the same way a lawyer would argue his case before a jury. Not angry, but persuasive. The case presented was always the same. For some reason my parents were afraid of the Forum. The Santa Monica Civic was okay. Even the Long Beach Arena, but not the Forum. "But Alison's parents let her go to the Forum and she's only thirteen years old," I argued. Alison was my best friend and a year younger than me. They liked her because she seemed intellectual, was always reading books and never got into trouble. I often thought they wished Alison was their daughter instead of me. "What's so bad about the Forum?" They couldn't come up with more than vague responses about the bad neighborhood. "There's going to be thousands of people there, what bad thing could happen?" They couldn't give me a response and my mom looked at my dad, who hemmed and hawed. I could tell they were breaking. My mom said, "You're too young to go there. There's no place to meet you afterward to pick you up."

My case ended in a mistrial because of a hung jury. Alison went to the concert with another friend who had more reasonable parents. I knew this disagreement would come up again and I was ready to seek justice. This was an unfair rule. I prepared by thinking of new

LET IT BLEED

arguments. "Alison's parents picked her up from the coffee shop next
door to the Forum after the concert that she was allowed to go to," I ca-
sually told my mother, knowing she would discuss this with my father.
Every Sunday the L.A. Times had concert ads in the paper. I'd cut the
ads out and paste them on my notebook, creating a decoupage. Every
time someone I didn't care about seeing played the Forum, I pretended
I wanted to go and acted resigned to not going. I would sigh loudly and
say, "My friends are going to see Grand Funk Railroad tonight but I
told them I couldn't go because it's at the Forum." This was an attempt
to garner pity. The next concert I wanted to go to at the Forum was
George Harrison! I was prepared to lie and sneak out if necessary. This
was not a concert I could miss for any reason. I couldn't contain my ex-
citement and dramatically held up the paper. "I will die if I don't see
him!" My father looked up from his book with eyebrows raised. He
liked the Beatles and took me to see Let It Be when I was ten years old.
"But I can't go, because he's playing at the Forum," I wailed, crying real
tears and dropping to the floor for dramatic effect. "Well, maybe we
could meet you at that coffee shop next door," my dad said. My mom
smiled and said she'd go to the Ticketron office at the May Company to
buy tickets for me. I was so happy I jumped around the room, saying,
"Thank you, thank you, thank you," like a dog excited you've brought
it a treat. The George Harrison concert was just the first of many great
shows I saw at the Forum. It only took six months of pleading my case,
tampering with the jury and presenting evidence.

BAMBI CONWAY, LOS ANGELES

Bambi's matter-of-fact tone has us in stitches every week along with
her deadpan delivery. Her parents seemed in tune with each other when it
came to the rules. It was my mom who doled out punishment at our house,
but she came to my defense when my dad's old-fashioned ideas threatened
the peace.

My daddy and I rarely argued. He left any kind of punishment for my mom to hand out to their only, adored child. I was sometimes grounded for staying out late, or for talking back, being insolent, obstinate or rebellious, and once my mom slapped me across the face for sassing her in front of a friend. Ooooh, she didn't like that one bit, and I never did it again. I did grumble about my dad's backwoods, down-South ideas about race and right-wing politics, but I didn't let that cloud my love for him, and usually avoided touchy topics to keep the peace.

Our biggest slam-bam blowup came when I was already out of the house and announced that my new roommate was a lovely fellow named Davy Jones (not that one), a wild, gangly, black, gay musician who I was writing songs with. My dad actually said the words, "Over my dead body!" and went on to lambaste my choices in a whirl of pig-headed bigotry—but this was one time I had to stand my ground and defend my dear friend Davy. My red-faced, blustering dad wouldn't bend until finally my mom threatened to leave him if he continued the tirade. "This is your daughter you're speaking to, Oren!"

My dear mama, also from the deep South like O. C. Miller, had somehow come out of Georgia with nary a racist bone in her five-foot, three-inch frame, while my dad actually called Brazil nuts "nigger toes"! Noooo! Absolutely not!

Finally, my six-foot Clark Gable dad had to back down, smoldering under his bygone beliefs, and slowly began to accept that his only daughter was forging a path that he might never quite accept or understand.

PAMELA DES BARRES

DO YOU HAVE "DADDY ISSUES"?

I didn't know I had daddy issues until recently when I started writing about him. Seems I have a few things to work out. Like the question, *did you admire him? A girl wants to admire her dad; she wants to believe that he is wise and always right. Like when I had my first Chicago apartment and called him to proudly announce that I'd killed the mouse in the kitchen and he replied, "There is no such thing as one mouse." Yep, turns out he was right about that one. Or when I was thirteen and pissed off that my mom had thrown him down a rat hole and he now lived in a shitty apartment with nothing but a few cans of Budweiser in the fridge and some hand-me-down furniture from God-knows-where, and he said, "Don't blame your mother, it's not her fault." Turns out he was right about that one too. I hated to admit it, but my dad was usually right about stuff.*

He used to say "People don't change."

"No," I'd argue with him, "people change," but he stuck to his guns. Of course, he wasn't referring to superficial stuff, like fat, skinny, rich or poor. He was talking about their character. Was he a shark? A lying jerk bastard scammer son of a bitch asshole? Cuz if he was now, he'd always be. "Wow, harsh toke, Dad."

This stuck with me. I was sure he was wrong on this one. People can change. That's what self-help books, life coaches, church and inspirational posters are for, to help people change and become better, new and improved, clean and purified. Turn that frown upside down, become a positive person—a better human being.

"People don't change." Was it just a good excuse for him to not try to change? Did he secretly say to himself, "No need to stop drinking or smoking or to start working or being nice, because no matter how hard I try, I'm not going to change. It's preordained, written in stone, an indisputable fact." Was this his crutch?

As I get older and look back on the relationships I've had the longest, I hate to admit it, but damn it, he was right. The real core of someone—the thing that matters most—doesn't really change. But don't ask me if this is true about me. I'll ignore the question.

KARI MCGLINNEN, CHICAGO

When you start writing these prompts, a sudden realization can hit you, like Kari's perspicuous reflection that perhaps ol' Dad was right about some things after all.

Polly Parsons lost her wild-living, iconic father, Gram Parsons, when she was a little girl, and her memories are few. There's so much she will never know. He was twenty-six when he OD'd, and his body was stolen from the hearse and burned in the Joshua Tree desert. She allowed her imagination free rein in this piece.

The refraction is the light inside a rhinestone. How much light it emits is measured by the cuts across its face. Daddy was covered in rhinestones when he died and was burned up in the desert. But I insist I was the one above his heart. And I'm sure I let go last as the embers hit the air. The room is number eight. The sheets are dark and dank. The party is on day three. And daddy is going to die today. The red-haired freckled girl can't shove enough ice up his ass to keep him alive this time. Maybe it was the day his daddy shot himself long ago. Perhaps it was the day of his mommy's suicide a few months later. Or maybe my tribe just has a hard time staying on the planet. Deep, dark crimson blood is the last thing to come from the needle prick on my daddy's sweet baby-fuzzed arm. It will be only moments now, as the songs buried deep inside his soul become the property of the Lord forever. Pulsing black tar heroin finds its way to Daddy's never-come-back place, and it is done. Daddy was a rock star. Run, Daddy, please run.

POLLY PARSONS, AUSTIN

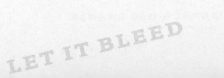

This is so poignant and heart wracking. The line that moved me to tears is "daddy's sweet baby-fuzzed arm . . ." Gram didn't get to live out his life; and perhaps his greatest songs remain unsung.

DO YOU HAVE ANY "MOMMY ISSUES?"

Although she has worked through a lot of her "mommy issues," Polly continues to struggle and strive. This piece about giving birth to Harper Lee, my great-goddaughter, shows how her difficult relationship with her mom has continued to echo throughout her life.

> *It's pitch-black in this room, the temperature in this boiling tub now reaching 110 degrees. I am naked, terrified and alone. Drip, drip, drip goes the honey down my chin for the tenth time in the eighteenth hour. Sweat pours down my face as my cries go unheard. I am giving up. I am exhausted. I am weak. I am growing resentful. There is no one on this planet who can stop the railroading pain and my mind snaps shut by the harrowing awareness of this fact. They finally pull my husband away from my screaming bloody body. I have left this realm.*
>
> *"She is presenting as an abused woman," says the midwife. "She said nothing about this; where is her abuser?"*
>
> *"She's in the living room," he offers meekly.*
>
> *Then I feel my mother's lips at my ear. I beg her for release.*
>
> *"Sweetheart, we are losing the baby's heartbeat. We will have to cut you now."*
>
> *"Please," I reply, "please, I beg you . . ." Within seconds I am sliced open, stem to stern. No drugs, just honey. A girl, to a tribeswoman to a mother. And it is done.*
>
> POLLY PARSONS, AUSTIN

As you're going along, what can you include in these exercises that shows who you are down deep? Are you generous? Loyal? Confident? A reminder—not every prompt or assignment will make it into the memoir, but doing them will help you reach into the corners of your cluttered brain and help to dig up unexpected treasures. This isn't the time for *shoulds* and *should nots*. Bury them with the same shovel you're using to dig up the hidden gold, and save the editorial thinking for later. As tidbits surface, you'll hopefully look at your life with a new pair of lenses and recall events that might be missed if you wrote only about adventures that easily pop to mind. Each memory can suddenly trigger another; forgotten experiences will spring up out of the ethers, demanding to be recalled and written down.

Stephen King calls drawing from memory "using your mental eyes" and "hypnotic recall." Briefly close your peepers and visualize the scene you're about to write. Instead of saying "It was 1973 when . . ." how about "Nixon was raging on about not being a crook when . . ." Or instead of "My father was over six feet tall . . ." remember how he had to stoop to get through a doorway. Let your reader hear with your ears and see with your eyes.

DESCRIBE A TIME YOU DISAPPOINTED YOUR MOM OR DAD.

WRITE ABOUT A DAY WITH YOUR PARENTS WHEN TIME SEEMED TO STOP.

My Austin writer Fannie elegantly expresses a perfect cross between torpid languor and nervous expectation in this melancholy remembrance. I can actually feel the pent-up listlessness mixed with anxiety while she waits for the darn phone to ring.

Waiting by the pay phone. My mother and I on a summer day. The sun is beating on us and we have nothing to do but wait. I have already finished the book I brought with me, and all that's left to read is the graffiti on the pay phone. None of it is that interesting, just names and the occasional curse word, but no great jokes or stories. All

LET IT BLEED

of it is terribly unfortunate, given that this pay phone is in the parking lot of the local library. Only twenty feet away is the entrance to my very favorite place in all of Chester, South Carolina. Once a week, more frequently when my mom allows, I get to leave with a stack of books that I will chew through in hours. I race myself to see how quickly I can finish each one. And I really do clock in a little quicker each time. If reading were a competitive sport, I could surely be endorsed for my efforts. But today is Sunday, the only day of the week that this library is closed. I live alone with my mom. At the end of a mile-long driveway, on a highway out of town, in a house without a phone. So when it's time to hear from Dad, he sends a letter telling us which day and time he will call on this particular pay phone. I think my mom chose it over the gas station closer to our house because it is safer. And no one is stopping by to buy beer or cause a fuss. But for me, waiting for the call is the ultimate in boredom. Combined with anxiety. I love hearing from my dad, or at least I did for a while. But he's told me too many times that he will move back with us when he finds a job. I know he's never going to live with us again. I just don't understand why he won't say so.

So I wait to hear the phone ring and hear his voice on the other end. To tell him how great my grades are and how many books I've read. And to apologize for not writing him more. Like I always do. I hate Sundays. And this pay phone. And having to sit in this car. Mom hates it when I leave the door open and hang my legs outside, but it's the only part I love. I stretch out across the seat and look out the window upside down. That world is always better and I imagine what upside-down me could do instead of waiting. She would run away to one of the beautiful houses on this block that are painted like cakes. And she would read stacks and stacks of books without ever having to wait for anything or anyone in the sun-baked parking lot of the library on the only day that it's closed. The phone finally rings and Mom and I look at each other. I don't move right away and she grimaces and moves toward the phone. I look through the window and wait to hear her call my name.

FANNIE GUNTON, AUSTIN

WHAT TRAITS DID YOU GET FROM EACH PARENT OR PARENTAL FIGURE?

HOW DO YOU VIEW YOUR RELATIONSHIP WITH YOUR PARENTS TODAY, WHETHER THEY ARE ALIVE OR NOT?

CHAPTER SEVEN

I

The Hormones They Are A-Changin'

These exercises about your teen years will help you pick up on overarching themes and turn over a good number of stones. (Be sure to look under all of them!) We'll cover topics about adolescence, transition into adulthood, teenage attitude and angst that relate to all kinds of metamorphosis and change.

One thing that helped me dredge up a few remarkable moments was to ask my friends if they'd saved any letters I'd sent them through the years. Reading through them completely popped my top! I had somehow forgotten that I went on a couple of dates with Gram Parsons, for instance, until Cynthia Plaster Caster send me a bundle of my handwritten missives tied with a ribbon.

When you come to a prompt that feels a little hazy to you, call on friends to help you recall forgotten details. They will float back into your mind like a parachute opening in midair.

As you're hurtling along with these exercises, remember that a memoir need not be chronological or cover all of life's events to be compelling or complete. Write it all down, but reveal only as much as you want to when all is said (written) and done. In one of my all-time fave-rave memoirs, *Chronicles: Volume One*, Bob Dylan carefully picked and chose times, places, events and situations that he wanted to share, and through these he created an absorbing account of his place in the pantheon of music. I can hear the cadence and tone of his voice, the urgency of his memories. I turn to it often, because it sounds like Dylan is talking just to me, and I keep hoping he really does complete the two additional promised volumes.

Dylan left Hibbing, Minnesota, as a teenager, knowing exactly what he wanted to accomplish. Here he describes landing in New York for the first time.

"When I arrived, it was dead-on winter. The cold was brutal and every artery of the city was snowpacked, but I'd started out from the frostbitten North Country, a little corner of the earth where the dark frozen woods and icy roads didn't faze me. I could transcend the limitations. It wasn't money or love that I was looking for. I had a heightened sense of awareness, was set in my ways, impractical and a visionary to boot. My mind was strong like a trap and I didn't need any guarantee of validity. I didn't know a single soul in this dark freezing metropolis but that was all about to change—and quick."

That one paragraph says so much about the young determined poet, the future American Shakespeare, who would let nothing stand in the way of his quest for immortality.

AT WHAT AGE DID YOU GET A SENSE OF WHAT YOU WANTED TO ACCOMPLISH IN LIFE?

DID YOU FEEL LIKE PART OF A GROUP OR WERE YOU AN OUTCAST AS A TEEN?

RECALL A TIME YOU WERE TERRIBLY MISUNDERSTOOD.

HAVE YOU EVER BEEN MADE FUN OF? RIDICULED? OSTRACIZED?

HAVE YOU EVER MADE FUN OF SOMEONE?

DESCRIBE THE DAY YOU FIRST GOT YOUR PERIOD.

HOW DID YOU LEARN ABOUT THE FACTS OF LIFE?

As I mentioned earlier, Brandy is a grade-school teacher, and I sure wish I'd had her for botany instead of the unremarkable Mr. Formsma! When she reads her pieces in our class, a riot of hysteria ensues. We all keep insisting she start her own podcast, sharing her class assignments with all and sundry.

DESCRIBE YOUR FIRST SEXUAL FEELINGS.

I was obsessed with getting a banana seat bike when I was eleven. (It's pretty much all I thought about, besides how much I really liked Keith from my sixth grade class and Cool Ranch Doritos.) I would stare at them at the Kmart when Mom had to buy stuff like paper towels and window washing fluid. I'd walk over and gaze at the bikes. I wanted mine to be purple with tassels to catch the wind. I'd pretend to be a velvet painting on the moon with a unicorn as I glided down the streets on my very own banana seat bike with tassels. So when Christmastime came around I heard a rumor that one of the pawn employees at my parents' store had built my bike. When the bike was bestowed upon me I was not massively surprised but I sure was elated.

I had to wait four long months to ride that bike due to the snowy onslaught that is Indiana, but it sure did pay off when I did. The first time I rode it over to my friend Christina's house because she was my bestie and her mom gave us Dunkaroos, which are long sticks of cake with dipping frosting and sprinkles. They would also let me dress up like a hobo and take pictures of me while I did a comedy show. (My hobo outfit consisted of a flannel shirt, a pool ring seahorse inner tube, a feather boa and a purple wig.)

So that first glorious day I was riding my bike to Christina's when I discovered bumps in the grass and the smooth sensation of my vagina gliding across that long banana seat. It was warm and misty like fields of exploding flowers. Oh my, I like that even more than dressing like a hobo, I thought. So I did it again. And again and again. And got to Christina's an hour late. It pretty much became my thing. My parents would take us on these long bike rides for family bonding time. I stayed in back, feigning that I was tired or some sort of preteen loner. But oh no, I wanted to rub on my special banana seat bicycle all by myself and I didn't want my weirdo brothers ruining the moment. It was just my banana seat and me, cruising hard forever in sweet delicious velvet vagina warmth.

BRANDY BATZ, LOS ANGELES

WHAT WAS THE FIRST BAND THAT DROVE YOU CRAZY? DID YOU HAVE A CRUSH ON ONE OF THE MUSICIANS?

WHO OR WHAT INFLUENCED YOUR WAY OF THINKING AS A TEEN?

RECALL A LIFE-CHANGING TEENAGE EXPERIENCE.

May 1971. The birds were singing, and the air was fragrant with lilacs. A small group of teenagers was idly hanging around the house of Victor Peterson. One of the boys wore a T-shirt with the number "714" on it. It seemed as though nothing could be wrong with the world after such a long, cold, snowy winter. And then an old VW Beetle putt-putted down the road, coming to a stop in front of the house. A boy named Joel Trefrey got out of the car and sauntered over to Victor.

"Hey, man, cops are going to bust me for boosting that TV. You owe me, man, and I'm here to collect."

Joel was a well-known drug dealer of the rip-off variety in high school, and Victor had relied on his seamy services too many times. The two boys circled each other warily, and only someone who knew Victor well could see that he was becoming upset and angry, by the redness climbing up his ears.

"You hear me, man? You'd better take this rap for me if you know what's good for you, fuckhead."

We all watched entranced as the two moved closer to each other, sensing the smell of fight in the air. Suddenly Victor bolted, running toward his house, slamming the screen door behind him. We looked at each other in bewilderment, as none of us had ever known Victor Peterson to back down from a fight.

Then—slam!—the screen door burst open and Victor was back with a large butcher knife in his hand. Before anyone could make a move to intercede, he stabbed that wicked knife into Joel's heart, scoring a perfect 10. Joel slowly dropped lifeless into the gutter, and the silence weighed heavy for a moment before one of the boys cried, "Hey, dude, you killed him!" He was just stating a fact. Joel was indeed dead, and we all stared in dumb shock at his exsanguinating body.

In the end, Joel went to the morgue, Victor went to the State Hospital for the Criminally Insane and we all went our separate ways, knowing we had been irrevocably changed.

LINDA LEATHER, LOS ANGELES

Linda can obviously still feel the emotion of that shocking experience all these years later. The odd little details peppering the description of that seemingly typical spring afternoon belie the horror of what's about to take place.

The final line of her story reminds me of the day Dennis McCorkell, the "bad boy" at Northridge Junior High, stole a car and died in a flaming crash. His brooding face was on the cover of the Valley newspaper the next morning, and I gazed at it, trying to comprehend that he was really and truly gone. I still think about him fifty-three years later. I even clipped his signature from my school annual ("Good luck with the boys, Dennis") and keep it in a little box with a crumbling dried flower I picked that day to commemorate him.

The first time we experience death is unforgettable and dramatic. Suddenly the safety net disappears, and we realize we are all vulnerable.

DESCRIBE THE FIRST TIME YOU WERE AFFECTED BY SOMEONE'S DEATH.

DESCRIBE THE DAY OF YOUR HIGH SCHOOL GRADUATION AND OF YOUR PROM.

HOW DID IT FEEL TO FALL IN LOVE FOR THE FIRST TIME?

WHERE DID YOU GO ON YOUR VERY FIRST DATE?

WHO WAS YOUR FIRST BOYFRIEND (OR GIRLFRIEND)?

DESCRIBE YOUR FIRST REAL KISS.

By age thirteen I had dabbled in chaste lip-locking but never with tongues. At that point, lolling on top of the maple bunk bed of my first real boyfriend, Darrell, I didn't even realize that the tongue could be involved in a kiss. Actually, there was another Daryl, in junior high, who I'd lightly smooched during a game of spin the bottle, but even though his mouth opened slightly, not even the tip of a tongue emerged from the safe place within our mouths. So imagine my surprise when I wound up alone in the backseat with an eighteen-year-old guitar player. This is my torrid teen awakening from *I'm with the Band.*

> *I could smell Robby's manly manliness; it wafted over me and I collapsed into his English Leather lapels with the giggles. I'll never forget this: He cupped my chin in his hand and pulled my face up to his lips, opened up my mouth with his tongue and slid it right in! What an amazing sensation! It was so wet, and he moved his lips all over, and his tongue poked around inside my mouth like it was trying to locate something. When I had to come up for air, we were in front of my house on Jamieson Avenue, and I felt like I had taken a trip around the world.*

DESCRIBE YOUR FIRST SEXUAL EXPERIENCE.

WHAT NATIONAL OR WORLD EVENTS DURING YOUR TEENAGE YEARS ARE MOST MEMORABLE TO YOU?

DID YOU EVER KEEP ANY SECRETS FROM YOUR PARENTS?

In his beautiful impactful book *The Untethered Soul,* Michael Singer says that if you look directly at the hurtful memories that keep revisiting you, and face them again and again without flinching, they can be expelled and won't color your reality any longer. I believe writing about your troublesome past helps it stay where it belongs. It can soften the blow, lessen the impact and put the hobgoblin back in his grave.

I have heard far too many horror stories from my girls about the violations they've been through and I'm always amazed by their bravery and forthrightness—and the graceful way they can often release the past as the words tumble onto the page. Praise Jesus, mine isn't nearly as harrowing as some, but this event stands out like a gloomy cloud in the otherwise glowing brilliance of '62 . . .

WERE YOU EVER ABUSED IN ANY WAY?

I was close to turning fourteen the summer a real live band started rehearsing in a garage across the street from my house on Jamieson Avenue. Already obsessed musically, I was delighted when these ravishing ebony-haired beauties allowed me and my friends to goggle at them as they sang and played their shimmering, sparkling guitars on my very street in Reseda. I got my first kiss from the guitar player; my first actual date was with the drummer—a trip to Pacific Ocean Park in a candy apple green Pontiac Bonneville (still my dream machine). I became close friends with the niece of the bass player, so when she invited me to visit her family up north in San Mateo for the weekend, I jumped at the chance for a sleepaway trip.

I don't remember much about that weekend away from home, except the heady pungent smells of Dutch Indonesian cooking, the closeness of the beds in the room where I slept with Trudy and her little brother, Raymond, and the predawn morning when Trudy's large-eared, pockmarked father whispered for me to get out of bed to come say good-bye.

I was half-asleep, and all was quiet as I tiptoed down the stairs in my shortie pajamas to meet this trusted patriarch of the family. Under half-lidded eyes, wearing just a T-shirt and undershorts, he pulled me onto his lap and began to rock me back and forth like I was a little baby, crooning in a foreign language, smoothing my hair, cooing and inhaling my virtue like a vampire. All was eerily silent in the house except for his heavy breathing; the tick tick tick of a wall clock counting the scary moments until he slowly slid me off his lap and told me to go back upstairs to bed. But I couldn't sleep. I knew something wrong had taken place. My untouched innocence had been tampered with, trust had been overturned, and what was left of my childhood quietly vanished.

PAMELA DES BARRES

LET IT BLEED

RECALL SOMEONE YOU CLICKED WITH IMMEDIATELY. ARE YOU STILL FRIENDS?

HAVE YOU EVER LOST A DEAR FRIEND DUE TO A MISUNDERSTANDING?

RECALL A TIME YOU WERE VERY JEALOUS OF SOMEONE.

When I was growing up I thought my friend and next-door neighbor had it better than me. She had a two-story house with a playroom. I had a one-story house with just my bedroom. She had an older brother and sister. I was the oldest with a little brother. In high school she had the cute, bad boy boyfriend. I hardly dated anyone. She got her mother's used car to drive to school. I had to ride the bus. Everything—her house, her looks, her car, her friends, her family—was better than what I had.

Then, one night, my dad called me at my work to tell me that her dad had committed suicide in their backyard while his wife was in the house. He had hung himself after being depressed for many years.

That night her sadness and despair was better than mine.

RHONDA ATKINSON, AUSTIN

Sometimes our envy and jealousy can color an otherwise ordinary experience. The folly of those negative emotions is summed up emphatically in Rhonda's final line.

WRITE ABOUT A THEFT. HAVE YOU EVER STOLEN ANYTHING? HAVE YOU EVER BEEN STOLEN FROM?

HAVE YOU EVER REALLY HATED ANYONE?

I'D LIKE TO PRETEND THIS NEVER HAPPENED . . .

II

She's Leaving Home, Bye Bye

For most of us the end of childhood is marked by moving out of our family home. As the Beatles so brilliantly encapsulated it, it can be a poignant and a liberating moment.

After doting on me as her only child, I knew my mama dreaded the day her baby bird decided to ditch the comfy family nest for digs of her own. It was a rainy night in North Hollywood when I trundled most of my earthly possessions out the door as my mom sat on the couch, her head buried in her hands. She couldn't bear to watch as I packed up my nineteen years of life in the Miller household and skedaddled for good, ready to take on the big bad world on my own.

I experienced that bereft feeling myself when my son, Nick, moved to Japan. As I waved good-bye at the airport I actually heard the apron strings snap. It was a piercing pang I'll never forget.

DESCRIBE THE DAY YOU MOVED AWAY FROM HOME.

HOW DID YOUR PARENTS TAKE IT? DID THEY GO THROUGH THE "EMPTY-NEST" SYNDROME?

HOW DID YOU FIND YOUR FIRST LIVING QUARTERS? DID YOU LIVE ALONE OR WITH ROOMMATES?

HOW DID YOU SUPPORT YOURSELF WHEN YOU FIRST LEFT HOME? WHAT WAS YOUR FIRST JOB?

WHAT ACTIVITIES FILLED YOUR FREE TIME OR HOURS AFTER WORK?

WHAT WAS YOUR FAVORITE BAR? ROCK CLUB? DESCRIBE A WILD NIGHT THERE.

WRITE ABOUT A NIGHT YOU GOT INTO TROUBLE.

As young ladies, we alternate between feeling like we've got it all figured out and wishing we were still in our backyard, happily making mud pies. You've come a long way, baby, but wouldn't it be swell to swim through time and whisper words of wisdom to your tortured teenage soul?

The next several prompts are for you dolls who chose to go to college. Even though I took a few college courses, I actually graduated from the College of Hard Rocks. Ha-ha!

WHERE DID YOU GO TO COLLEGE? WHY DID YOU CHOOSE THAT PARTICULAR SCHOOL?

DID YOU LIVE ON CAMPUS OR OFF? WHY, AND HOW DID IT AFFECT YOU?

HOW DID YOU PAY FOR YOUR COLLEGE EDUCATION? WHAT WAS THE IMPACT IT HAD ON YOU OR YOUR FAMILY?

WHAT WAS MOST IMPORTANT TO YOU IN COLLEGE: YOUR STUDIES OR YOUR SOCIAL LIFE?

DID YOU GRADUATE? DROP OUT?

DID YOU STUDY ABROAD?

WHO WAS YOUR FAVORITE PROFESSOR?

HAS YOUR COLLEGE EDUCATION ENHANCED YOUR LIFE?

WHAT ADVICE WOULD YOU GIVE TO YOUR NINETEEN-YEAR-OLD SELF?

You won't be weird forever. We'll come to embrace the fact that being "weird" is without a doubt better than being a popular prom queen— we being the daydreamy folk, the misty-eyed believers, the artists that know that the times they are a-changing. You won't always live in this town, mostly because you know you're destined for the otherwild. Some people will try to turn you into a house of toothpicks, as if you're some kind of mystery that needs solving. What they—and what you— don't see yet, is that it's important to leave a little bit of you for—you. Other people's energy might feel consuming and confusing, so make yourself a coat of armor or an umbrella kaleidoscope to protect you, because you'll need it way more than a mask.

Every relationship will be important because they were present for a time that mattered, the girl who is like the Joan Jett to your Cherie Currie but may never meet you at that sweet spot where curiosity and compassion make for a lasting relationship, or lovers who lash out and say the wrong thing at the wrong time—they will all exit, some with ease, some with difficulty, some with pockets of feelings they hope you'll carry into the desert for them.

Go to that Bob Dylan concert alone and dance your ass off with the ladies in the leopard-skin pillbox hats. Remember the rule of three: grace, compassion and dignity. Write it in eye pencil on your bathroom mirror.

Thank the men in your life, like your dad and your brothers—they too are teaching you to be a strong, opinionated, artistic, convicted

LET IT BLEED

dreamer. It doesn't mean there won't be nights when the phone doesn't ring. Lonesome, dark periods are necessary too. Don't fight those waves, just ride them out until morning. Sad songs won't always feel sad; they'll turn into the best songs you ever heard in your life. Mark my words: no one can taint Zeppelin for you.

Your idea of growing up will change—dress however you feel, wear what makes you exhilarated, never apologize for feeling taller than you seem or feeling smaller than you really are—don't be so hard on yourself! We are all on Spaceship Earth, floating in the galaxy like rocket waves of atoms—a part of the tide. You are heard. Nurture your mind with books, music, film, and always write. The future is uncertain, so says Jim Morrison, but we both know you're an old soul who has much to do.

KIM HOFFMAN, PORTLAND, OREGON

Kim's clever line "you know you're destined for the otherwild" not only creates a brand-new word (remember Kerouac's "crazy dumbsaint of the mind"?), it foreshadows her cosmic Spaceship Earth attitude.

CHAPTER EIGHT

I

Grown-Up Blues

Do you remember when you were suddenly an "adult"? When everything became sternly serious and you had to act like a *grown-up* and make important decisions? What did that mean to you? Some mornings I wake up, stunned that I'm not just going to put on a pair of shorts and ride my bike down Jamieson Avenue to get some SweeTarts and cherry-flavored Lik-M-Aid! Hopefully some of that joyous childhood freedom still resides in our womanly hearts.

DO YOU FEEL "GROWN-UP"?

My group of writers in each city spans the ages. In Chicago my oldest doll is almost eighty-three. We all listen rapt as she shares bohemian tales about her beatnik days in Greenwich Village and what it was like to be ballsy before feminism was even a thought. My youngest in that class is twenty-one, a singer-songwriter with her own set of angsty issues and a much older rock boyfriend. Margaret is a feisty liberal woman in my L.A. class who went to junior high and high school with me, now in her mid-sixties, and my youngest is sweet Sara at twenty with a fairy-tale voice, a crimson past and high dreamy hopes. They all have one thing in common: they want to write it all down, figure it out and share their lightning bolts.

123

LET IT BLEED

And when they do, every woman in the room can relate to the truths within the words—whether she's been on the planet for two decades or eight. Time after time, it just proves that age doesn't truly divide us like we often perceive it does.

DO YOU ACT YOUR AGE?

DO YOU FEEL YOUNGER OR OLDER THAN YOUR YEARS?

Money, money, money, money—*money!*

She works hard for it, honey! At least most of us do. When we have to start supporting ourselves, it sure feels like we've entered adulthood! I've had my ups and downs with the Queen of Pentacles, and now try to see money as an exchange of energy, freely given and joyously received. Let's take a hard warm look at how you and Ms. Money get along—whether you're close friends or she's off gallivanting in a distant land.

IMAGINE MONEY AS A FRIEND OF YOURS. CREATE A CONVERSATION BETWEEN YOU AND MONEY THAT SHOWS WHAT KIND OF RELATIONSHIP YOU HAVE. DO YOU ARGUE? GET ALONG?

ARE YOU FINANCIALLY COMFORTABLE, OR DO YOU WORRY ABOUT YOUR FINANCIAL SITUATION?

WHAT WAS YOUR BEST JOB? WORST JOB? MOST UNUSUAL JOB?

Back in the '60s in my beloved Berkeley, folks regularly sold their artistic creations on Telegraph Avenue. This was particularly true at Christmastime and I was hired to help produce little faux stained-glass windows that would hang in real *windows. Christy, the owner, had* manufactured molds of different kinds—flowers, butterflies, the sun and stars—which would be laid out on long tables in a freezing, poorly ventilated garage, and I'd then mix the chemicals that would fill the molds.

Christy oversaw her workers with zealous vigilance, as if she were one of the great masters supervising the parts of a project left to journeymen.

The mixing itself was singularly unpleasant since the chemicals gave off noxious, surely toxic fumes, and we had to wear bulky face masks, like scuba divers, that immediately began dripping our sweat into the goo.

Our rubber gloves were only semiresistant to the quickly hardening glop and began to dissolve almost immediately. We worked as fast as we could, since the stuff had to be poured into the molds while it was still liquid and Christy docked our pay for waste.

First came the "outline," which used only black plastic; then, after the hours it took them to dry, we'd pour colors. The end results were "stained plastic" window decorations selling for five dollars apiece at Christy's table on "the Ave."

A usual "workday" lasted as long as Christy said it did and left workers frozen, exhausted, short of breath, with pounding headaches from the overpowering chemicals.

Despite my continuing need for money, I could only rejoice when Christy informed us her Christmas gift to herself was to shut down the shop. That was the same week I discovered my wonderful guitar at the Ashby BART Flea Market and joyfully brought it home. I soon realized that the many instances of the fiercely abrasive chemicals melting my gloves had left my fingertips so raw and tender I wasn't able to play it until Valentine's Day.

MARGARET FARRELL, LOS ANGELES

DESCRIBE YOUR BEST BOSS. YOUR WORST BOSS.

IF YOU ARE A BOSS YOURSELF, WHAT KIND OF BOSS ARE YOU? HOW DO YOU RELATE TO YOUR EMPLOYEES?

HAVE YOU EVER STARTED A BUSINESS?

HAVE YOU EVER FREELANCED OR BEEN SELF-EMPLOYED?

WHAT WOULD YOUR DREAM JOB BE?

HAVE YOU EVER GONE FROM RICH TO POOR OR VICE VERSA?

HAVE YOU EVER BEEN COMPLETELY BROKE? IF SO, HOW DID THAT CHANGE?

HAVE YOU EVER BEEN STUCK SOMEWHERE WITHOUT ENOUGH MONEY?

My dad always stopped to pick up pennies in the street. He wasn't cheap, or a miser—far from it. I used to tease him about it and say, "It's only a penny." He'd give me that smile that looked sweet but also meant "How could my kid be so dumb?" and say, "It's only a penny until you need it—then it's money."

When I got a little older my mother would send me to the corner store—yes, we had one—to pick up a loaf of bread or carton of milk. She'd give me the few dollars it would take, and off I'd go. But I'd take the long way, past the streets of stores we called the Avenue, then duck into the drugstore to buy something small, like a candy bar or magazine. Or I'd get a soda somewhere, just enjoying being on my own. I'd make sure I had enough money left to cover what I was supposed to buy. It always worked out.

Except for that time I miscalculated. I had entertained myself up and down the Avenue and was heading for the corner store for milk when I realized I was six cents short. Six cents. Such a tiny amount, but it might as well have been a thousand dollars, because I didn't have it. I heard my dad saying, "When you need it, it's money," and started searching the ground. The store was still a few blocks away, so I kept walking, head down, focusing, praying a little. It had to work. I couldn't go home empty-handed. And sure enough, by the time I reached the store, I had six grimy pennies clutched in my hand.

I kept the story to myself for a while, but eventually I told my dad the story of the six pennies. It made his day. After that I never made fun of him when he stopped for pennies, and when it became harder for him to bend down, I was happy to pick them up for him.

On my kitchen counter I have the plastic tub I found in his room after he died, filled with pennies. It's money, if I ever need it.

SHEVA GOLKOW, NEW YORK

DO YOU CARRY DEBT? IF SO, HOW DOES THAT AFFECT YOU?

ARE YOU THE MAIN BREADWINNER IN YOUR HOUSEHOLD? HOW DOES THAT MAKE YOU FEEL?

ARE YOU NOW OR HAVE YOU EVER BEEN SUPPORTED BY SOMEONE ELSE'S MONEY?

My L.A. writer Lucretia, a collector after my own rockin' heart, nabbed herself a piece of history! Money well spent, in my humble opinion.

127

WHAT IS THE MOST EXPENSIVE THING YOU EVER BOUGHT BESIDES A HOUSE OR CAR?

I invested two thousand dollars in a limited edition copy of the infamous Jimi Hendrix Plaster Cast, signed and numbered (and as beautifully packaged as Jimi's package) by the artist herself, Cynthia Plaster Caster.

The cast is true art. It is weighty with the artistic media of plaster, and heavy with musical legacy. The feeling I had as I held the cast in the palm of my hand was profound, at once both ephemeral and tangible; I felt the vibes in the cast. I knew it wasn't the original plaster cast, so Jimi's member hadn't really been inside the cast I held in my hands, but I knew it was a cast of where his penis had been, and it felt real to me. I thought about what it was like for them as they made the art together, how he had sex with the goo as it dried, and how Cynthia was too shy to sleep with him so she made art with him instead. I thought about all the strings he had plucked, what it might be like to be her making the cast, or to be him onstage, or to be with them in the hotel room. I wondered if auras can leave just a little bit in the art or song for us to linger over and love, even in the copies of originals. I heard his music in my head. I thought about how music and art can make revolutions.

Maybe it was the power of my own imagination, or the power of all the words I'd read and all the music I'd heard through the years about the two legends—SuperGroupie artist Cynthia Plaster Caster and legendary musician Jimi Hendrix. I felt the power traveling through my own personal history as the package of his cast had traveled from windy Chicago to sunny California, to me in a hilltop house I painted purple, holding a cast of his penis in the palm of my hand. Or maybe vibrations live in the grooves.

I don't know for sure. But I know this: I suddenly felt experienced.

LUCRETIA TYE JASMINE, LOS ANGELES

**WRITE ABOUT DISCOVERING YOUR FAVORITE THRIFT STORE/
GARAGE SALE/FLEA MARKET FIND.**

**DO YOU GAMBLE? IF SO, WHAT ARE YOUR FAVORITE GAMES?
HAVE YOU EVER WON OR LOST BIG?**

**DO YOU INVEST IN THE STOCK MARKET? HAVE YOU EVER
GAINED OR LOST BIG?**

II

Sweet Nothings

Enough already with the weighty financial prompts. Who cares about dough when passion is rising? Let's get down to the real nitty-gritty heart of the matter!

Ah, romance . . . I've had my share. So much of our prime time is squandered and trammeled in our frantic search for *love*. No other feeling compares to the feverish flutter of the expectant heart, swelling inside your chest like your rib cage might crack. Does he love me? Does he not? So much of my youthful energy was spent chasing down Cupid, that capricious little f**ker

Here's another little ditty that almost made it onto the GTOs album.

> Where is romance?
> The kissing of hands?
> Boys down on one knee
> Wasn't it grand?
> Dropping perfumed handkerchiefs

Blowing kisses from across the room
Make us swoon

Where is romance?
Whispering sweet nothings
Into little pink ears
Has it passed with the years?
Two straws in a bottle of pop
Sipping together at the soda shop
And a walk in the park . . .
Get me home before dark!

You don't even walk us
To the door anymore

Looking back upon my well-lived life full of glowing, agonizing, tempestuous relationships, I realize that despite all the times I believed I was truly in love, the Real Thing only happened to me five times. Two Aquarians, two Sagittarians and one Taurus!

HOW MANY TIMES HAVE YOU REALLY BEEN IN LOVE?

True love? Once. I've had boyfriends I truly cared about, and more that I didn't, but I've never felt that "in love" feeling that you read about in fairy tales. Does this bother me? No, to be honest. I couldn't care less, because I have me. Yes, that's right. I am in love with myself. In fact, there is little about me that I don't love. I don't claim to be flawless or that I don't struggle, and sure I wish my thighs were smaller and that I could make decisions easier and not worry about every little thing. But if it really bothered me all that much I could get a gym membership. Maybe my inability to make quick decisions is a blessing in disguise. I've only ever really needed myself, and okay, maybe the support of my family and some great dolls. When I don't have a man in my life I never feel lonely or less of a person because I haven't found my other half. I never worry about finding Mr. Right because I am Mrs. Right and I am fabulous. While I'll gladly welcome any deserving man into my life, whether it happens now or never, I can honestly say none of my time will be spent waiting for him.

LYNX, TORONTO

Brava! So nifty how Lynx turned this prompt on its rear end. Jesus said, Love your neighbor as yourself, you may recall. But it's the *yourself* part most of us have trouble with.

HOW DID YOU MEET EACH OF THE PEOPLE YOU'VE TRULY BEEN IN LOVE WITH? WRITE TWELVE MINUTES ON EACH.

HAVE YOU EVER BEEN ON A BLIND DATE?

DO YOU BELIEVE IN LOVE AT FIRST SIGHT? HAS IT HAPPENED TO YOU?

Ages ago I had an alt-pop band in need of a lead guitarist. A free ad in the Recycler *was the way to find musicians back then. We spent a long time wording the ad so it reflected exactly the style we were going for—lots of jangle, harmony and sixties good vibes. A twelve-string Rickenbacker would be ideal, if you played one.*

The night got away from me, and Giorgio, who had answered the ad, called to see if he could still come by and get the cassette tape of our music (I told you this was a long time ago).

"I'll be right there to pick up the tape. Please don't go to bed!" he pleaded.

131

There was something about a total stranger pleading with me not to end my day just yet, begging me to let him be part of it, to make a cameo appearance at the very end, to catch me before I went to dreamland and reset the clock and reset the day and didn't wake up until it was tomorrow. Something haunting came down the phone line. I told him I'd wait for him to arrive.

I needed to look somewhat cool, as he'd no doubt be deciding whether to join our band based on his opinion of the lead singer. I kept my full outfit from the evening's nightclub jaunt on—shoes, makeup and all. It was the '80s, and my hair was bigger than big. I flipped my head upside down and then whipped it back just to make sure my 'do was big enough to impress.

The knock came. A respectfully quiet knock, so as not to disturb my neighbors so late at night in this cheap Hollywood apartment building with its echoing barren courtyard and paper-thin walls. I swung the door open.

The door frame held him perfectly in its rectangle, backlit from the yellowish courtyard lighting. The perfect silhouette with skinny legs and all. His large dark eyes blinked at me from under his deep brown curls.

The resounding words filled up my mind as if another person was announcing it. Another person from another place or time who knew way more about what was going on here. It was a pure, unadulterated recognition, a knowing on a cellular level that filled my core like melty toffee. Sweet, thorough familiarity. A smile filled me from the inside out, as the delighted voice inside my head greeted the person I'd spend the next two years with:

"You're here!"

KATHRYN SMITH, SEATTLE

All the distinct, vibrant details, such as "echoing barren courtyard and paper-thin walls," take you right to Kathryn's Hollywood apartment as she's about to meet a True Love. And how about her core being filled "like melty toffee"? Can't you just feel that creamy rush?

WHAT WAS YOUR BEST DATE EVER? THE WORST?

DESCRIBE MEETING THE PERSON YOU BELIEVED WAS "THE ONE."

HAS SOMEONE FALLEN IN LOVE WITH YOU BUT YOU DIDN'T FEEL THE SAME WAY?

DO YOU BELIEVE YOU CAN HAVE MORE THAN ONE SOUL MATE?

DESCRIBE YOUR DREAM RELATIONSHIP.

OSCAR WILDE SAID, "I see when men love women they give them but a little of their lives: but women, when they love, give everything." WRITE THE PROOF OF THIS.

My longtime student Lorraine and her hubby, Harv, have the most enviable marriage of all my coupled pals. With four sons, two of them grown, they somehow keep the romance alive and well after almost three decades of togetherness. The term "joined at the hip" is a cliché, but it describes them to a T. (Another cliché! Ha-ha!) Harv's job takes him all over the country, and once when he was stuck in a different city for several weeks, Lolo seriously pined.

DESCRIBE THE FEELING WHEN YOU'RE APART FROM SOMEONE YOU LOVE.

Upon all of us a little rain must fall, so the saying goes. Just a little rain? That's how I feel, right here, right now, under the umbrella, waiting . . . waiting . . . waiting . . . for the rain to stop. I feel trapped

133

between the present and future, just waiting. Can't move forward into the unknown, frozen in the present. What's next? Afraid to change anything because it might rock the boat. The strain is unbearable . . . I curse the gloom set upon us. Whoever said absence makes the heart grow fonder was a liar. Absence makes the heart hurt, hate, question and accuse. It's not easy to be apart; it's the hardest thing I've ever done. Something I swore I would never do. But be careful with your words. Sometimes they come back to taunt you. These are the seasons of emotion, and just like the wind, they rise and fall. Love, hate, hurt and yearn. This is the wonder of devotion. Alone here, still yours, still painfully in love. So I'm waiting. Under my heart-shaped umbrella. After all . . . it's just a little rain.

LORRAINE COLE, HOUSTON

DESCRIBE YOUR MOST MEMORABLE SEXUAL EXPERIENCE. WHAT MADE IT SO SPECIAL?

What is the exact chemical reaction when a want turns into a need? When any action can be justified to acquire that thing or person that will satisfy you? I could hear the hum of the amps and the buzz of voices as I walked up the street to where my need had located himself that night. Make an entrance, pay cover, get myself a drink and pretend that I'm not looking for him. He can come to me. The joint was crammed with people, the space so electrified that the swing of the door letting in the frigid January air couldn't cool it down. Windows glazed with fog, shielding all our sins from the outside world.

We found each other before his set. Picked up where we left off with subtle flirting and niceties before they plugged in and lifted off with their glorious sound and vision. I requested my favorite song. He obliged. They cracked open the room with a wail of guitars and his voice rang out over all the loud talking, the sounds of glass clinking, feet shuffling and coins hitting the inside of the till. I moved to him like I always knew how to. And when the set ended, the electricity, still feeding the room, threw us into each other. We passed through the crowd, past the bathrooms, down the hall and into the only private place in the whole bar—a dingy closet. Boxes upon boxes, old logos tacked onto chalkboards, empties, all things not necessary. But we were necessary. And this was our chance.

Ripping off each other's clothes, we gave in to our craving for each other. Tasting his mouth, from where that sweet voice echoed, was pure ecstasy; his hands feverishly grabbing every inch of my body, commanding my pleasure. He turned me around and threw me up against the wall, taking me from behind while I moaned a re-sounding "yes" from deep within myself. The music of "Dear Prudence" hung lightly over the hot air as we took our final thrusts together. Disoriented. Warm. Buzzing. We said good-bye.

KAITLYN KELLY, TORONTO

A standout in this piece is how the joint is so freaking hot that even the frigid air coming through the swinging door can't cool the flaming energy down. And "They cracked open the room with a wail of guitars" perfectly describes the jolt that transforms a club when the band starts to play.

WHAT'S THE KINKIEST THING YOU'VE EVER DONE?

I've had some sex. Good, bad, whatever. But the sexiest moment of my life was becoming a submissive at an S&M dungeon in L.A.

I was Genevieve.

I'd never worn a corset before, so three of the doms took me aside. Two of them held me steady in my six-inch stripper heels. I was like a fucking baby giraffe trying to balance in those things. Real graceful. Real sexy. (Eye roll.)

135

LET IT BLEED

The other laced me up so tight that I could practically taste my spleen. But damn. With legs like mine, the eighteen-inch waist I was left with and my tits pushed up to my nostrils, I was something to see.

My first session was actually a group session with a dom and a client. She was five-foot-ten when flat-footed. But no. Claire also liked to wear six-inch heels. She was much more graceful than I, of course.

She tied my arms together and fastened the rope to the suspension hook above my head. I was a baby giraffe again, swaying about as she tied my ankles.

Then she blindfolded me.

I didn't know what to expect. I couldn't see, could barely stand and could rely only on my hearing. But suddenly Claire was dragging her nails across my skin, starting at my ankles, the fabric of my fishnets tickling my now overly sensitized skin.

I swear I came.

Then she was running her fingers across my collarbone and arms. I barely recognized the wanton moan that escaped from my throat.

Then she removed my skirt.

I sensed her moving around me, like the proverbial lion stalking its prey. Then I felt the sting of the flogger against my bare ass cheeks.

No orgasm can compare to being flogged.

She made fast work of removing my corset and bra, and the licks of the flogger resonated up and down my torso.

I was glad for that blindfold. I was in my own head, having this experience that defined erotic, sexy, taboo, wrong!

It was only me, my Amazon Claire and her footsteps, and that flogger, leaving its delicious licks all over my body.

When she was done, she removed my blindfold, wiped the tears from the corners of my eyes, smoothed my hair down and brushed her lips ever so gently across mine.

I came again.

There was a client in the room? I hadn't noticed.

NATALIE RODRIGUEZ, LAS VEGAS

Whooooee! Natalie wound up her twelve minutes with a zinger, didn't she? A perfect ending that depicts how entangled she was in that all-encompassing, steamy spiderweb. Natalie's a newly-minted law enforcer in the great state of Nevada and looks pretty darn bitchin' in her spankin' new uniform.

DESCRIBE A TIME YOU WERE SEDUCED.

DESCRIBE A TIME YOU SEDUCED SOMEONE.

DO YOU HAVE A HEALTHY ATTITUDE TOWARD SEX?

RECALL A SPECIAL MOMENT WITH A LOVER.

I usually woke up with my nose nestled into his right armpit, snug as a kitten, smelling his man scent, stretching into awake as we disentangled from wet dreams that were mostly real. However, this morning slid through the blind, and I found myself alone, my nose nestled into nothing more than the sweet, sea-smelling, love-wrinkled pillowcase that late last night had been under my fanny making my tiny body easier for his big one to get at and into . . . wet dream indeed. Yum.

I did smell the familiar aroma of toast on the other side of the big red room. He padded over to bring the crispy pieces of white bread to me, dripping butter and strawberry heaven jam just like his mama used to make and still did. He went back for our tea and brought that to me in bed as well. This morning felt special and was already tingling with something that we hadn't experienced before. He said, "I want you well fed, and all tea'd up. I have a surprise that I want your ears for." I sat up in bed and crunched at my toast and sleepy-eyed him over the rim of the hot mug of tea. His dark curls fell loosely to his shoulders, and his neatly trimmed beard glistened like polished ebony in the morning sun. He looked like he was steaming from where I sat, the air before him wobbly from his heat. My legs stretched out to meet the floor; it was cold and I thought we should snuggle back in and pick up where we left off last night, all warm-to-hot in that soft, cuddly bed with the perpetually wrinkled sheets, never made, always ready to jump back into. "Come on, you! Up now, come listen!" I wrapped the top sheet around my naked body toga style and followed him up the stairs.

The big white room held a shiny black and very regal baby grand piano, a big cushy armchair that you could disappear into and a bench behind the piano. That was it. The light filtered through the curtains, shafts of light on Shaftesbury Avenue. He looked at me, his big brown eyes melting into mine, his mouth curled into that smile, and said, "Sit down and listen. This is for you, my love."

Then he started to sing in that strong, spun sugar voice . . . "Oh, baby, baby, it's a wild world, and it's hard to get by just upon a smile, girl . . ."

PATTI D'ARBANVILLE, TRYON, NORTH CAROLINA

Yum indeed, with his "spun sugar voice." Cat Stevens (now Yusuf Islam) wrote an entire album for my Lady D'Arbanville, entitled *Mona Bone Jakon*, a reflection of his captivating muse. Lordy lord, there's nothing like having a song written for you. My first true love, Chris Hillman, wrote a song about me, called "The One That Got Away." If I was the type to use clichés, I'd say it meant the world to me! He got away from me too, but I believe in reincarnation, don't you know.

> That's why I'm sighin' in the night
> Her dancing eyes laughin' so bright

Swoon . . .

RECALL "THE ONE THAT GOT AWAY."

DESCRIBE THE WORST BREAKUP YOU'VE BEEN THROUGH.

WHO WAS THE FIRST PERSON TO SHATTER YOUR HEART?

DESCRIBE THE FEELING OF LOSS AND HEARTACHE AND HOW YOU'VE HANDLED IT.

IF YOU'VE EVER BEEN ENGAGED, DESCRIBE YOUR MARRIAGE PROPOSAL. IF NOT, DESCRIBE YOUR FANTASY VERSION OF BECOMING ENGAGED.

HAVE YOU EVER BEEN MARRIED? IF SO, DESCRIBE YOUR WEDDING(S), AND IF NOT, YOUR DREAM VERSION.

DESCRIBE YOUR HONEYMOON.

HAVE YOU EVER BEEN DIVORCED?

THIS IS THE DIFFERENCE BETWEEN MEN AND WOMEN . . .

RECALL AN ARGUMENT WITH YOUR SPOUSE OR SIGNIFICANT OTHER.

I am not you. My daughter is my love. I watch her make Jesus cakes and dance in Christmas plays at church. She needs rich soil and constant pruning with small metal spades. She needs you to create perfect rows, with hand-painted seed signs and home-made scarecrows to scare the crows away. Instead you tear me down. We dance in the moonlight. You pit her against me because

I don't know fourth grade math. You tell me I am not much better than the mother who raised me. But what I do know, you cannot take away with your redneck confusion and half-truths. If we are to raise a balanced child, we will need to be thoughtful about our differences and wise beyond our ages. She is stardust flying across the universe for only a short time, and each of us is just powder on her wings. Too little of one and she will be forever confused. Too little of the other and she will be broken. Elevating to a higher plane as parents is the only solution. Alas, you are too busy ripping me to shreds to join me.

POLLY PARSONS, AUSTIN

When Polly read this aloud in class, we were all wiping away the tears. The line "each of us is just powder on her wings" made me gasp. It says so much about the fleeting nature and preciousness of childhood.

III

Teach Your Children Well

Polly's piece above leads squarely into this section for those of you who've experienced the scalding joys of parenthood. If working for a living didn't usher you all the way into adulthood, being responsible for a tiny person's precious life will grow you *right* up! Crosby, Stills and Nash had groovy advice in their song "Teach Your Children," and I know I've done my darnedest to always support and uplift my boy, Nick. But people have long speculated as to why parents aren't handed a guidebook from heaven before making the most humongous decision of their lives. It's impossible to really prepare for the brand-new human being that suddenly appears in your atmosphere, no matter what color you've painted the nursery.

> May you grow up to be righteous
> May you grow up to be true
> May you always know the truth
> And see the lights surrounding you
> May you always be courageous
> Stand upright and be strong
> May you stay forever young . . .
>
> BOB DYLAN

I was at Moon Zappa's tenth birthday party when my water broke, dribbling down my miniskirted legs. Gail happily drove me to Hollywood Pres, where I had secured a "birthing room" and planned to give birth "au naturel" without drugs. Curled in the back of Gail's snazzy Rolls, I bleated that I was sorry her leather seats were getting all wet, but she laughed and chirped, "It doesn't matter! You're having a baby today!"

Here is a clip from my second book, *Take Another Little Piece of My Heart*, about the birth of my son, Nick.

I waved good-bye to Gail, who promised to return when the baby came, and finally climbed into bed, my eyes crossed with spellbound attention to the matter at hand. I became an animal, alone with my womb; a wordless, focused hunk of primeval wildlife. . . . When Michael tried to caress me, I grunted like a beast, flailing at his fingers like they were pesky flies on my fur. . . .

. . . Because it was my first baby and since I was only at three centimeters, [they said] I was likely to be in labor for several more hours.

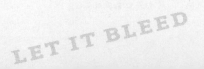

LET IT BLEED

I took in this information and discarded it instantly as fiction, knowing I would prove [them] wrong. Even though the pain was beyond mortal thought, I wanted to feel, feel, feel *it all wrapped around me like swaddling clothes. I pushed hard and felt something give. . . . "Michael, call a nurse." . . . The stunned angel of mercy found I was now at nine centimeters and when surprise flattened her features, I felt a divine sense of power wash over the careening agony. For a split second I was ferociously immortal. I felt like baying at the moon. . . .*

. . . The contractions had become constant, so I was one with the experience; one about to become two. Me and my shadow, strolling down the avenue. I prayed for a perfect baby and shoved like the brute creation I was, sounds coming out of me that had been heard only in the wild or maybe at a very large zoo. . . . "It's crowning! I can see the head!" That was my cue to thrust and heave with supersonic force, propelling the tiny, slippery being out into the big, brand-new world. The final push felt like a wrenching, all-consuming, full-body orgasm, with a choir of angels tossed in for good measure.

DID YOU CHOOSE TO HAVE CHILDREN? IF NOT, WHY NOT?

IF YOU ARE A PARENT, DESCRIBE YOUR PREGNANCIES.

IF YOU HAVE CHILDREN, DESCRIBE THE DAY EACH OF THEM WAS BORN. WHAT KIND OF CHILDBIRTH DID YOU CHOOSE? WAS YOUR PARTNER WITH YOU?

DO YOU FEEL YOU CHOSE THE RIGHT PARTNER TO RAISE YOUR CHILD OR CHILDREN?

Sitting around a campfire one night about a dozen years ago, I made a joke about my dad not remembering the seventies. A girl I'd just met laughed and said hers didn't either. "Yeah," I said, "but your dad is Alice Cooper." My dad didn't have a cool excuse for his excesses, but we all have our demons, and mine was at the camping trip with me. I'd always had notoriously bad taste in men, and had really outdone myself this time. Like most parasites, he was part of an infestation, so always had other freeloaders around him, but Calico, who had only recently met them, was super cool.

My daughter, who was around twelve at the time, happened to be wearing an Alice Cooper baseball cap that night. She was so embarrassed when she realized his daughter was camping with us. She thought it seemed like she'd worn the hat to impress Alice's daughter, but Calico encouraged her to leave the hat on and be proud of it, so she did. Because my kids were such big fans of her dad, Calico arranged to send us tickets and backstage passes to an upcoming concert in our little seaside city.

My kids were so excited. I let them get off school early, and they'd told all their friends. When I picked them up, their backpacks were filled with memorabilia for him to sign, which is a trait they inherited from their greedy, record-store-owning father. I'd been having a really rough time of it, and was so poor that I'd actually had to eat condiments as my meals. I was supporting two kids and one parasite on my no-degree salary in Southern California, and this led to late Christmas presents and not being able to provide basic needs, which was depressing and humiliating.

The parasitic friend of my parasite boyfriend was supposed to deliver the tickets to us that night, but he never showed up. He kept the tickets for himself and took the same friends he'd taken to an Alice Cooper concert the night before. None of them were even fans. My kids were crushed, but I took it even harder. I was emotionally invested in being able to do this for the kids, and now they were dejected

and would be humiliated at school. I could not stop crying. They
ended up consoling me, and I just felt like a bigger asshole.

GINA COVARRUBIAS, LAS VEGAS

Sounds like Gina's answer to this prompt was a resounding "No!" Describing her parasitic boyfriend and his freeloading pals as an "infestation" shows great imagination, and even a touch of biting humor.

WAS THERE SOMETHING YOU HAD TO GIVE UP BECAUSE YOU'RE A PARENT?

ARE YOU RAISING YOUR CHILDREN THE SAME WAY YOU WERE RAISED OR DIFFERENTLY?

HOW WOULD YOU DESCRIBE YOUR PARENTING STYLE? ARE YOU OVERLY PROTECTIVE? EASYGOING? A DISCIPLINARIAN?

HOW WOULD YOUR CHILDREN DESCRIBE YOU AS A PARENT?

WHEN YOU ARE (OR WERE) AWAY FROM YOUR KIDS, DO YOU MISS THEM OR FEEL RELIEF?

WHAT'S THE MOST TERRIFYING PARENTING MOMENT YOU'VE BEEN THROUGH?

The jet pulls from the gate and I'm in the back row, phone pressed to my ear, trying to hear the doctor—he's prescribing urgent surgery, urgent and exploratory—he can't figure out why my teenage son's bile duct is blocked, why he has a blinding five-day fever, why his eyes are glassy.

We only get to see him in photographs, online. We can only hand write letters. No phone calls. His letters make me chuckle and cry. They make him real again.

I search the photos for details . . . His clothes are dirty, hanging. His skin is covered in dust. His hair is dull. His eyes . . .

I can feel the stewardess moving down the aisle, pre-check. Now she's looming. People are buckled in. Cell phones off. I hold up one finger, as if that's going to make her go away. The doctor is telling me he wants to inject Connor with dye, the last option before surgery, but one that comes with a bit of a mortality rate.

Connor was an easy baby. Golden curls, deep blue eyes, laughter. Always laughter.

When did he drift away?

Before he started hanging with a new crowd. Before he took the bus south, before he took his skateboard and escaped like smoke into the ganja crowds of Venice.

Before he fancied himself a tagger, just this side of a banger.

"You're a white kid from a wealthy hood," I'd remind him as I'd pat down his pockets.

He was now DESER, his name in ink all over the west side, failing out of ninth grade and in trouble with the law. His dad and his stepmom were done with him. All of our lives had become unmanageable and we couldn't see the end of it—not a good one, anyway.

His dad floated the idea of Aspen Achievement Academy in Utah, built around the philosophy that when you pit groups of troubled kids against the wilds of Utah, everybody wins. Unless you develop a mystery illness. And now, thirty-eight out of forty-two days into it, Connor is really in trouble.

The captain drones into his microphone, "Sunny skies and a

smooth climb all the way, folks." I look out the window at that great expanse of sky—clear blues and white whites. My stomach is a fist.

Lose Connor, lose me.

When I land, the doctor tells me that Connor is gone. Not gone, gone, but back to the wilderness camp gone. He had a miraculous recovery while I was in the air.

They hunt him down in the pine scrub for me (where he's perfected the dinner—fire fueled by jack rabbit poops), and this is what he tells me—after he reminds me that I'm not allowed to call—"I want to finish this, Mom. I'll see you at graduation."

As we hang up, I see a cop car behind me and check my rental car's speed. The desert between Las Vegas and Utah—it's a beautiful night.

VICKI WHICKER, LOS ANGELES

Vicki's writing is suspenseful and spare. Being the mom of a nonconformist myself, *my* stomach was a fist until her motherly agony turned into glorious relief. All was beautiful again. Her boy was safe.

WHAT'S THE PROUDEST PARENTING MOMENT YOU'VE HAD?

WHAT IS ONE PARENTING MISTAKE YOU REGRET?

IF YOUR CHILDREN ARE GROWN, HOW CLOSE ARE YOU NOW?

DO YOU, OR WOULD YOU, SUPPORT YOUR CHILDREN FINANCIALLY IN TIMES OF TROUBLE?

DESCRIBE AN ARGUMENT OR BATTLE YOU'VE HAD WITH ONE OF YOUR CHILDREN.

WHAT DO YOU FEEL IS YOUR CHILD'S OUTSTANDING ATTRIBUTE? WHAT DID HE OR SHE GET FROM YOU AND YOUR SPOUSE?

HAS HAVING YOUR OWN CHILDREN AFFECTED YOUR RELATIONSHIP WITH YOUR PARENTS?

IF YOU'RE A GRANDPARENT, HOW DOES IT DIFFER FROM BEING A PARENT?

IV

Truth or Dare

Regrets, I've had a few. Not really—I don't even believe in regrets. Does it count if I regret something I didn't do? I try my best to share lovely moments with my fellow man and woman. I play fair, tell the truth unless it's going to mess someone up for life, and try to be some sort of glowing example for my loved ones and the many delightful (and sometimes not so delightful) people I encounter in my busy dizzy life. I throw a lot of parties and often it's a thrill being the center of attention, and other times it's exhausting and I want to lie down in a dark room and pull the covers over my head. Are you social? Antisocial? Fascinated with fame? Do you listen to your unwavering inner voice? Or as that fabulously corny country song asks, would you rather sit it out or dance?

DO YOU LIKE BEING THE CENTER OF ATTENTION?

OR ARE YOU SHY? BASHFUL? INTROVERTED? IF SO, HOW DO YOU FEEL IT HAS AFFECTED YOUR LIFE?

RECALL A TIME WHEN YOU WERE FORCED TO BE THE CENTER OF
ATTENTION.

DO YOU EASILY TALK TO STRANGERS?

HOW DO YOU BEHAVE AT PARTIES? ARE YOU A WALLFLOWER OR
THE LIFE OF THE PARTY?

DESCRIBE THE MOST MEMORABLE PARTY YOU GAVE.

DESCRIBE THE MOST MEMORABLE BASH YOU ATTENDED.

HAVE YOU EVER HAD ANY BRUSHES WITH FAME?

HAVE YOU EVER INTERACTED WITH A CELEBRITY?

DO YOU EVER PERFORM IN PUBLIC?

HAVE YOU EVER BEEN ON TV? IN A MOVIE OR DOCUMENTARY?
IN THE NEWSPAPER OR ON THE RADIO?

HAVE YOU EVER BEEN INTERVIEWED? ABOUT WHAT?

WOULD YOU WANT TO BE FAMOUS? IF SO, FOR WHAT? IF
NOT, WHY?

RECALL A TIME YOU LIED OR WERE LIED TO AND THE
REPERCUSSIONS.

I let a tiny creature die.
I let a parakeet die and told the easy lie that it had just—died.

As small pets do.

I was twenty-three and I didn't want the bird anyway.

It was a gift from my young husband, who had given it as a way of honoring the young me, the little girl with too few happy memories to share.

Peppy, the bird I'd loved when I was eight, had been killed by home perm fumes when my mom had forgotten to relocate him far enough away from her de facto beauty shop in our dining room.

No one lied about that. It was just what happened.

So now I was twenty-three and had a baby and a new bird. His name was Ian. He had a beautiful handmade cage. Her name was Ava and I had no idea what to do with her.

Recently, like a familiar dream where you turn a corner to find you're suddenly in some sinister place you've never seen before, I'd found myself living in East Texas where I had no connections at all but where the young husband had been hired to teach school.

I put the elaborate birdcage on top of the refrigerator to keep little fingers away and spent my days following the careening baby around the kitchen, out the back door, down the ugly rental house porch steps, past the fire ant mounds and, way too many hours later, into her little bed. Then I'd stand in the dark at the stove, or stare into the bathroom mirror for long minutes, having no idea who I was or where I was. It was during one of those quiet moments when I heard Ian hit the newspaper layers at the bottom of his cage like a dirty bomb.

KRIS KOVACH, AUSTIN

How about that thwack of a simile at the close of Kris's gutsy piece? Ouch. When the little bird hit the bottom of the cage, it must have actually been just a tiny thump, but for Kris it sounded like not just a bomb, but a loud, nasty blast. After she read this aloud in class, there was a

moment of silence, and the image of Ian, the tragic bird, stuck with me for a long time.

DESCRIBE A RELATIONSHIP (OF ANY TYPE) THAT YOU SCREWED UP AND HOW YOU COULD HAVE DONE IT DIFFERENTLY.

DESCRIBE THE LAST TIME YOU HAD YOUR FEELINGS HURT BY A CLOSE FRIEND OR FAMILY MEMBER. HOW WAS THE SITUATION RESOLVED?

WHO ARE THREE PEOPLE WHO CHANGED THE COURSE OF YOUR LIFE?

WHICH AUTHOR/WRITER HAS SPOKEN DIRECTLY TO YOU?

Hunter S. Thompson has added layers onto my life from the very first sentence. Reading him is a rush of heat to the cheek, a never-ending repeat of the same liquid fast words spilling over my mind. Gonzo writing is intense, stark, mean, real and speed-ridden.

It hits me so quick I can smell the exhaust, the taste of rusty copper in my mouth as its very essence enters every fiber of my being and makes me lean back. You cannot copy or pretend with his work; it is not your plaything, your id or your ego. It's all movement and should shock you into never attempting it yourself, its purified noise of truth should make you gulp. "It never got weird enough for me" is a direct dose of honesty, a go-to whenever I'm in doubt, it has driven me past my previous boundaries like an ambulance off a cliff—there's some security in there, but falling through the air just feels so good. Especially that first time.

The more I write about it and try to get to the orange red core of it, I lapse and stray further from the root. It is not the Man—it is

*what his life stood for. When sent to cover the Kentucky Derby he
ended up with a piece called "The Kentucky Derby Is Decadent and
Depraved," along with a color illustration of the discombobulated
heads and white heat of fat, bald, repulsive men betting on animals
they didn't give a shit about, galloping in the baking heat. He entered
himself into the center of it and became one of the mutants. He once
said the way you can tell a Republican from a "real Republican" is if
they look like a lizard when they get angry.*

*This is all over the place because there is no place to start . . . or
end, just hopefully enough here to make you enter into the moment
of an experience like Thompson did, instead of just being an observer.*

ADAM BRETHERTON, FAIRMOUNT, INDIANA

As I mentioned earlier, I invite men into my Fairmount, Indiana,
workshops. Adam isn't actually from Fairmount, but a young British James
Dean fan from Manchester who returns year after year like I do. He's
loaded with passion for the rebellious people who inspire him. In this
piece, he manages to give us the same smell of exhaust and the coppery
taste he feels while immersed in Thompson's words.

WHO DO YOU CONSIDER A HERO?

*I immediately want to go to familiar subjects: my grandparents, a
courageous friend who just went through her husband's illness and
death, or maybe the Dalai Lama. What's the definition of a hero?
Someone who has shown great courage, who has accomplished extraordinary things. A couple years ago I helped catalog a collection of
Holocaust materials at an academic library, ranging from well-
known books, like Elie Wiesel's* Night, *to lesser-known memoirs and
essay collections to actual artifacts and Nazi propaganda. I became
preoccupied reading the memoirs and testimonies and was awestruck*

LET IT BLEED

by the courage and heroism of everyday people living in extraordinary circumstances. The father who kept his family hidden while reporting to a train that would inevitably take him to a death camp, the child who tried to keep his sick parent alive by giving him tiny rations of bread, the soldier who fell in love with a seventy-pound girl with prematurely white hair he'd rescued from a camp and brought to new life in America. It made me stop and look at the people around me. The student or professor from a war-torn country, the immigrant working in the cafeteria. What heroism might be living within them, invisible to me as I pass them in the hallway?

LYLAH FRANCO, NEW YORK

The term is now a cliché, but "cut to the chase," when it was coined by silent filmmaker Hal Roach Sr., meant to skip the dull dialogue and get to the exciting chase scene—or *get to the point*, which perfectly describes Lylah's effective take on this prompt.

WHAT BRINGS YOU THE MOST JOY? RECALL ONE OF YOUR MOST JOYFUL EXPERIENCES.

GO THROUGH YOUR PHOTO ALBUM AND FIND A DOZEN PICTURES WHEN YOU APPEARED SELF-CONFIDENT. WRITE TWELVE MINUTES ON EACH.

WHEN DO YOU FEEL MOST AT PEACE?

WHEN ARE YOU THE MOST AFRAID?

DO YOU HAVE ANY PHOBIAS? IF SO, WHAT ARE THEY AND HOW DID YOU DISCOVER THEM?

RECALL A TIME YOU LONGED FOR SOMETHING. WHAT DOES LONGING FEEL LIKE?

ARE YOU LONGING FOR ANYTHING RIGHT NOW?

RANT ABOUT SOMETHING THAT REALLY PISSES YOU OFF.

DO YOU FOLLOW YOUR GUT FEELINGS? DESCRIBE AN INCIDENT WHEN THAT PAID OFF.

RECALL A TIME YOU DIDN'T TRUST YOUR INTUITION.

It's one thing to be in a relationship you shouldn't be in, but not knowing how to extricate yourself because you're being held hostage is another thing. I knew I should flee, but the resounding throb of my heart and pussy kept telling me otherwise. I met him at a club. He was very young, cute, tall, long-haired and played guitar, and he wanted me to be his girlfriend. Why did I feel annoyed? I thought I wanted to dive into deep, dark, sensual and musical adventures and feel the psychedelic, gothlike merging of the yin-yang. And so I got my wish, following what was sparking me, what was hip and cool in my peer group, and not trusting my intuition. I was involved in this thing called "rock 'n' roll" where I could live out big, overstuffed, H.R. Pufnstuf snakeskin Marshall stack dreams, with pink spandex and Doc Martens. Yes, I was in deep and that's how I liked to play it.

I wasn't good at paying attention to red flags. He still had a girl-friend, he drank and smoked a lot of pot, he enjoyed tripping and some of his friends were losers. Then we started having sex. That sealed the deal.

LET IT BLEED

Even though I had higher aims and personal goals like law school and writing, I somehow got sucked into thrash metal, alternative grunge excitement and intrigue. He pleaded to move in with me, but I had many crushes on other guys, one in particular. He found out about it when he read my diary, and announced his anger ferociously.

Even though I had given him everything—all my love, half of my apartment, my warm support and my body—the treason of me wanting another made me the sitting duck for five thousand years of patriarchal scapegoating. Surely I should be burned as a witch or put in irons in the town square and endlessly ridiculed.

I bought it. I didn't know how to get out. I was an addict for our miserable love. I lost my self-esteem and took no interest in life.

Point: if your intuition tells you no, listen.

LAURA GILMORE, NEW YORK

RECALL A TIME WHEN YOU DIDN'T LISTEN TO YOUR "INNER VOICE."

I was cursed and blessed being born into an Italian Catholic family. This entailed many things: learning how to curse in a Sicilian dialect (where every profanity involved an animal, a vegetable or a trip to Naples), having Sunday macaroni dinner every week of my life and being dressed in too much lace and white as if my First Communion was being perpetually celebrated.

It also meant that my mother expected that I'd marry young and live at home, unsullied, until the day of my wedding.

By my late twenties I was still unmarried. I was never the little girl who dreamed of her wedding day and I certainly was not the adult who dreamed of finding that perfect man.

I don't know if it was the imprint of my mother's hand-wringing guilt, the bleakness of being alone in the midst of a city of eight million strangers or the desperation of thinking that I'd never meet someone—and always be alone.

But I met someone, and we dated, and he asked me to marry him, and I said yes. I said yes and I knew it wasn't what I wanted and I knew I didn't want him. But I wasn't brave or self-confident or any of those other qualities that I had always admired in strong women. I was attracted to his intellect. I was attracted to that New Year's Eve poster for the Saint Mark's Poetry Project where his name sat next to Yoko Ono's and Allen Ginsberg's. I was attracted by the old photograph he showed to me, of a kind small boy feeding a stray dog.

But I knew this relationship was not right. There was something off. Awry. He and I were wrong together. Where one plus one equaled nothing. I never wanted to hold his hand or have his arm around me or kiss him in public. I didn't even care for sex with him. It was tepid at best, and at its worst, I just ticked off the minutes until it was over. But I felt I could do no better . . . and I thought that no one else was out there to love me.

The day of our wedding got closer and more oppressive. And though I knew it was a mistake, a wedding takes on a life of its own, building its own crushing, suffocating momentum.

There is something deep in our dinosaur brains that gives us intuition and prescience. Is it chemical? Instinctual? Divine? Do we sometimes smell the invisible aroma of someone's pheromones and it telegraphs a desire to fight or take flight? I knew that I should flee, but instead I acquiesced. Why didn't I listen to myself? Why didn't I believe that I needed, deserved, desired better.

I married a man who devolved into a hate-spewing, lying alcoholic, a somewhat talented PhD with a super-ego but not enough talent to warrant it. A jealous pedagogue who abused me verbally and emotionally and then financially when after ten long years I divorced him.

I'm a firm believer in not having regrets about decisions you've made. A regret only bathes you in melancholy and since you can't go back in time to change anything, it serves no purpose.

I messed up myself. I didn't listen to that inner voice that tells you to run as fast and hard and long as you possibly can—to save your identity, your sanity and your soul.

I learned to listen to that voice.

LINDA RIZZO, NEW YORK

Miss Linda is a spitfire New York DJ who isn't afraid to pour her mistakes onto the page and reveal how she's learned from them. Even though this relationship was a hellish one, she's realized that regret "serves no purpose." And her doozy last line completes the picture with elegant aplomb.

CHAPTER NINE

I

Livin' on the Edge

Most writers are metaphysical outlaws.
—TOM ROBBINS

Many of the women drawn to my books get up to all kinds of their own titillating tomfoolery. Here are some prompts to help you recall those heady moments when you threw caution out the back door and blithely entered the danger den.

HAVE YOU EVER DONE SOMETHING TABOO OR FORBIDDEN? WHAT WAS IT? HOW DO YOU FEEL ABOUT IT TODAY?

I was at this club called 7969 on Santa Monica Boulevard. It must have been fetish night because there was a hairy, overweight, middle-aged man walking around in a leather thong that reminded me of an adult diaper. He was wielding a paddle like some kind of hideous-yet-kinky man-baby, so it probably wasn't disco night. He kept asking people to paddle him, and I did when it was my turn, but being a

LET IT BLEED

dominatrix bored me when I was doing it for money, and doing it for free was even less exciting.

I got up on a table, like I always did in my twenties, and I was dancing wildly in a minidress and platform sneakers. I was drunk, probably off of overpriced Heineken, and I don't remember what music was playing. Some Hollywood-in-the-nineties thing.

This hot guy got up on the table and started dancing with me. I think he had long hair and he may have been wearing a trench coat, like he was lost on his way to play Magic: The Gathering. We started getting into it, grinding and gyrating against each other. Then I turned around and he stuck his hand up my dress and began fingering me. I bent over and let him. Whatever I was doing, no matter how public, it was still less of a spectacle than the groveling leather baby.

I lost touch with reality for a little bit, and at some point I returned and I realized the man with his finger inside me was not the same guy I had been dancing with. It was some other guy I'd never seen before. I think he was Mexican, and he looked like he was pretty pleased with himself. I just pretended I hadn't seen him and I turned back around and kept dancing. I didn't really care whose finger it was anyway.

GINA COVARRUBIAS, LAS VEGAS

Hideous kinky man-baby! What an unforgettable image! It sounds to me like Gina feels dandy-fine about her "taboo" experience today. There's no point in hanging on to guilt or feeling shame about anything. Forgive yourself, forgive others and move on down the line. And then write about it!

DESCRIBE A TIME YOU DID SOMETHING THAT WAS COMPLETELY OUT OF CHARACTER.

Uptown, Friday night. Streets that eons ago were laced with crack vials, bullets and the sorry carcasses of unemployed actors were now teeming with a potpourri of tragic hipsters and hipster wannabes. As I played my music off a shiny silver MacBook, virtual turntables grinding through thousands of almost long-lost pieces of someone's soul, the bar's front window sported a garish cheap-beer neon sign, casting an otherworldly glow of color onto my hair (not to be confused with the otherworldly blue-green color that it already was).

"Lost Dream" by the Electric Prunes fades into "Don't Press Your Luck" by the Shags.

The club was so dark that it gave everyone and everything a slightly out-of-focus patina of mystery and beauty. The glare from the lights inside the DJ booth rendered me somewhat blind and all I could see at a distance were the outlines of sawed-off guitar necks subbing for beer tap handles and silhouettes of the throngs at the bar. Long hair. Long hair. Shaved head. Long hair. Ponytail. Shaved head. The pattern repeated itself like a string of misbegot, style-challenged paper dolls. And then the pattern was broken, and my heart stopped.

He'd stand out in any crowd, because he's lots of a little too much. A little too much hair, too much black leather, too much metal, too much guy-liner. And I was a little too much . . . what? In love? Definitely, a little too much in lust.

"Ain't That Love" by the Cords mixes to "It's You" by Mickey and the Milkshakes.

I thought we made eye contact. It was too dark and I couldn't really tell, so I smiled and winked anyway. Oh jeez. I hoped my flirtation hadn't bypassed him and hit the big ol' biker dude next to him. The biker dude who always requested that I play some "Bad Brains!"

"Sixty Minutes of Your Love" by Love Affair segues to "Every Minute of Every Day" by Mal and the Primitives . . .

And when I looked back up from the mixer he was smack in front of me. All fucked up shaggy layered hair and crooked smile and dimples and shit.

"Flirting with the biker dude, eh? Should I be jealous?"

As he finished his bottle of beer in one gloriously long and deliberately sultry swallow, I was struck deaf and dumb. Besides the fact that he had on honest-to-God Beatle boots, Cuban heels and all, he was wearing velvet pants. Black. Velvet. Pants. Very tight . . . black velvet pants . . . with a lace-up fly. Shall I stop now?

Oh, sweet baby Jesus. Let me get this out of the way now. Bless me, Father, for I have sinned. It's been about twenty years since my last confession . . .

I couldn't help myself. "Nice pants, babe."

I lined up a massive amount of songs from my "I Wanna Punk You Up" playlist. I switched to automix and did what I had only fantasized about. I took his hand in mine and walked to the back of the bar, imagining we would do what countless others had done before us. I opened the door to the most hideously graffitied and poorly maintained bathroom, and beneath the snarling yet knowing photographed gazes of Joey, Johnny, Stiv and Sid, to the opening one-two-three-four count of "I Wanna Be Loved," he pulled me inside . . .

LINDA RIZZO, NEW YORK

WHAT IS THE MOST DANGEROUS THING YOU'VE EVER DONE?

WHAT IS THE RISKIEST THING YOU'VE EVER DONE?

ARE YOU GUILTY OR ASHAMED ABOUT ANYTHING YOU'VE DONE?

WRITE ABOUT A SECRET RENDEZVOUS.

ONCE WHEN NO ONE WAS LOOKING, I . . .

Tom Robbins, author of breakthrough irreverent novels like *Jitterbug Perfume* and *Even Cowgirls Get the Blues*, once said that humanity has advanced "not because it has been sober, responsible and cautious, but because it has been playful, rebellious and immature." Sometimes we just have to follow the voice of unreason.

THE VOICE IN MY HEAD TOLD ME TO DO IT . . .

The first time the Voice said, "Why not? Just try it," I lined up for a cattle call to be a movie extra, one of about three thousand people who submitted a photo. But I kept hearing about Travolta filming all over town, and I just thought, "Oh well, I guess I didn't get the part."

The second time: I was sitting at my desk at work, a very hectic day in March. The phone rang and a casting assistant asked if I could be at Gruene Hall at seven the next morning and commit to eight days on set. Talk about bad timing. My car was in the shop, we were trying to close on a house and my first marriage was at the beginning of the end. I love Gruene Hall. Damn. But the voice in my head came out of my mouth. "Sure, I'll be there." Then I hung up and said out loud, "Oh God, how am I gonna do that?"

Turned out I was one of about thirty extras in a bar scene that started off with a dance that turns into a fight. We had to dance to "Chain of Fools," and a few of us would get chosen to dance with the main star: John Travolta.

They didn't want us to look too "dancer-y," and I made it to the final twelve to run through the scene with the choreographers. Then Travolta himself crashed the audition and said, "No way I'd miss dancing with twelve women!"

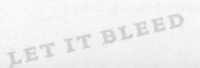

He danced with each of us and that voice in my head said, "Smile!
Smile! Eye contact!" I was one of the final eight chosen—by him—to
dance all around and with him. My job was to stand near him for
hours on end while lighting guys, gaffers and cameramen set up shots.
The fight scene took six twelve-hour days to shoot, so we got to cut up
a lot, and let me tell you, that totally beat the shit out of a desk job!

Blink and you miss me in the actual movie, and I almost lost my
job and my marriage over it, but I'm glad I listened to that voice and
still break out in a big grin whenever I hear "Chain of Fools."

LISA GOUVEIA, AUSTIN

Here's another response to the same prompt, which just shows how we
all travel to the beat of a different drum, as the divine Linda Ronstadt once
crooned. By listening to that voice in her head, Lisa created a funtastic experience. Tory, my youngest Austin doll, hears a very different kind of voice,
and describes the torment of depression impeccably. When she says the
voice in her heart was "crying like a newborn," I got those full-body chills.

It wasn't me, I swear. I want to live. I promise. But the voice in my
head told me to do it. The voice in my head told me I didn't want to
live anymore. Then it told me all the many ways I could commit
suicide. I ruled out the most physically painful ones. The voice in my
head ruled out ways to die like I was planning a murder investi-
gation. I was planning my own murder. The voice in my head told
me to do it.

Then the voice in my heart spoke up. It was crying like a newborn.
Don't do it, baby girl, be the one to stand up and shock this system.
But when I'm alone, the voice still comes out of the dark. I try to keep
myself busy and say Get out of here, bitch-ass thought! But sometimes
I succumb to the voice in my head telling me I'm not good enough,
that it's too painful to care.

Then the voice in my head told me to start living. And I mean really living every single moment I'm given. If I want to die anyway, then why not go for it? Go for life, go for love, go for dreams. Go ahead, kid, fill up your empty heart with bliss. Reverse psychology is the hidden key. The voice in my head told me to do it, so I've been living every day like I'm seriously dying.

TORY HARGROVE, AUSTIN

DESCRIBE THE FIRST AND LAST TIME YOU DID SOMETHING.

RECALL A MEMORABLE STONED EXPERIENCE (IF YOU CAN, HA-HA!).

The first and last time I ingested peyote in this particular way, I swore it would be the last time. My roommate, Harvest, had envisioned a marvelous money-making scheme, which called for her to hitchhike to New Mexico, hook up with a guy she'd met at the Dead concert, and buy peyote buttons he'd told her were available there. These she would then sell for a tidy profit—keeping a few, of course, for our own spiritual questing.

Things began well enough; she got a ride right away and called us from Tucumcari the next afternoon. "God, they're amazing looking!" she told us excitedly. "This is going to be so outta sight!"

Two days later she arrived back in Berkeley, tired but still excited about her bright financial prospects. She'd brought back a whole grocery bag full of the mysterious buttons, which somewhat resembled butter squashes, but sort of purple and bruised.

"I guess we just eat them," she said blithely and plucked one out of the paper bag. She took a smallish bite and immediately gagged. "It's fucking horrible!" she choked out and ran for water. "We've got to cover up the taste somehow."

163

LET IT BLEED

We searched the kitchen but found very little to mitigate the bitterness of the buttons. Then we looked in the freezer and saw the ice cream.

"How about a milk shake?" Strawberry, our other roommate, suggested as she came downstairs. "And it's my favorite flavor!" she laughed, turning to wink at her old man, Chocolate, lapping enthusiastically at his ear with her tongue.

"That's it!" I said, and Harvest got the blender. Twenty minutes later we were all fighting over the two toilets, trying not to throw up on each other.

"I told you not to put all that Hershey's syrup in it," Straw admonished me, thus setting off another tidal wave of nausea and projectile vomiting.

Admittedly, the psychedelic experience that followed the storm of puke was quite lovely, but none of us cared to follow that particular road to enlightenment a second time.

The next day, Harvest, now in a rather more businesslike frame of mind, set about making her scheme pay off by spreading the word about the groovy opportunity to partake of fresh-picked, Don Juan–worthy peyote buttons. Potential buyers asked awkward questions, like, "What's the best way to eat them?" One guy said he'd buy one to try, but reconsidered when she told him they were two dollars apiece, saying they looked nasty anyhow.

And the truth was that they did look nasty—and looked nastier still, every day. Harvest had stored them in her closet, and soon her clothes smelled much like our compost heap. Then a week or so later, she noticed her shoes sticking to the floor and discovered that the bottom of the grocery bag had dissolved and the rapidly decomposing peyote buttons were now just a gluey unhealthy mess of rotting goop all over her closet floor.

Summoned to this disappointing scene, all I could do was pass her
a joint and observe that the goop looked pretty trippy.

MARGARET FARRELL, LOS ANGELES

HAVE YOU EVER EXPERIMENTED WITH DRUGS? IF SO, WHAT KIND AND FOR HOW LONG?

For many years my best friend was a Latina named Marijuana. I
first heard about her in junior high when she was someone the bad
boys invited to all their parties. I knew they were all too wild for me
at thirteen or fourteen, and I steered clear. A few years later, though,
she basically moved into my house. My brother knew her well, and
we all spent many hours in her cheerful company.

When I eventually started convening with her directly, I simply fell
in love. Marijuana had a wonderful sense of humor, and she led me
to join with music in a way I had never imagined possible. It came to
be that even when we were not actually together, her influence fol-
lowed me—I made ever more imaginative associations in my or-
dinary life, and became infinitely more inventive and joyously creative
and full of deeply felt insights about home decor, calculus, and the
everpresence of God.

I was intimate with Marijuana almost every day for ten years. I
see her rarely now, but my debt to her for the liberation of my mind
and spirit is vast, though she will never expect or understand the
concept of repayment. It delights me now that my daughter has also
come to know the joys of Marijuana. Her legacy will never die.

PENELOPE THRASHER, CHICAGO

It's so comical and clever the way Penelope chose to "humanize" Miss
Mary Jane! I can almost picture her dreamy bloodshot eyes.

LET IT BLEED

II

Regrets, I've Had a Few

Many of the tales you include in your memoir will be full of heartrending woe, maybe even tinged with shame or regret—experiences you wish hadn't happened. You may feel reluctant to write about some of the screwy choices you made and the folly that followed. Don't dwell on the events or give in to self-judgments, just go with the prompts. There's a lot of strength, required and generated, in spilling your guts all over the page. If you decide later to burn your words in a fiery Wiccan ritual, so be it.

WHAT WOULD YOU WRITE ABOUT OR INCLUDE IN YOUR MEMOIR IF YOU HAD NO FEAR?

I'D LIKE TO FORGET ABOUT . . .

I'd like to forget about the smell of pipe tobacco and lumberyards. More correctly, planing mills and lumber camps. The wood smoke, sawdust, the scent of wine or Four Roses always lingered around him. His beard was scratchy as it rubbed against my face. His hands were hard, callused, strong, insistent, determined. He felt soft and spongy in my tiny hand, then suddenly . . . not. I'd like to forget about plaid wool shirts, work pants and suspenders. Again, the smell of sawdust from the planing mill, but this time a clean, sweet smell. Coupled with shy touches and an innocence seemingly out of sync with a man of his age. He never meant harm.

I'd like to forget about the stuffy winter smell of the heater in the old Buick. And the musty blankets in the backseat.

I'd like to forget about the particular bulge in the zipper area of blue jeans. That cow barn smell that I loved, and the acrid sweat from a hard day's work.

I'd like to forget about the catechism lessons in the kitchen while everyone else watched Lawrence Welk in the living room. I remember how that particular bulge pressed against my eight-year-old cotton-pantied crotch, as he whispered, "Wouldn't it be nice if this was real?" thrusting against me as he swung me around the kitchen, my legs wrapped around his waist.

I'd like to forget about the taste and smell of Freon. The feel of an unfamiliar object entering my body. The crying, the disbelief, the assault, the lasting pain.

But no blood. Not a drop. I didn't bleed for any of them.

DIANNE SCOTT, AUSTIN

Miss Dianne has written several times about her abuse and abusers, and through the painful process of reliving and sharing, the long-ago nightmares don't hold sway over her life any longer. She has even read "Not All Wounds Are Visible" (a saying in the PTSD community), a piece that stemmed from a prompt in class, at a Tertulia (Spanish for "a social gathering with literary or artistic overtones") in the Continental Club Gallery. The applause was deafening! Dianne also has the distinction of being the longest-running female bouncer at any club in the U.S. of A. Don't even try to sneak in the back door of the Continental without being on the list!

I CARE TOO MUCH ABOUT . . .

I care too much about you.
All the ones that came after you could never quite fill the
    void. If not for you I would never have a word to write.
Now, it seems I am running out of words to write.

But maybe I can summarize you.

You . . .

Make my head hurt

Make me cry

Make me laugh

Make me want to write

Inspire me

Depress me

Make me feel love

Make me feel hate

Make me contradict everything I say & feel

Make me insane

Center me

Love me

Hate me

Fuck me

Deny me

Welcome me with open arms

Push my buttons

Thrill me

Teach me

Bring me to life

Kill me

It is time to end this.

I think it's time to end you.

But if I end you I would also be ending myself.

BRIANNA WIRTH, LAS VEGAS

Whoa! Haven't we all been caught up in this same conundrum? When you care more about that bad boy than you should? When the playing field is woefully uneven? Brianna captures this deadly dance of back-and-forth with point-blank precision.

WHAT IS SOMETHING YOU'VE HAD TO LET GO OF?

My father died in Vietnam. Ten years after the war, he finally got around to killing himself. My childhood swung like his fists, in a drunken desperate balance—equal parts fairy tale and nightmare—between my mother and my father.

I feel the ache of my father's regret. It reaches me like the light of a star that burned out thirty years ago. It wasn't until middle school when I realized the Vietnam War had actually ended. I even had the nerve to argue with my teacher. At first I was insistent. And then just embarrassed. Because my dad had talked about the war every day. He talked about his men. He talked about shrapnel. He uttered strange foreign phrases like "dinky dau." And about how we had landed on the moon the same day he lost half of Bravo Company. I never realized the war had ended. Somehow I had missed this crucial fact.

"But there are still men over there!" I told my teacher. She looked at me sadly. I felt my face flame. Please don't ask, I hoped, as the realization washed over me. Don't ask me about him.

I went home and cried. I wondered what else I had gotten wrong. I could hear his voice like it had never been silenced. And so I pushed it away.

It wasn't until my grandmother, his mother, had passed that I heard his voice again. In a closet on the second floor of that house on Washington Street was a box pushed way to the back. On it was written the name "Jaw," my father's nickname from an ugly scar earned in some far-off land. The box was full of letters by a poet sent to war. And at the bottom, a war journal . . .

LET IT BLEED

I dove in. I read them all, saving the journal for last. I read every word. I thought about him hanging from our second-floor balcony, the rope silencing him, save for his voice in my head, and I understood. I read his words and I understood. It was too much, just too much.

I put the letters away. I put the top back on the box and pushed it to the back of the closet in final grateful surrender.

JESSI GUNTER, NASHVILLE

Often I'm amazed at how my girls get down to the real nitty-gritty in the twelve allotted minutes. Jessi's powerful, painful remembrance proves it can be done. She manages to convey the ache of loss, the anguish of schoolroom embarrassment, the horrors of war and, finally, the acceptance of her father's suicide.

HAVE YOU EVER FELT LIKE YOU WERE ON THE OUTSIDE LOOKING IN?

Often in the past, I've felt real displacement and dislocation, but now that I'm older, I feel more "in" than I ever have—which means living more in the Nowness, since surface level and appearance no longer matter so much, if at all. I am at home in the strange, more so than in the familiar.

Painfully, a place where I definitely did not belong was my small hometown in Hillbillyland, where I felt I was born into the wrong situation. When I was gang-raped by people I knew, I split in two: me and what was happening to me—two very different entities. That split was, of course, a coping mechanism. In order to continue to survive, I had to operate that way.

Another such split was after my drowning accident and "out of body" experience when I looked down at my mother sobbing over the gurney where my skinny little eleven-year-old self lay, and I made a conscious decision not to leave her because she'd suffered so much over the death of my older brother thirteen years earlier.

In early grade school when I first ventured from the pastoral safety of my childhood farm life, I may have seen what I was lacking by comparing myself to others—such as not having running water or heat. But I was very young and wanted more to fit in and be like the other kids than to possess any one thing.

Thankfully, though, I was treated abysmally in my youth, or I might never have left that gossipy, stuck-in-time environment. Instead, what a rich life full of loving memories I've made along the way—mainly because I was/am different.

TERRY MORELAND HENDERSON, LOS ANGELES

Despite all the difficulties Terry had to endure growing up, she's been able to put her life into perspective and has even found strength and goodness in her experiences. Writing about these episodes has actually given her a sense of gratitude for the woman she's become.

ONE THING I KNOW FOR SURE IS . . .

One thing I know for sure is that I'm in love with him. The difference between then and now is that it doesn't matter anymore. Because the second thing I know for sure is that he's a liar. He's a good liar. He's a liar in the way that Holly Golightly is phony. He doesn't lie to you to hurt you, but because he believes his lies. I used to believe them too. I understand his lies but I don't believe them anymore.

They're like games. He says he loves me and I say I love him too. He says let's get married and I say okay. He says he's coming to visit me and I say I can't wait. I know none of it is real but I play along,

LET IT BLEED

get caught up in it, and sometimes for a minute, it feels like real life. But I know it's not.

I don't think I'll ever not be in love with him, and I like it that way. I don't care anymore if it works out or not, if the ups and downs are heartbreaking, if he's here one minute and gone the next. None of it matters. It's trivial. Because after seventeen years, I still haven't met anyone that comes close to him. There's no runner-up.

If I hated him, which I have, I'd still be in love with him. If I loved someone else, I'd love him more. I still smile every time I hear his voice. I have thirty-seven voice mails from him that I've accumulated for the last few years. I didn't save them to listen to over and over again, but because I want to hear his voice after he dies. I want that long four-minute rambling voice mail so I can laugh out loud when he's gone.

I've been waiting for him to die for over a decade. I've seen him through rehab more times than I can count. I don't think he'll ever be sober. He's not a sober guy. He gets clean for a few months and those months are great, but then he relapses and it's a fucking nightmare. It used to hurt so bad. I'd cry and plead and try to save him. Now it doesn't hurt because I don't expect anything different. I don't even think of him as a real person anymore.

There have been months when I've purged my life of him because it's been too much. The broken promises, the hollow words. Once he told me he was dying of cancer when he wasn't. Another time he locked himself in my bathroom and did heroin, and when I kicked him out, he took back all the books he'd ever given me on his way out the door. It was my birthday and he told me he'd never trust me again. He's already broken my heart. He's done all the things to make me walk away from him. And I always know what to expect.

He left me a voice mail two weeks ago that I listen to every night, sometimes twice. It almost sounds like real life. It almost sounds like he means it and I should believe him. One thing I know for sure is that I'm in love with him. I always have been and I always will be, and it doesn't mean a thing.

BONNIE FROMAN, SEATTLE

It's incredible what we'll endure when we are *in love*. Most of us have been in the sticky insufferable situation Bonnie describes with an almost fly-on-the-wall objectivity. You can tell by her long-suffering tone that she's accepted the utter truth of the situation, her broken heart be damned.

WRITE ABOUT A BROKEN PROMISE.

RECALL A TIME YOU CHANGED YOUR MIND.

RECALL A TIME YOU WANTED SOMETHING DESPERATELY—A RELATIONSHIP, A JOB, A THING—AND DID NOT GET IT.

III

A Change of Scenery

As a preteen I was enthralled with the movie *Around the World in Eighty Days*, starring the debonair David Niven and his clownish sidekick Cantinflas, who got them into a plethora of tricky situations all over the globe. I hadn't been out of California yet, except for the flatlands of Dayton, Ohio, and the Technicolor view from the airborne balloon held such eye-popping possibilities that I vowed that Pam Miller would *go places*!

Any change of scenery takes us from everyday humdrum and our same old worries to a spanking new landscape where something unexpected is

LET IT BLEED

bound to happen. Let's explore some of the wheres on this wild planet that *you've* visited!

DESCRIBE AN UNFORGETTABLE VACATION.

We got up early. He likes to fly after ten a.m., but the flight was early, so early we went. I travel constantly, but still have nerves when boarding, and even more so at takeoff. Higher and higher, the clouds engulfed us. Thank you, Xanax. Fast-forward six hours and our legs are no longer cramped. Bathroom, luggage, rental car.

We arrive and are greeted with cool towels for sweaty brows and glasses of minty iced beverages. Sailboats docked in the marina are easily viewable from our guest room balcony. Pillowy down comforters and chaise lounges gently occupy our time. My tanned daughter dives effortlessly into the pool at night with the heavens shining down on her and the stars watching over her as she glides seamlessly from one end of the pool to the other.

While driving, I notice that the sky looks different here, like God took everything that was blue and lifted it overhead. The sand is soft like cotton, but granular like sugar—and just as sweet when your toes seep in. The man of my dreams and my daughter run to the edge of the surf and let waves lap at their heels. He finally convinces her that here, the ocean water will make you smile, and I hear her giggle from my warm spot on my beach towel. Their heads bob like whack-a-moles up and down in the distant ocean.

On the drive back we stop where the pineapples grow. Their sweetness lingers on my tongue long after I swallow. The fields are red like Zion Canyon, and the tops of the fruit are like Christmas trees sticking out of the soil. We pause at a fruit stand where they cut and bag our fruit and it dawns on me then: These people are living the good life, the desired life, a contented life.

Back in our hotel room, my daughter takes a book and heads for the balmy balcony. I've never seen her look so grown up, yet so filled with wonder. I want her to appreciate things and people and experiences.

We walk downtown at one p.m. for dinner and opt for breakfast foods. French toast and fresh-squeezed juice never taste as good anywhere else as they do in Hawaii.

JJT, LAS VEGAS

DESCRIBE YOUR FIRST BIG TRIP WHEN YOU TRAVELED OUTSIDE YOUR COUNTRY, STATE OR HOMETOWN.

HAVE YOU EVER HITCHHIKED?

WHAT'S YOUR BEST TRAVEL STORY?

YOUR WORST TRAVEL STORY?

WHO IS YOUR MOST MEMORABLE TRAVEL COMPANION?

HAVE YOU EVER TRAVELED WHERE YOU DON'T SPEAK THE LANGUAGE? IF SO, HOW DID IT WORK OUT?

HAVE YOU EVER BEEN LOST? REALLY LOST? HOW DID YOU GET FOUND? WHAT HAPPENED TO YOU WHILE LOST?

IF YOU COULD GO ANYWHERE IN THE WORLD ON A VACATION, WHERE WOULD IT BE?

LET IT BLEED

CHAPTER TEN

I

I've Got the Music in Me

As you can already tell, most of my writers are slightly music obsessed, and I have found that musical prompts take my girls to a liberating place when they describe what the music does to them, inside and out. Very little thinking gets in the way as they blast back to a live concert or the first time they heard a certain song.

A fun place to start is with a question that pops up on Facebook every once in a while: "What was your first live musical experience?" I always feel like I'm the winner because my first concert was the freaking *Beatles*!

It's a forever memory engraved inside my pupils because I can blink and see it all again, just like waving a magic wand and landing in the fifth row at the Hollywood Bowl, August 23, 1964. James Paul McCartney's side of the stage. I am determined not to shriek, wail and sob like the other Beatlemaniacs, swooning all around me. I am piercingly focused, holding my head high, my hair coiled up on my head with a long-ringleted piece of fluff streaming down my back— very mature for a fourteen-year-old. I am bedecked in a blue-checked mini outfit, carefully chosen, chiffon, tight, short and sassy, gazing hard at the Cute Beatle, knowing for certain we will make eye contact. Knowing. Knowing. Knowing.

And we do. His bedroom browns lock onto my baby blues. The moment shimmers, the world spins and spins, rollicking inside me. The screams cease. True tunnel vision. One second. Two.

I know he's seen me like I know his first name is really James. That Ringo was born Richard Starkey, that John's birthday is October 9, that Paul's mother died when he was only fourteen, that he was named after his dad, Jim, who played the trumpet, that he has the longest, leanest legs in rock and roll . . . Slowly, slowly, the oh-so-familiar music comes back to me, barely discernible over the howls and yipping of my besotted compatriots. The Beatles played for twenty-three minutes and then they were gone. Girls are fainting and holding each other up beside me as I numbly walk out of the Bowl. My Beatle friends talk loudly, animatedly, about the show, but I am silent and sure and wildly alive. I have been seen.

PAMELA DES BARRES

So now it is your turn. I was one lucky duckling to have the Fab Four be my first, but we're all one in our love for rock and roll. How much can you remember about the very first live music experience that shook, rattled and rolled you?

DESCRIBE YOUR FIRST LIVE MUSICAL EXPERIENCE.

Here are a few more to start your heart racing and get those musical moments onto the page! Sheva's uplifting piece captures my feelings about how certain concerts have taken me to the true church, connected to the souls of twenty thousand compatriots. Four hours of Springsteen?! Give it to me!

DESCRIBE THE IMPORTANCE OF MUSIC IN YOUR LIFE.

If you believe in magic—and I know you do—and you believe music is magic—well, of course it is—then you know that concerts are a

LET IT BLEED

hallowed place where magic happens. They represent the holy joined with the profane, the exquisite with the mundane. They are sacred and special.

Going to a concert is like a July revival meeting in a tent in Mississippi. Hot, sweaty; arms outstretched. Bodies pressed together, focused on the priests and priestesses onstage. Heads thrown back and eyes closed in ecstasy. It's prayer and sex brought gloriously together, with all the splendor and ritual appropriate to such an event.

The true believers gather in the front; the skeptics hang back. The lights dim, the chatter ceases and for a moment everyone breathes as one.

Then they appear. The magicians. The shamans. The holy rollers. The preachers, the teachers, the tellers of great truths. The best of them—the ones you lose your heart and soul to—glow as if lit from within.

The bass booms and throbs right through you, merging with your heartbeat. The guitars ring and rock, singing sweet and high or reaching down, way down, into that secret place inside you. As one song gives way to another, you are a disciple, a devotee—you shake and dance, clap your hands, laugh and cry and offer up praise.

These are the moments I live for. I come alive, abandon all cares and worries and immerse myself in the music as if in the mikveh, *the Jewish ritual bath. I sing and pray and give thanks, and emerge with my spirit cleansed and my faith renewed.*

My life was saved by rock and roll. Wasn't yours?

SHEVA GOLKOW, NEW YORK

DESCRIBE THE AHA MOMENT WHEN YOU HEARD *YOUR* MUSIC FOR THE FIRST TIME.

WHAT WAS THE FIRST ALBUM YOU BOUGHT?

The first album I bought with my own allowance money was Alone with Dion *(sigh) and I still have it. Once in a while I pull it out, gaze at the come-hither cover and briefly become the thirteen-year-old girl who proudly carried her Dion Fan Club card. It was his first foray into a solo career, having left the Belmonts behind, singing on the street corners in the Bronx. I would sit in my room and study Mr. DiMucci's eyes smoldering into the camera, a pair of hot-pink-satin-clad arms wrapped tightly around his torso, and wonder who got to embrace my hero and how long did she have her arms around him? How tall was he? What did Dion smell like? He's a study in nonchalance, so relaxed, the utmost in cool. And the album features the song "Lonely Teenager," which still ranks very high on my personal hit parade. Not only was he crazy handsome, and crooned with yearning angst, "What can I do? What can I say?" He understood me!*

I recently made the pilgrimage to the Bronx and wandered the wide streets, past Italian markets and garlicky scents wafting yummily all around me, ate in a restaurant that Dion still frequents, and stood in the foyer of the very building on Belmont Avenue where Dion and his Belmonts doo-wopped their way into the Rock and Roll Hall of Fame. My friends and I tried to re-create the poppin' harmonies, but anyone strolling by probably wondered where the racket was coming from!

It's remarkable how certain things that happened during our pubescence still hold such tender sway in our lives. Yes, Bobby Rydell was suave, Fabian was cute, but Dion was smooth and he wrote his own songs. I'm proud of my good teenage taste in music.

At seventy-seven, Dion continues to perform brilliantly, and I still drive hours to sit enraptured in the front row and glow. When he sings "Runaround Sue," I have to get up and dance, and sometimes he spots me and his eyes twinkle behind his überly cool shades. It still feels good to be seen.

PAMELA DES BARRES

LET IT BLEED

My Austin writer Rhonda doesn't remember her first album purchase quite as fondly.

It was the time of skating at Playland on Friday nights. It was the time of . . . disco! I bought the C'est Chic album on a shopping trip with my parents from the record bin at Tom Thumb. I liked one song—"Freak Out." It was played everywhere and constantly: at the skating rink, on the radio, at slumber parties, on TV shows like Solid Gold.

That one song was fun and upbeat. The rest of the songs on that album, I soon found out, were jibber-jabber to my eleven-year-old mind. I didn't understand the whole world of Studio 54, and the "you can't get past this rope because you're ugly" thing. I wasn't going to admit it to anyone that I didn't even like disco. But being naive, I didn't realize there was anything else out there for me. Changing the station wasn't an option because the cool kids listened to disco, so I went along with it, but longed for something more. Something I could understand. Something not superficial, "Let's dance all night and be cool." Or as I later learned, "Let's dance all night because we're on cocaine." I didn't have any way to tell people that it made me feel . . . empty. My parents couldn't help. My dad listened to country, for Pete's sake. Another no-no in my crowd.

So for the next year or so, I endured and pretended I liked it, until disco died a tragic death. R.I.P. I know that album is still in my storage unit somewhere. I may get it out one day and listen. But probably not.

RHONDA ATKINSON, AUSTIN

As I mentioned before (Dylan freak that I am), "Like a Rolling Stone" actually altered my consciousness with its insistent demand, "You shouldn't let other people get your kicks for you"—advice I took, and still take, very seriously. We all have a song that opened a brand-new space inside us, making room for a radical way of thinking.

WHAT IS A SONG THAT CHANGED YOUR LIFE?

When I hear Stevie Nicks singing "Gypsy," I go into this deep, sacred, primal, childlike hole where darkness is nothing to be feared. And manifesting all my dreams and desires feels like the only way to live and survive. At Fleetwood Mac's Portland show I burned my thumb on my lighter, peed my pants and lost a great pair of navy blue, steel-toed cowgirl boots. I was drunk off the energy in the arena—drumming, thumping, music pouring from the stage. Mick's unforgettable solo lasted forever as he shouted into the night and we ravenously joined in. Lindsey's enormous roar, swiveling his hips just so, Stevie inviting us into the renewal of all rock-and-roll rituals—unearthing tears and taking us into a cavern of thunder. It was mid-summer and after that concert I felt a knowing about myself, that Portland had found me, and I had found my gypsy. I have no fear, only love, the lyrics say. Sometimes it all does come down to you and you know it.

    KIM HOFFMAN, PORTLAND, OREGON

Remember our metaphors and similes lesson earlier? This is a peachy keen exercise to help you get a new kind of pizzazz into your narrative.

DESCRIBE A LIVE MUSICAL EXPERIENCE USING TWO SIMILES AND TWO METAPHORS.

I wait for the first note to begin. My favorite artist. I listen to him every day. The band has moved onto the stage and picked up their in-struments. The lights are low, and the show is ready to begin.

Then there they are: the first four notes struck on a keyboard as though from the gentle hand of an angel. The song begins traveling from the speakers, through my ears and into my very being. I feel my bones begin to resonate. The sound is Bliss. It crashes over me like an ocean wave. I feel myself floating away from the rest of my life. Concerns and fears dissolve in that safe space he creates with his sounds. I see the universe, and it is me. The surface of my skin is alive with dancing sparks. Like ethereal fingers glancing up and down my arms, my back, and over my head. A current of energy runs in a widening path where my spine used to be.

The projector shows a girl walking slowly through a multicolored desert with no destination. She moves easily without care, and I, too, am lost in that space. That space may feel bleak and lonely when you are captured by fear, but is so freeing when you let go and allow life to be. This music is my guide, the compass to point me toward my Truth. My reminder that all is as it should be—myself included.

FANNIE GUNTON, AUSTIN

Ah, the glory of just the right music at just the right moment! I counted at least three metaphors and three similes. Did you find them?

DESCRIBE WHY YOUR FAVORITE SONG HOLDS SO MUCH MEANING FOR YOU.

On Sundays, we would listen to three, sometimes four albums all the way through before Mom finished ironing or it was time for dinner. Lady Sings the Blues, Tapestry, anything Johnny Mathis. These were just a few of the Sunday afternoon selections that became part of me.

One album gave me quite a thrill every time it played—The Don Ho Show! A live recording of his concert in Hawaii. Dad humming, Mom singing once in a while. I remained mostly silent, examining album covers as spray starch fell, tickling the backs of my legs. Until track 18—"Sweet Someone." The one song all of us would sing together.

Fast-forward to the summer of 2014, our first full day in Hawaii. My mom's mind is quickly declining. Dementia is a thief; my mom its victim. She asks me to take a walk on the beach. The ocean on one side, high-rise hotels and condos on the other, we walk a few yards in silence. I point out a colorful catamaran. She stops to look, then turns to me. "Reese, are we in Vegas?" Without missing a beat, I say, "Nope. We're in Hawaii, Mama. It's so much better!"

We link arms and continue our walk. But I'm too slow for her. She follows the path around a lagoon. I sit on a bench and cry. I get myself together as I walk the path to meet her. An old guy with an old guitar sits on a wall, singing. "I wonder if he takes requests . . ." I wonder aloud. A few steps beyond him, my mom, unprompted, begins to sing that old Don Ho song, "Cast your memory now—Sweet someone . . . whoever you may be . . ." Arms linked, we sing the song as we walk back to our condo.

I don't know where it came from inside her, but it came at the right place and right time.

RISSA DODSON, LOS ANGELES

Rissa's lovely piece reminds me of *Alive Inside*, the award-winning documentary that explores the astounding healing effects of music on dementia patients, especially songs from their youth. They come to life on-screen, sing along and seem lit up from within.

WHAT SONG ALWAYS UPLIFTS YOU?

WHAT SONG CAN ALWAYS MAKE YOU CRY?

It's just incredible to me how meaningful lyrics will stick with us all our lives. My Fairmount writer Cathy uses lyrics by Billy Joel and Paul Simon to sum up her frustration perfectly.

LET IT BLEED

I'd like to forget about life for a while—and how long ago I first heard that Billy Joel lyric. I need someone to see my writing in the Chronicle Tribune *and say, "Man, what are you doing here?" the way people say to Billy in his song "Piano Man."*

I saw Billy Joel in concert three times, twice in Indiana and once in London. I was a small-time groupie and remember waiting for Billy to come out of Wembley Stadium after the concert, but he ducked down low in the seat. Or maybe that wasn't him in the car at all. So my kids know Billy from my Greatest Hits DVD and they sing, "Sing us a song, you're the piano man," and their friends don't know who he is. Billy's old now and his voice may be raspy, but I remember and love his lyrics, "I felt the stranger kick me right between the eyes," about the stranger in ourselves. My favorite these days is "Don't forget your second wind . . . You're only human. You're supposed to make mistakes." I'm counting on that second wind as I look at all my mistakes. Billy makes me believe there's always hope. Maybe those mistakes and sadness and tough life lessons will all turn into something beautiful. Some days, I think they already have.

It's the everyday stuff that's memorable, like that footage I saw of Simon and Garfunkel's reunion in Central Park. A few years ago, I took my kids to see Art Garfunkel in recital. My favorite lyric from "America" had always been "Kathy, I'm lost, I said, though I knew she was sleeping." Maybe that's me talking to myself. My dreams are all good, but sometimes I don't want to wake up to a harsh reality. "I'm empty and aching and I don't know why," Art sang for me.

For some reason, sad songs speak to me. I was working at a tiny resort one summer during college and Willie Nelson and his band checked in. After they played at the state fair one night, they came back and gave us a free concert. "On the Road Again" was good. But "You Were Always on My Mind" was my favorite. "Girl, I'm sorry I was blind," Willie crooned.

People talk about when Kennedy was shot, but I remember when Elvis died. I was driving alone in the car with the radio on. It was my dad's birthday. My favorite song Elvis sang isn't "Blue Suede Shoes" or "Hound Dog." It's "You'll Never Walk Alone." I need to send the kids to YouTube where Elvis still sings "Though your dreams be tossed and blown, walk on, walk on, With hope in your heart."

CATHY SHOUSE, FAIRMOUNT, INDIANA

WHO IS YOUR FAVORITE MUSICIAN AND HOW HAS HE OR SHE AFFECTED YOUR LIFE?

Several of my L.A. writers have been coming to my workshops for years. Sara has written many times about how a particular musician has enhanced her reality beyond measure. She'll call him up out of those dark ethers whenever she gets the chance. It doesn't matter what kind of music rocks your soul.

This man is my greatest love. Now and forever. He saved me when my young mind wanted to live no more. He's crazy, insane, eccentric, and you can hardly understand him. He has many names, and some imply that he is a satanic follower.

This is most certainly not the case.

His voice alone pulled me up from the dark recess of my basement, giving my minuscule life meaning when I could not otherwise find one.

Because of him I developed a style, a personality, fearlessness and caution. He saved my life and he may never know. He inspired my

future and may never know. He is forever engraved on my skin and in my heart with an undying love that is so fragile.

With him as my guide, I went through a traumatic rebirth, in a good way. I became an entirely different person overnight; no longer was I a Mary Poppins–like creature with buttons done up to my throat. No longer was I the conservative white sheep of the family.

Nothing comes close to the first sexual fantasy you have as an emerging young woman. He was there first and he comes first. Over and over again this mumbling musician is my savior.

I love you, Ozzy Osbourne.

SARA STARDUST, LOS ANGELES

HAVE YOU EVER MET ANY OF YOUR MUSICAL IDOLS?

DESCRIBE A ROMANTIC NIGHT WHEN MUSIC ENHANCED THE EXPERIENCE.

The '80s was my favorite decade. The music, the dancing, the night-clubs, the clothes, the figure I'll never get back, but especially the music (the Cure, Depeche Mode, Psychedelic Furs, and of course Robert Plant's solo albums). A club I regularly visited had country night on Tuesday, so instead of fingerless lacy gloves, stirrup pants and jackets with padded shoulders, I wore cowboy boots, size 0 jeans and any lacy top that could subtly show off my tatas. That's how I met David.

Not the kind of guy I'd normally date, but I felt safe with him. He was stocky, his arms were muscular, his voice was deep and he adored me. We'd often lie on his sofa and he'd sing country songs to me with his beautiful voice. "There's No Way" was my favorite: "There's no way I can make it without you. There's no way that I'd even try . . ." I was in heaven; I felt at home.

But our lifestyles were different, our crowd was different, our primary taste in music was different, so it was inevitable. We parted ways and he moved to Georgia.

Several months later, on a Tuesday night, I was dancing with Martin, a tall, thin boy with blond hair and breath that always smelled like he just drank a glass of milk. We were dancing to "Amarillo by Morning."

There's always that awkward moment when a slow song ends and another begins and you wonder if you'll keep dancing. The next song was "There's No Way," and when Martin held me closer, I wondered about David. Would Martin sing to me with his high voice and milk breath? I wanted to cry. I closed my eyes. I danced.

Suddenly, a strong hand was on my arm. I opened my eyes and saw David: he was cutting in! (How?! How did he get here? He's supposed to be in Georgia! Am I dreaming?) Martin looked at me, puzzled and sad, and I said, "It's okay." As David took me in his arms, he whispered, "You're my girl, and this is our song."

I felt like I'd experienced a moment so surreal it could never happen in real life—but the people in the club paid no attention, they had no idea how romantic that moment was, but I did, and so did he. He sang in my ear as we danced.

JULIE GERUSH, AUSTIN

RECALL A LIFE-CHANGING MUSICAL EXPERIENCE.

I wasn't sure if we had broken up because I wasn't sure if we had been dating. But there we sat at the Ryman, watching Neil Young move across the stage—first the acoustic, and then the organ, playing the same two note pattern repeatedly for what seemed like a solid ten minutes. I leaned over and whispered irreverently, "Damn it, Neil, that's driving me crazy . . ." and we giggled, the tension between us

LET IT BLEED

easing a bit. Yes, we had fought, horribly we had fought! But here we were, drawn back together perpetually as if by some dysfunctional bungee—the story of our existence ever molded by music, working on us as always like some crazy astronaut glue.

I began to try to remember all the shows we had seen at the Mother Church. I glanced around, looking for ghost couples of us, the spaces where we had sat . . . that magical front-row night for Dylan, or dancing wildly at the back of the hall for Levon's Ramble. So many shows. So many ghost couples of us, a littering of memories . . .

You leaned over and said something about Neil's tone, and I nodded like I understood. And then, I looked at you. And saw something I'd never seen in nearly twenty years knowing you. You were quietly crying. You took my hand and touched it to your face, and I felt all of those ghost selves of me scattered around that lovely hall jump into my body, catching me in the moment—catching me up to the moment . . . with you. Just us. And we were no longer ghosts.

JESSI GUNTER, NASHVILLE

The beauty of Jessi's final paragraph took me to a similar night when my ex Mike Stinson took me to see Willie Nelson, Merle Haggard and Ray Price in Las Vegas. The miracle that three of his heroes were together on-stage was overwhelming, and he silently wept, which, of course, brought me to tears. Catching me in the moment—catching me up to the moment . . . one of the purest I've ever experienced.

WHAT WAS YOUR FAVORITE SONG AT AGE SIXTEEN, AND DOES IT STILL HOLD VALUE FOR YOU TODAY?

When I was sixteen, the United States was at war in Vietnam, four students were killed at Kent State, my parents got divorced and I was a high school cheerleader. I took an elective class, Shakespeare, and became Juliet. I put down the pom-poms and fell in love. With Romeo. Our teacher put us in groups and assigned us a scene from the play. Ours was an eclectic group:

Juliet: Myself, a skinny rah-rah cheerleader with olive skin and long, thick, dark brown hair.

Romeo: A surfer with gentle brown eyes and sun-bleached hair swept to one side of his tan face, wearing wheat-colored corduroy jeans and a short-sleeve button-down shirt with a white tee peeking out. And desert boots.

The Nurse: Well endowed, with curly blond hair and glasses who dressed conservatively but was a liberal free spirit.

Mercutio: His eyes were always half-closed, and he interspersed slurred radical prose into the Shakespearean verses.

We met at night to rehearse our scene. Some had done LSD and mescaline. I was a goody-two-shoes cheerleader, who hadn't yet smoked my first joint, and they were determined to get me high. In a pot-infused VW bug, we roamed the Valley as I stuck my head out the open window, shouting my lines: "Romeo, Romeo, wherefore art thou, Romeo?"

We did our scene and got an A. Then Romeo asked me to a party in Laurel Canyon where the band Spirit was playing. We got there as a half dozen police cars screeched up, so we drove on and ended up at Zuma Beach, where we smoked a joint and made out for hours in the sand. A radio somewhere was playing Bread's "Make It with You."

We saw each other a few more times before he graduated. He said he was going up north, either for college or to live on a commune. In my yearbook he wrote, "To my dearest Juliet." Over the decades, whenever I hear that song, I feel the beach sand on my skin, smell the salty sea air, see the stars over the water. And in my heart I hear the beautiful words of Shakespeare.

CHERA THOMPSON, NEW YORK

LET IT BLEED

The way Chera opens her piece solidly places it in time and instantly takes us to that revolutionary, conflicted era before drawing us into her very personal teenage tale.

HOW HAS YOUR MUSICAL TASTE CHANGED OVER THE YEARS?

DO YOU PLAY MUSIC YOURSELF? HOW DOES IT FEEL? WHAT DOES IT MEAN TO YOU?

IF YOU COULD BE ANY KIND OF MUSICAL SUPERSTAR, WHAT DO YOU IMAGINE YOUR LIFE WOULD BE LIKE?

CHAPTER ELEVEN

I

Inspiration Information

In this section we look at how religion or spirituality may have colored your reality. Whether you're a Buddhist, a Christian, a Wiccan, a Muslim or an agnostic—no matter what label is used, we've all been touched by the Divine in one way or another. Mother Nature is always on display. The majesty of a mighty tree has caused me to swoon with joy. Watching a busy bee collecting the nectar that winds up in my coffee fills me with sudden gratitude.

From a young age, I've had an inner itch, knowing there was more to this life than met my blue eyes. Even though my parents weren't religious and didn't go to church, where I grew up, the only possibility open to me was Christianity. I sought out Jesus and studied his crimson words that blazed throughout my white zippered Bible.

I was doing homework with my next-door neighbor, Kathy Standifer, when the glowing blue figure of Jesus appeared at the foot of her twin bed. His arms were outstretched, and the neon blue wavered like pulsing water in the air. We both saw him and weren't afraid. I was eight years old.

It's a long—actually, a lifelong story—but Jesus and I have had quite a stormy relationship. A few years ago, I finally made it across the world to Jerusalem to see where he calmed the storms, turned water into wine and walked the stations of the cross on his way to becoming the most revered and misunderstood human being who has ever lived. When I reached the Church of the Holy Sepulchre and got down on my knees in front of the holy hole where the cross once stood, inhaling the billowing frankincense, I almost passed out among the myriad candles. Talk about a memorable moment! I have come to realize that Jesus was an awakened master, but not the only one, and that he wanted to show us that we can all attain the same sublime state of consciousness. He ain't heavy. He's my brother!

This chapter is about your inner journey, discovering your truest self. These prompts are mirrors for viewing your mystical soul from all angles, revealing the intuitive experience of what it's like to be the real you deep down inside.

WERE YOU RAISED WITH RELIGION OR LEFT TO YOUR OWN DEVICES?

"God Is Spirit." Words written in childish print above a page as white as pure light.

Scowling face hovers above the page. "Your Sunday school assignment is to draw a picture of God." Her voice is filled with judgment.

Well, sometimes I get confused. I'm only ten, after all. I'm not sure what she wants from me, but the message is clear. Not this.

I sink into my deepest place, the safest place I know. Within I find the truth: the one thing I understand about the teachings I've inherited. There is but one God, creator of all that is. I certainly can't draw a picture of everything that is.

She hands me back the clean white paper entitled "God Is Spirit," filled with nothing and everything. It stares back at me with no opinion of its own. Only acceptance, openness and a promise of limitless possibilities.

Oh, and a large red F on the upper right corner.

SAMANTHA VANDERSLICE, AUSTIN

DO YOU ADHERE TO A RELIGION? WHY OR WHY NOT?

DESCRIBE GOING TO YOUR PLACE OF WORSHIP.

DO YOU BELIEVE IN A HIGHER POWER?

I don't know who that is anymore. I'm reluctant to give it a name. All the names that have been used are . . . used. Tarnished. Logic would tell me there is nothing. I don't believe there's an entity. An individual. Rather I hope it is a collective made up of us. Of just people. I don't pray every morning and night like I did as a child, but I do when I'm really in need, or thankful, or afraid. It's not formal, no kneeling or clasping hands. Usually just a silent thought or wish. A feeling that something could be paying attention to my small moment. Maybe deep inside us there is a flame, a gas, a force that we can access, that can be joined and combined. Created to grow into something more than just you and me. Invisible connective tissue, ether, threads of humanness. Sub-sub-sub-atomic level of basic matter. Reaching outside of ourselves, to others, entwining in the skies, spreading across lands, seas, planets, galaxies. Swirling in the cosmos, making the big bang, kicking off life. I believe we are God if we choose it. Actively together. It would be nice if it were true. It would be nice to not be alone.

    JULIE BOT, TORONTO

DO YOU PRAY? SAY GRACE?

No, I don't pray. Ideas on how to begin come in false spits and starts.
    I obsess to a fault. I can never quite quiet my mind. Inner monologue, hum. It's a constant prayer. For this or for that. For him or for him or for me. Or for me to have him. Wanting. Hoping. Obsessively

LET IT BLEED

reliving and reworking every pleasure and painful turmoil. My pulse rises. Humming always to myself.

Every airliner I saddle, I make bargain promises with a God I'm not afraid to talk about but can never get behind. The one-sided conversations are informal: "I'll be really pious if you can just deliver me to the ground under the pilot's intended control." And then we land safely but that never seems like enough proof.

"A fish walked out of water; he talked. That means there's no God," I hear the radio say. The burden of proof that only faith can argue against. I imagine Stephen Hawking's heart breaking when he formulates the absence of God. Einstein too.

Nothing.

"I just pray for you guys," she said after the lecture about how my evils have ruined her life. Bullshit, I think. I hear that sentence coming from so many people I loathe. You pray us ill. You prey us ill.

P-r-e-y. That's more like it. As a noun I visit the word time and again, and I've had my share of verb application.

I cut onions and cry, but the tears are as alligator as any prayer I could make. Somehow, I get by.

MICHELLE PIE, NASHVILLE

I pray and count my blessings every day. Even though I get dragged down in the darkest pits and forget I have these blessings, I try to find that glimmer of sunshine. I pray for my mother and her safety and peace of mind, believe me I pray for her. I used to pray for her love and I know it's there somewhere. I hear her voice now as I pray. I pray for my children I pray for happiness I pray to be thin I pray for money I pray for guidance I pray for the preyers—the people who prey on us all. I pray to be a better person. I pray to find my voice. I pray for the children I teach to be able to grow up. I pray they stay out of jail I pray that they're safe at home right this minute I pray no one is hurting them I pray someone says I love you to them. I pray someone says I love you to me again and means it. I pray for a hand on my knee I pray for companionship. Sometimes my prayers are answered. A little glimmer may come through, maybe it's purple in the sky, or a song on the radio that suddenly speaks to my heart right where it is, or Spotify rolling the dice and coming up with an answer, maybe it's a smile from a stranger or three green parrots squawking on the telephone wire above me. Lately the well has been deep and lonely and fattening because I am not caring for myself, so I've been praying for me. I pray to the mother deep down in the earth to make me feel whole so I don't need anyone else to make me feel whole and I pray that I see my goodness and value my gifts. I pray to let go of things that hold me back. I pray that I forgive myself for everything I've done wrong I pray that I can help more people I pray that I live up to the talents I was given. I pray to write I pray to create to get out of bed. O goddess mother help me release my fears help me become myself O father sun thank you for your warmth and blessings O dear Buddha God Muhammed please find love in everyone's hearts please let me be part of the cure and not part of the problem please help me not to be greedy help me to be prosperous help me to be organized please help me to hold everything with open arms so that love can flow in and love can flow out. Thank you. On my knees, thank you.

LILY WELCH, DRIPPING SPRINGS, TEXAS

It's interesting that both Lily and Michelle mention "prey" in these assignments about prayer. Michelle questions the validity and the potential hypocrisy of prayer, while Lily's piece actually turns into a prayer. She also effectively bypasses punctuation, à la Kerouac, to stress the constancy and desperation of her prayers.

HAVE YOU EVER HAD A PRAYER ANSWERED?

I've always believed in God and Jesus, but six years ago I had an awakening. It was really early in the morning and I thought, "Oh, I hope the dope man is out." We called the dealers "gym shoe boys," young guys who spent all their money on gym shoes.

I had walked a block, copped the bag of dope and poured the dope out onto a mirror. I raised the straw to my nose, handed the mirror to my man, lit a cigarette and gazed out the window. I was dope sick and knew I'd feel better in a couple of minutes and would go out to hustle.

"I don't want to do this anymore," I mumbled. He tried to hand the heroin back to me, and I said, "Nah, I don't want no more," and walked out of the house, looked up into the sky with tears in my eyes. "God, please help me. Help me, Lord."

I headed downtown to Banana Republic, where it was easy to steal, thinking how much I hated my life, and when I got busted with the stolen goods, it was that moment God helped me. Oh yeah, I went to the penitentiary and did my time, but to this day I haven't touched any kind of drug or taken a sip of alcohol. God heard me say, "I don't want to do this anymore."

I never really understood the teachings and thought it was all myth, but I did believe. Now I truly understand, and I find myself one with the shorelines of beaches and water. I sit on the pier behind my apartment before the sun rises every morning, no matter if it's raining, snowing or warm summertime. I love to look out onto Lake

Michigan from the beautiful north shore of Chicago. As I drink my coffee I reflect on my life, and always thank God for saving me. After all, it is a miracle that I didn't die in the streets from a drug overdose. And all those years in prison.

Suddenly the sun peeks out in the distance and the sky is filled with pinks, blues and radiant reds. The sun begins to flicker and the reflection shines upon the huge body of water. I know for sure that it's God's way of talking to me. The beauty is so blinding, but I don't dare move my eyes away. I stare straight into the sparkling sunlit water and watch until the waves crash elegantly onto the sand of the lonely beach, grateful for so much.

BIANCA ANGALIA, CHICAGO

Coming from Bianca, this piece is revelatory. A former gang member, she fought with heroin addiction for decades before landing in the slammer for twelve years. She's now a dedicated servant for peace and sobriety, helping at-risk youth, working with the University of Illinois organization CureViolence (formerly CeaseFire), and is an inspirational, brutally honest public speaker. When she reads her stories in class, she leaves nothing out, despite the horror involved, and it's heart chilling. The next moment, she'll have us laughing. What a survivor! I'm so proud of her. Bianca is spilling her pain and redemption in a memoir, cowritten with my Chicago hostess, Linda Beckstrom, entitled *In Deep*. They met in class, which warms the cockles of my heart. (According to Merriam-Webster that idiom means "the core of one's being.")

I ALMOST LOST MY FAITH WHEN . . .

The night before a tour with my band, I had a dream. In that dream two tires blew on the way to Montreal, in my hotel room a pigeon

landed on my head in the middle of the night and the drummer went missing between sets. I woke up with a feeling of dread, and that I should just quit, pull the rug out from under the whole thing. But I had faith . . . faith that one thing would lead to another, that all would be well, so I should go.

Then, one by one, what I had foreseen began to fall into place. Two back tires on the van blew out just east of Kingston, halfway to Montreal. Three days in, a pigeon trapped in a wallpapered-over stovepipe vent pecked its way out, landed on my head and died. I almost lost my faith, but then there were good days that turned into great weeks and the band was getting tight. Then, on the last night of the tour, in St. Jerome (in northern Quebec), the drummer disappeared before our last set. I almost lost my faith, but saw no choice but to get back onstage. The crowd seemed to love us, and didn't seem to care. I found the drummer at the end of the night, in jail, busted for smoking a joint made from remnants that had fallen onto the floor of the van. I almost lost my faith, but the cops lost the evidence. And after all, I had a dream.

AMELIA BRIDGESTONE, TORONTO

DO YOU COUNT YOUR BLESSINGS?

DO YOU MEDITATE?

DO YOU MAKE EFFORTS TO FOLLOW THE GOLDEN RULE (DO UNTO OTHERS . . .)? WHAT DOES IT MEAN TO YOU?

DO YOU BELIEVE IN HEAVEN AND/OR HELL?

DO YOU BELIEVE IN PURE EVIL? IF SO, HAVE YOU EVER ENCOUNTERED IT?

Most of us believe what has been rammed down our psyches for eons: that committing a sin is a big, naughty crime against God. But the original Hebrew translation will surprise you. It simply means "forgetfulness"—"to miss" or "to be absent." To not be awake, or present in your life, you are missing the truth, beauty and potential of the moment. The Buddha called it "mindfulness." Krishnamurti said, "Pay attention." I say snap out of it! The real sin is to straggle through life with blinkers on and a head full of blather, keeping you from experiencing the moment you're in.

WHAT DOES "COMMITTING A SIN" MEAN TO YOU?

||

Into the Mystic

I'm sure you've experienced unexpected moments of grace and transcendence that you think cannot be put into words. Here's where we're going to change that notion by calling on the mystic within you to come forth and bay at the full moon.

DESCRIBE AN "OTHERWORLDLY" EXPERIENCE, A MOMENT OF WONDER YOU'VE HAD.

I have had so darn many seemingly otherworldly experiences that I am working on a book, *Sex, God & Rock and Roll*, about my spiritual life. But what happened in London, 1996, remains a resplendent standout—unexplainable and downright incomprehensible in the "real world."

Working on my third book, Rock Bottom, *was a difficult and painful journey, delving into some of rock and roll's most tragic* moments. I was in the thick of compiling tales about Pink Floyd's lost genius soul, Syd Barrett, and after a sorrowful interview in London with one of his old friends, I stopped into a bookstore on my way back to my rented flat. I needed a dose of purity and grace to temper the choking madness. Ah, William Blake! A perfect respite from such troublesome tales. I settled in bed with a cozy cup of Earl Grey and turned to one of my favorite poems, written long ago, in 1794: "The Tyger," one I'd read many times before. On this night, however, the familiar words were brand-new to me, leaping off the page like red-hot arrows, and when I got to the fifth stanza, all heaven broke loose.

> When the stars threw down their spears
> And water'd heaven with their tears:
> Did he smile his work to see?
> Did he who made the Lamb make thee?

There have been endless scholarly explanations about this mysterious poem, but on that stormy London night it imbedded itself in my soul, woke up a slumbering fire within my solar plexus, and I became one with its author as if I held Blake's quill in my own hand. I began spurting tears of total understanding (back in the '70s, if we really "got" something, we "grokked" it—a descriptive word unlike any other from Heinlein's Stranger in a Strange Land), as if I'd composed "Tyger, Tyger, burning bright, / In the forests of the night . . ." To me, it was about the glory of creation in all its extravagant and unimaginable majesty.

Suddenly through my flying tears, Blake's quill appeared about a foot in front of me, as a 3-D hologram, slowly spinning in front of my eyes, a gift from the past, sent to me through time, a soul connection *that landed smack-dab in the Now. As I fell deeply asleep that night, I was expanded and wide-open to whatever the universe had to show me.*

I have been studying the true meaning of playing cards for decades. They were invented eons ago as a divining tool, but that had to be hidden from the powers-that-be, so it was played as a game. Each card has a meaning, and I often find one in the street, look the card up in The Power of Playing Cards: An Ancient System for Understanding Yourself, Your Destiny, and Your Relationships, *cowritten by my friend Geraldine Sullivan, and get a mini reading. The next day I was in line at the tube station buying my weekly travel pass, and as I got to the window I looked down and an entire deck of playing cards was at my feet. Wow. Was I somehow being followed by a cosmic jester? I snatched up the box and, when I was settled into the train, opened it up and gasped, hardly believing what I was seeing. Each of the fifty-two cards was emblazoned with two tiger heads, with the words "Tiger, Tiger" on both ends. I kid you not. I still have the cards as proof of that impossible moment, and whenever I question our Universal connection I pull them out of the drawer and gaze upon those double tigers with awe and wonder.*

PAMELA DES BARRES

DO YOU BELIEVE IN REINCARNATION? KARMA? IF SO, WRITE ABOUT A PERSONAL EXPERIENCE THAT PROVES IT TO YOU.

HAVE YOU EVER HAD A PSYCHIC EXPERIENCE? A PREMONITION THAT CAME TO PASS?

DO YOU BELIEVE IN PSYCHIC PHENOMENA?

DO YOU BELIEVE THERE IS LIFE ON OTHER PLANETS?

HAVE YOU EVER FELT THE PRESENCE OF GOD/THE DIVINE?

The summer I was eight years old I spent two weeks at Girl Scout camp, my first experience at overnight camp. I was unhappy for most of that time. It turned out my cousin was there as well, and the staff thought it would be good for us to be in the same tent—a disastrous idea. My cousin was a year older than I was. Blond, skinny and always one of the leaders of the most popular girls, she was my polar opposite, and we'd never gotten along. Not content merely to torture me herself, she encouraged the other girls in our tent to do the same. They made fun of my weight, my clothes, my failure at pretty much anything athletic and my overwhelming shyness. One day my cousin went through my things and found a letter from my father, in which he addressed me by his pet name for me. She found this hysterical and pinned the letter up where everyone could see it. It was unbearable. The counselors weren't much help; there wasn't much they could have done about it anyway.

A couple of days after that, I was off by myself when the sun began to set, and we heard the call for dinner. Girls were streaming toward the mess tent in small happy groups. I hung back, then followed along, slowly, until I came to a big hill. The sunset was at its most beautiful, spreading brilliant streaks of color across the sky, and I started to cry. I felt all the pain of those last few days bubble up inside me and spill out, replaced with something I couldn't name. I felt ag- itated and peaceful all at the same time, and knew that these were good feelings. I remember throwing my arms open wide, as if trying to gather the glorious pink and orange sky close to me; I even spun around like Julie Andrews in The Sound of Music. *And in that moment, I felt G-d with me, felt G-d all around me and inside me, in a way I hadn't before. The tears were still coming, and I was thanking G-d for all that beauty, for loving me, for watching over me. The rest of camp went by quickly. I carried the memory of that sunset, my sunset, with me, and survived.*

It was the first time I felt the power and glory of G-d in nature, all alone. It would not be the last.

SHEVA GOLKOW, NEW YORK

It's so life affirming that despite the harassing and bullying Sheva experienced at camp, this moment of gratitude made the petty put-downs pale in comparison. I find it fascinating that many people in the Jewish faith believe that not spelling out the entire name of God is a sign of respect. The custom stems from the commandment in Deuteronomy 12:3–4 that affirms that God's name should not be erased, destroyed or written down.

DESCRIBE THREE OF YOUR MOST VIVID ACTUAL DREAMS DURING SLEEP.

DESCRIBE A TIME WHEN YOU KNEW ALL WAS RIGHT WITH THE WORLD.

RECALL A JOYOUS MOMENT WHEN TIME SEEMED TO STAND STILL AND YOUR HEART TOOK A PHOTOGRAPH.

WHAT IS THE PURPOSE OF MANKIND? WHAT IS MY PURPOSE?

Here we are on the edge of everything that is known or can be known. The West Coast of the United States, Los Angeles, the place where the

LET IT BLEED

magic happens, where there is little left to the imagination. We know too much about how the world works. The only true secrets are held in the death grip of history or in the deep recesses of the soul. So, why are we here? Why am I here? I can tell you what the purpose isn't, but I don't think anyone has the time or patience to be reminded of all the mundane things we do to pass the time. The universe doesn't care what kind of clothes we wear, or if we wear clothes at all. The universe isn't concerned about houses, credit, diamond rings, social affiliations, the cure for cancer, HMOs, HOAs, PTAs, PTSD or AIDS. The universe doesn't count us by color, religion or political party. It doesn't understand no or yes, give or take. The universe just is. We can't seem to wrap our heads around just being. You are. I am. I am Bobbie? I am a daughter? No. I am.

We have created social order and disconnected ourselves from the creator. I can't get to my purpose with all of the layers acting as barricades. My job, my identity, my needs, my name, my roles, my debts, my riches, struggles, triumphs, responsibilities, obligations, my freedom, my expectations, fears, worries, happiness, pain, joy, confusion, my hope, my peace and my search for what is true and eternal. Can I not just be? I don't imagine the creator walking in circles, worrying, racing to the next self-imposed finish line. The creator just is. Call the creator by any name, but the creator remains unchanged.

The keys of fulfillment are not held by the number on the scale, the name of our God or the cars we drive. Peace is not obtained by filling and freezing every line on my face, the size of my jeans or the age on my driver's license. Enlightenment cannot be found in the man I love, the prescriptions I take or the weed I'd like to smoke. The answer to my prayers cannot be summoned through a crystal ball, a deck of tarot cards or the flame of a candle. Life is not a race, there is no winner, there is no loser, there is no finish line and no trophy. Life just is.

The only thing that really matters is what I hope to carry with me beyond my purpose here. The father recuperating in the hospital bed, the mother who has long since passed away, the brother across the ocean, the faces of my niece and nephews, my girlfriends, the animals I care for and the man I will love.

If you look closely enough and are quiet enough, you can see your purpose mirrored in the eyes of others, human and animal. Be silent, be peace, just be, then look into the eyes of the universe. There is your purpose.

BOBBIE BEEMAN, LOS ANGELES

I was very moved by this piece, how Bobbie starts off in the seemingly shallow city of Los Angeles and winds up discovering her true purpose reflected in the eyes of her loved ones—pets included. Is there anything sweeter in life than a smiling dog or a purring kitty?

HOW DO YOU IMAGINE THE UNIVERSE WORKS?

The universe has a mind of its own and we cannot control its movements. Even psychic mediums like me can only do our best to predict, but we'll never truly know the inner mysteries that have been guarded for eternities. The universe gives us peace, war, feast and famine, but no one knows what its next move will be. We have to learn to roll with the universe and embrace its rhythm. So day to day we do the best we can to become one with our reality. It's been said that if you overanalyze the world you will miss its message. Mother Earth and her skies above, along with the cosmic wheels that make her turn, will never be fully understood by us. So let us accept the

LET IT BLEED

small pieces of enlightenment that we are given, one piece at a time,
until we discover our own personal rhythm within this unknowable
universe.

MIKI CORAZZA, TORONTO

I appreciate this piece from Miss Miki, a highly regarded psychic in Toronto. Despite her gift of insight into the confounding human condition, she accepts and respects the unfathomable mystery of the cosmos.

CHAPTER TWELVE

I

Let's Get Physical

Oddly enough, Olivia Newton-John's pop hit was one of Nick's favorite songs when he was a mere tot, so I often found myself dancing around the living room to that masterpiece while the record spun on his Sesame Street record player, along with the Go-Go's and Sparks, his other faves. When he was at school, I flopped around in my tights, watching tapes of Jane Fonda, who insisted that I "feel the burn," while doing endless leg lifts to get rid of my "dingle-dangles." I was an early adherent to fitness, joining the Beverly Hills Health Club before it became the Sports Connection, then several other gym joints before blossoming into L.A. Fitness, where I now strut and squat, huff and puff, flinging myself around in my Zumba classes three times a week.

The way society has viewed women for the last hundred years or so, demanding impossible perfection, it's no wonder we have issues! Sheesh! At least we don't have to cinch our waists to eighteen inches à la Scarlett O'Hara or the original 1959 Barbie doll. It was just last year that Mattel gave Barbie realistic measurements. Yes, we have come a long way, baby! And since we only get one body to carry us through our adventures during this lifetime, let's take an honest look at your relationship with yours!

HOW DO YOU FEEL ABOUT YOUR APPEARANCE? ARE YOU VAIN OR INSECURE?

DO YOU EXERCISE/WORK OUT/PLAY SPORTS NOW?

DOES YOUR STYLE REFLECT WHO YOU REALLY ARE? DO YOU HAVE ANY STYLE ICONS?

IF YOU COULD LOOK LIKE ANYONE ELSE, WHO WOULD IT BE AND WHY?

WHEN DO YOU FEEL THE MOST BEAUTIFUL?

I feel beautiful when I have taken care of myself, truly pampered and unrushed. Really long shower, taking time to shave my legs way more carefully than usual. Way more conditioner has been left on way longer than necessary, in hopes of smoothing down the ever-unsmoothable hair. Then a special whoosh of the blow-dryer to make sure my most private areas are completely dry. Face slathered with moisturizer—not skimping to stretch it like I do in ordinary moments.

The dress is of the most flowing material—some kind of postwar rayon that has exactly enough weight to hang smooth and yet swirl wide if I give a little twirl. The way it feels swishing around my knees is sexy and luxurious. I feel it with every step.

The bodice of the dress is cut perfectly—deep enough to be tantalizing, yet modest enough that I don't have to give one iota of thought about whether the wrong person is looking down my cleavage.

Because there is only one man I want looking down my cleavage. The night he fell in love with me, standing side by side at a concert at the Wiltern, he took full advantage of his vantage point (being taller than me). He looked down my shirt and said with all sincerity, "Your breasts are luminous." Of course it takes a writer to pull off such a

phrase—a phrase and a moment that have stuck with me fourteen
years and counting. It was the night that clinched my love for him too.

He is waiting for me up there now, up the tight spiral staircase
that makes me walk with great care in my just-high-enough heels. I
don't mind the extra care on the steps because it lengthens my grand
entrance, extends the breathless moment before I present myself to
him. I see the smile slide across my husband's face—slide right up
into his blue-blue eyes—and hear him say, "Wow, you look won-
derful."

It's the way he says "Wow" that really makes me feel beautiful.

KATHRYN SMITH, SEATTLE

With snazzy descriptions, from the whoosh of the blow-dryer, the
slather of moisturizer and the swish of fabric, Kathryn playfully pulls the
reader into her romantic toilette. And she seductively conveys how a
certain someone's appreciative gaze can light you up like a bottle rocket!

Margaret's piece on the same topic reminds us that beauty is indeed
in the eye of the beholder. Or as Franklin said back in 1741, "Beauty, like
supreme Dominion, / Is best supported by Opinion." Ol' Ben was a highly
quotable fellow.

The stone on my mother's grave bears a quotation from a story I once
read. In it, a little child is found lost and sobbing. He has become sep-
arated from his mother and is inconsolable.

Being a very little boy, he knows his mother only as "Mama"
and has no idea of either her actual name or his address. All he can
do is keep repeating that his mother is the most beautiful woman in
the world.

Since the village is not very large, those gathered around the child
are puzzled to think that a great beauty has lived among them in

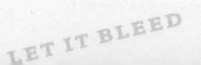

anonymity. Several minutes of questioning elicit only more of the little boy's tears and continued assertions of his mother's loveliness. Suddenly a burly, red-faced woman comes pushing her way through the crowd, untidy braids swinging and her large feet treading on un-suspecting toes.

The little boy leaps immediately to his feet and she scoops him up in her meaty arms, crying aloud with joy.

"I told you!" he exclaimed to the astonished onlookers. "I told you she was the most beautiful woman in the world!"

When I see myself in my own son's loving eyes, I do feel beau-tiful.

And my own beloved mother's tombstone reads, simply, "Daisy, the most beautiful woman in the world."

MARGARET FARRELL, LOS ANGELES

WHAT DO YOU CONSIDER YOUR BEST FEATURE?

WHAT IS YOUR WORST FEATURE?

TELL THE STORY OF HOW YOU GOT ONE (OR MORE) OF YOUR SCARS.

HAVE YOU EVER LOST OR GAINED A SIGNIFICANT AMOUNT OF WEIGHT? IF NOT, DO YOU WORK AT MAINTAINING YOUR WEIGHT OR DOES IT JUST HAPPEN NATURALLY?

LOOK AT YOURSELF IN THE MIRROR STARK NAKED AND WRITE ABOUT WHAT YOU SEE.

Milky white softness and plenty of scars. Pink and pouty comfort resides between undulating lines. Dimples and folds, freckles and

moles. Beauty marks jiggle. Sandalwood, roses, oils and hydration.
Peach-fuzzy warm invitation. Faint lines and suspicions, better
see a dermatologist. Plump backside better to sit with. An ass
man's woman, I've always sat well with it. I might not be twenty,
but I'm not ninety either. If hotties invite, divine things must be
there. Big thighs I once cursed are what get me around, so my
curse is reversed, now gratefulness abounds. I'd like to tighten,
and whittle and wax . . . but until then this abundant goddess
gonna relax.

ASHLEIGH DANIEL, AUSTIN

Whenever I give this assignment in class, there are always plenty of
groans. If only we could be as accepting of our beloved bodies as Ashleigh
seems to be. Even while describing what she once saw as flaws, she now
finds comfort in her dimples and folds. I believe all women are god-
desses!

**HAVE YOU EVER THOUGHT OF YOURSELF AS A GODDESS? WHY
OR WHY NOT?**

DESCRIBE YOUR RELATIONSHIP TO BATHING SUITS.

**HAVE YOU EVER LET FEAR ABOUT HOW YOU MIGHT APPEAR
HOLD YOU BACK FROM DOING SOMETHING IN LIFE?**

DO YOU WEAR MAKEUP? WILL YOU GO OUT WITHOUT IT?

**DO YOU DYE YOUR HAIR? WHY OR WHY NOT? DO YOU CARE IF
PEOPLE KNOW?**

WHAT IS ONE BEAUTY LUXURY YOU CAN'T DO WITHOUT?

LET IT BLEED

DO YOU HAVE ANY TATTOOS? DO YOU PLAN ON GETTING ANY? IF NOT, WHY NOT?

I didn't need an alarm clock because my parents blasted us out of bed with CCR, Deep Purple, Janis Joplin, the Guess Who . . . Looking back, they were pretty cool.

One Saturday the teenage neighbor came over to show my parents the Physical Graffiti *album he'd just bought. I was in my room and could hear the music streaming throughout the house, as usual. But this music was different, so I just stayed on top of my covers, listening intently. I tried to imagine what this group of musicians looked like and how they played (in the '70s most of that remained a mystery until you were lucky enough to catch them on* The Midnight Special *or* American Bandstand*). I wanted to know how they came up with the incredible lyrics—and how on earth could the lead singer moan like that?!*

After Physical Graffiti *played in full, the boy returned with* Houses of the Holy. *"Oh oh oh oh ay ay" (from "D'yer Mak'er") drifted in the air. It haunted me; I was entranced. I wondered, "Who is this band and where do they live?" and my parents explained, "Led Zeppelin; England." From that moment, I was obsessed. With England, and with the band.*

I didn't know what the band looked like until I saw the movie The Song Remains the Same, *and the obsession reignited.*

John Bonham died when I was in tenth grade, so I never got to see Led Zeppelin live. I've seen Robert Plant every time he tours, and I saw Page and Plant together. When the opening chords of "Tangerine" started, I screamed it out while most of the audience was trying to recognize the song. Robert Plant sang to me. I swear. He moaned and bowed and made eye contact throughout the entire song. I was crying and tearing at my clothes. My brother was fanning me and saying,

"Keep breathing." Even the audience members noticed—"He's singing to you!" It was an unbelievable three minutes. I screamed, "I love you," and he put his hands beside his ears and said, "Oh. Pillow talk!" I could have died at that moment and not minded a bit. How could any tomorrow top that?

When I see Robert Plant's face now, it's like family. He's that familiar to me. Since he's been such a part of me, I wanted a tattoo of his symbol, a circle with a feather in it. It needed to be on a place on my body that wouldn't stretch or sag, and a place where I could see it.

It took me years to decide. When it finally hit me—inside my left forearm—I got the tattoo the very next day. It reminds me to be true to myself and to always appreciate music. To me, the feather symbolizes writing, the circle symbolizes infinity and of course it symbolizes music, Led Zeppelin and specifically Robert Plant.

JULIE GERUSH, NEW YORK

I wonder how many tattoos Robert's feather symbol has inspired? I took a friend to meet him backstage in Arizona, and she proudly showed him the tattoo of his symbol on her ankle and asked him to sign his name right above it. He kindly obliged and she went the very next day and had his signature turned into another tattoo! A signature is a good way to honor your heroes. I've seen too many unrecognizable inked monsters that are supposed to be Dean or Elvis, or even Mickey Mouse! I have James Dean's signature on the back of my neck, Elvis Presley's is spread across my back and I am about to get both of my Walter egos—Whitman and Disney—scribbled on me somewhere. That'll make seven.

My L.A. writer Linda wound up with three.

It was high summer in Wisconsin, July 1976, meaning very hot and humid. I lived in halter tops and cutoff shorts.

I was at a party one night that happened to be next door to a DIY tattoo parlor. The tattoo artist was a notorious biker named Gordy, a convicted rapist who proudly rode a hog with a coffin sidecar.

As the drinks went down, so did caution. People were heading next door and coming back with some enviable ink. Finally, I couldn't stand it anymore. I had to get a tattoo!

I brought a guy named Bubba with me as a bodyguard. Bubba had a fit when I began enthusing over the idea of putting a teardrop next to my eye. "You aren't going to fuck up your face!" he said loudly. Today I thank God that I was with someone who'd had a little less to drink and a lot more sense. I don't think I'd like that murderers' row look.

I looked and looked and found my perfect tat: a little broken heart with a vine growing through it. Trying to keep in mind Gordy's criminal past, I decided to get it on my right shoulder, a body part that didn't seem likely to inflame his passion.

Even Bubba was happy with it. And there's never been a day that I've regretted getting it. Especially since I walked back to the party and didn't wind up in Gordy's gruesome sidecar.

Not until 2000 did I think to do it again. My husband and I were vacationing on Martha's Vineyard, in a Victorian inn that was—again—next to a tattoo place. Browsing the tats, I saw a little seahorse that I just knew had to be part of my body. I've always considered the seahorse my spirit animal and now he lives right above my right ankle.

The third and last tattoo is my least favorite. I consider it to be the "gratuitous" tattoo, as after my second one I was lusting after another, so I got a Mandarin language "think" on my left leg. And I "think" that's just enough tattoos for me!

LINDA LEATHER, LOS ANGELES

HAVE YOU HAD (OR WOULD YOU HAVE) PLASTIC SURGERY?

RECALL A TIME WHEN YOU FELT YOU LOOKED YOUR VERY BEST. WHAT DID YOU WEAR? WHERE DID YOU GO?

WHAT IS THE BEST COMPLIMENT YOU'VE EVER RECEIVED REGARDING YOUR LOOKS?

DESCRIBE YOUR FAVORITE PHOTO OF YOURSELF. RECALL THE MOMENT IN DETAIL.

||

Rockin' Pneumonia
and the Boogie Woogie Flu

We all want to be hale and hearty and dance through our lives in tip-top shape—but our bodies don't always do what we'd like them to. Such as stay tight, toned, burnished and healthy. Hopefully you are in fine fettle, but eventually in all our lives, a little pain must fall. How have you faced illness, ailments and accidents through the years? For me, sleep is paramount. If I don't get enough shut-eye, the world is fuzzy and fraught with complexities.

DO YOU SLEEP WELL? ARE YOU ABLE TO SLEEP THROUGH THE NIGHT? DO YOU HAVE INSOMNIA?

DESCRIBE YOUR WORST ILLNESS OR HEALTH ISSUE.

Thankfully my relationship with the sandman is usually pretty copacetic. I did, however, have to face my childhood boogeyman when I got breast cancer twelve years ago. (Cancer free today!) When something dire happens, writing about it helps to calm me down. Here's the opening page of my ten-part series that appeared at Dishmag.com.

Have you ever been in a car accident? When every cell in your entire being goes into High Alert? Smash! Crash! Crunch! You can almost hear the hum in your charged-up blood pressure as it surges to the shocking occasion. Whatever you may have been blithely daydreaming about shatters like your once-perfect windshield, and you know that for weeks, and perhaps months to come, you'll be dealing with fickle insurance companies, cagey auto mechanics and all types of people you would never encounter in your everyday life.

The same thing happens when you're told you have cancer. The Big C. One minute you're blissfully unaware of the impending drama, and the next, your whole existence takes an unexpected turbulent roller-coaster U-turn into retailored territory.

I was on the phone, excitedly gabbing away with my dear friend Catherine, when another call beeped into our sex-charged chat. When I didn't recognize the number on my call-waiting, I decided that telling her all about last night's orgasm-festival with my new boyfriend, Mike, was infinitely more important. On and on I went about his magical, adoring tongue. But this insistent unknown caller kept beeping into our flow, so begrudgingly, I told Catherine to hold on and clicked over.

"This is Kristi Pado," the interrupter began. "I'm sorry to have to tell you this on the phone, but the test results came back. You have cancer." Dun-duh-DUN-dun . . . Every single cell vigilant and on

fire. Brain unable to compute. Eyes wide and unblinking. Mouth hanging open and powerless to utter simple syllables. Heart slamming like I'd just been rear-ended by Mötley Crüe's tour bus going eighty zillion miles an hour. The first word to finally form and blow out of me like fear itself was, "WHAT!!?!" It's probably the initial sound that most people expel when given such cataclysmic news. And it was news I was definitely not anticipating.

HAVE YOU HAD ANY SURGERIES?

ARE YOU ALLERGIC TO ANYTHING? IF SO, HOW HAS IT AFFECTED YOUR LIFE?

HAVE YOU SPENT MUCH TIME IN DOCTORS' OFFICES? HOSPITALS?

HAVE YOU TRIED (OR WOULD YOU EVER TRY) ALTERNATIVE HEALING METHODS?

DO YOU TAKE MEDICATION (OR HAVE YOU EVER HAD TO)? HOW DO YOU FEEL ABOUT IT?

HAVE YOU EVER BEEN IN AN ACCIDENT?

WHAT IS THE WORST INJURY YOU'VE HAD?

ARE YOU CONCERNED ABOUT AGING? IF SO, WHAT ARE YOU DOING TO STAVE IT OFF?

LET IT BLEED

III

People Are Strange

Aren't we? One woman's pleasure is another's pain. And vice versa, of course. "When you're strange, faces come out of the rain," crooned the Lizard King decades ago. "When you're strange, no one remembers your name."

WHEN HAVE YOU FELT MOST ALONE?

DESCRIBE A TIME WHEN YOU FELT LIKE YOU DIDN'T FIT IN.

WHAT ISSUES CAUSE YOU THE MOST STRESS?

HAVE YOU EVER BEEN ADDICTED TO ANYTHING? DRUGS OR ALCOHOL? SEX? FOOD? GAMBLING?

Like any true addict, I think anything good is worth overdoing. For me, that would be drugs, particularly opiates.

The constant throughout my life has been narcotics, ever since my mother began dosing me at three years old with codeine. In those days it was possible to buy codeine over the counter, and by the time I went to kindergarten, I was unaware that I was a baby addict.

As I got older, I began taking speed, barbiturates, Quaaludes, along with any hallucinogens that came my way. I wanted to know not only what it felt like to be Lucy in the Sky with Diamonds, but how it felt to feel okay about myself.

The summer of 1975, the speed became a problem. I was taking a handful of Black Beauties, the tolerance going up daily. According to the people around me, I was "acting crazy" and needed to switch drugs, so at an after-bar party someone offered me a hypo full of liquid opium as a special birthday present.

It was the gift that never stopped taking. Within days, I turned my nose up at the "garbage" I'd been gobbling—the Percodans, uppers, 'ludes, the brown-and-clears. I was shooting my drugs now—morphine, Dilaudid, crystal meth . . . I learned fast how to do myself and a new stage was reached. And yet, it was the first time I felt I belonged to a group of people. Even though they were a bunch of junkies, they were my junkies. Unfortunately this feeling never lasted longer than the high itself.

Fast-forward through years and years of six a.m. methadone clinic visits and endless travel hassles. Nothing like being in an Icelandic airport and having air personnel pull out that big baggie full of liquid methadone bottles and demanding, "Vot dis?"

So, on January 31, 2012, I finally surrendered. I went into a rehab program in Malibu, not completely sure I was serious, because as impossible as it became to live with the drugs, I couldn't begin to imagine living without them. It was far from the first time I'd been to rehab, through detoxes, mental hospitals and even, once, Jesus. At age fifty-six, it might be late, but it was definitely time. I'm not sure what was different, but I became committed to it, and I found support people who made a huge difference in my life. And I have to admit, my life has become manageable now that my every waking thought isn't consumed with "I need more, more, more, more!"

A huge reason for the drug abuse epidemic is because when the feelings aren't inside you, you can take a pill . . . or a drink . . . and feel so much better about yourself. Until it stops working—and it does stop working. This coping method is no longer open to me, and sometimes I miss it so much.

LET IT BLEED

These days, I have to be enough for me, and I have to believe that I have all I need inside me without resorting to better living through chemistry. Some of us bloom later than others and I am one of them. Life is good.

LINDA LEATHER, LOS ANGELES

My favorite line in this forthright piece is "the gift that never stopped taking." Such a sharp switcheroo. I'm dead chuffed when common phrases are turned upside down and given an entirely different meaning. It takes bravery to admit that she misses her hell-bent coping method, but Linda makes it clear that she's still in bloom.

DO YOU HAVE AN ADDICTIVE PERSONALITY? IF SO, HOW HAVE YOU DEALT WITH IT?

DO YOU FEEL MENTALLY SOUND MOST OF THE TIME?

HAVE YOU HAD AN EXPERIENCE THAT MADE YOU QUESTION YOUR SANITY?

HAVE YOU EVER BEEN AFFECTED BY MENTAL ILLNESS?

HAVE YOU TAKEN ANTIDEPRESSANTS? OR A SIMILAR MEDICATION?

HAVE YOU EVER BEEN IN THERAPY? IF SO, HOW DID IT WORK FOR YOU?

HOW DO YOU COMBAT NEGATIVE THOUGHTS?

HAVE YOU EVER FELT SUICIDAL?

Well, she sits on my shoulder like a whisper every day. A strange comfort that the choice is always there. She's bossy too. And sometimes she almost wins. But so far, I've been victorious.

It all started in sixth grade. There was an argument in church about my all-loving god. A god who would not love me anymore if I committed suicide. I think I wanted to find out if that was true. I mean, how could this god of such great love that had been drilled into my head week after week not love someone whose suffering became so great they had to end it?

I felt tricked. Like Santa all fucking over again.

I did not feel worthy of love. I still don't. Even my own. I can tell you every fault because she's always there sitting on my shoulder whispering in my ear. "You're fat, you're lazy, you can't jump hurdles, your men left you. You are alone! Your kids don't even want to be around you. You have no money, no talent, you're worthless."

My question is, Who is it that sits on my other shoulder? The force that let me hang on till Christmas as a child? I don't know what to look forward to now, but the same force is here with me right now. To keep me on this earth. It might be the next song I hear or the next step I take or the sparkle in my only granddaughter's eyes.

The star shining through the tree last night gave me a handhold to make it through the night. Writing this now might make me last another hour. I do not know every day who will come out on top. The fight goes on. And it can be exhausting on this hunt for joy.

LILY WELCH, DRIPPING SPRINGS, TEXAS

221

LET IT BLEED

IV

This Is the End, Beautiful Friend, the End . . .

Thanks for another chapter heading, Mr. Morrison. The last time I saw him, right before he left for France, he seemed strong and sober, excited about moving to Paris and getting a brand-new start. Sadly, as we all know, that wasn't to be. I often marvel about the stunning resilience of humankind, knowing that at any moment the persona we're holding fast to will disappear like the moon in the morning. We are finite, yet we plow ahead every day with meetings, workouts, romances, jobs, events, concerts and parties. We continue to have worries, concerns, rages, agendas, challenges, secrets, hopes and wishes, knowing full well it will come to a screeching halt one day, and we don't even know how, why or when! I say brava and bravo to the stalwart human spirit! But since we all have the same exact fate, why the heck can't we accept our seeming differences and come together, right now, over me?

Ah, well, let's delve into that final taboo, the consummate mystery, the one true thing that we all have in common.

WHO IS THE OLDEST PERSON YOU'VE KNOWN AND WHAT DID YOU LEARN FROM HER OR HIM ABOUT LIVING YOUR OWN LIFE?

HAVE YOU EVER HAD TO CARE FOR A VERY SICK PERSON?

My parents were both very heavy smokers for fifty-odd years. Then, as luck would have it (theirs and mine), within a year they both got diagnosed with lung cancer. His & Hers, just like everything else since their high school sweetheart days. His was stage 3 squamous non–small cell, hers was stage 4 adenocarcinoma. We were told three to six months for both of them.

It's all about role reversal. The parents become the kids and vice versa. But instead of growing up and getting stronger, they got weaker, moodier and more difficult to please. They threw childish tantrums, insisting food didn't taste right and I'd somehow "messed it up." (And cue long-simmering Issues that I had to keep to myself with gritted teeth.) At one point Mom clamped her mouth shut as I tried to give her her meds.

Hospice care is hours and hours, days and days, weeks and weeks, not just meds and meals, but hand holding, tear wiping, laundry (so much laundry), housework, grocery shopping, mail. You know—the stuff they used to do for me. My world narrowed to theirs, which had narrowed to their bedrooms, computers and TVs, and trying to keep them as comfortable as possible.

Unfortunately, the intro hospice session hadn't prepared me for the constant feeling that I was failing them both.

When Mom had a "good" day, it was an extended slumber party, and she was almost cheerful, wanting Chinese food and ice cream. We watched old movies and she told all the stories she wanted us to remember. Those days were the silver lining.

Dad had what the hospice nurses politely called "end-stage agitation." He was irritable, snapped whenever we asked him anything and totally abandoned any effort at personal hygiene, including adult diapers. Our second-to-last conversation—on Father's Day, no less—was a shouting match because he refused to let me change him or the bed linens, and I'll just say it was beyond horrible. I kept staring at the emergency morphine, wondering if I could dope him enough to clean him off. But the nurse had warned I'd be accountable for every *pill and drop, and I didn't want to screw it up and kill him. Some days I was tempted to give* myself *the emergency morphine!*

Five days after the shitty shouting match, so to speak, I peeked in to ask if he was ready for his Dr Pepper and meds, and he'd passed in the night. I touched him three times before my brain could process it.

Mom overexerted herself attending his graveside service, went into a downward spiral, then joined him, exactly one month later. She slipped away peacefully with my sister and I holding her hands. I felt her pulse flutter briefly, then simply stop.

I get angry at the portrayal in movies and books that this time is magical and honorable, suggesting terminally ill people are plugged into the spirit world and will tell us special things. I feel ripped off because we had none of that. The closest thing to an epiphany was when Mom said, "I shouldn't've let him treat me like that. I shouldn't've let him treat y'all like that. I don't know why I put up with that so long. I'm sorry."

LISA GOUVEIA, AUSTIN

Lisa's austere tone tempers the despair of her situation, but it's still an unsparing look at the day-to-day details of watching a loved one die. Even though she doesn't see her mother's apology as an epiphany, it rings like a bell in the midst of all the suffering and struggle.

I've been blessed with my mom's unaddicted genetic code, but my first two memoirs cover quite a bit of rocky ground about my attraction to people who are attracted to various substances. Seems like most of us wind up with one of these blasted afflictions. Both hurt like the devil's pitchfork.

HAVE YOU EVER BEEN AFFECTED BY A LOVED ONE'S ADDICTION?

My father allowed me three or four passes at the stack of nearly four hundred record albums in the musty garage; everything from Herb

Alpert to the Doobie Brothers, basically the Kennedy era until right after Nixon got booted. All of the important stuff.

My parents had plenty of Elvis, Little Richard, Platters, Chuck Berry and the Killer. But this treasure trove completed my rock education seamlessly from 1960 to 1975. After that, I could and would fill in the blanks and own the whole story for myself.

The records had belonged to my dad's next youngest brother, Larry, who had put a pistol to the soft spot under his chin the previous Easter. Pulling the trigger that left a house for his mother to clean up, and these hundreds of musical messages for a niece he never really spoke to.

I was nine; it was the Bicentennial. I stood in the dim light of the funeral parlor, the only kid there, eye level with the weird, rubbery repair substance that had been sculpted onto my uncle's neck. The adults above me had a different perspective and murmured the things adults always say about how good he looked. I kept thinking about waxed fruit, which I'd never see the same way again.

Back in the hot and hazy garage, I flipped through the real stack of wax, taking as many records as I could carry: twenty or thirty clutched in my skinny arms.

Some I took because I knew they mattered or were already familiar, like Dylan or Simon and Garfunkel; some because of the artwork, like the original Tommy, *or* Goats Head Soup. *And at least one because of the title alone:* The Soft Parade. *All these years later, I still think about the ones I left behind, especially the eponymously named* Blind Faith *album, with the naked freckly girl in early puberty holding a toy airplane. She looked too much like me, with her unfortunate red hair, watery blue eyes and swollen nipples. I couldn't tuck the terrifying thing back behind the old records fast enough. Later I came to love that disk and the little girl on the cover.*

By the time he took his own life at the now clichéd age of twenty-seven, my uncle Larry was well beyond the help and solace his music might have offered. But when we assumed the loan on his house, because it was in "a better school district in a safer neighborhood," and when the other kids wouldn't befriend me, making an X on my back with a stick dipped in dog shit, and when I stood wordlessly at the top of the stairs and saw blood being pulled into the carpet cleaner out of the dark green shag that my dad was too cheap to change, Uncle Larry's music came to save me—fifth grade me at the window, who sang, "I am a rock, I am an island," while the pretty girls with good hair walked on by below, never seeing me.

It's a damn good thing Uncle Larry didn't have any Janis Ian records in his collection, only a bunch of angry, crazy rebel boys to inspire me . . . oh, and the ubiquitous Carole King, who sat in her own window with her own bad hair and looked like she probably had lived some of my secrets.

KRIS KOVACH, AUSTIN

From comparing her uncle's embalmed body to waxed fruit to the realization that even his music collection couldn't have saved him, there is so much to take away from this boffo piece. Kris always seems to be able to wind up her twelve minutes with some kind of astute pronouncement, probably because she's learned to empty her chatterbox mind and let the memories surge through unimpeded.

HAS YOUR LIFE BEEN TOUCHED BY SUICIDE?

HAVE YOU EVER BEEN WITH SOMEONE WHEN THEY PASSED? IF NOT, DESCRIBE THE MOMENT YOU LEARNED OF A LOVED ONE'S DEATH.

I was blessed to be at the bedside of both my parents when they made their transition into the Great Unknown. My mother and I wrangled for decades about her demonic tobacco habit, but despite her many attempts to quit, the two big Cs took her out—cigarettes and cancer. Margaret was so devoted to her cigs that when the doc showed us the massive swath across her lung X-ray and told her she had a few weeks to live, she defiantly lit up.

A month or so earlier I had an overwhelming desire to put my head in Mama's lap and have her stroke my hair like she did when I was little. Despite all the delirious turns my life had taken, she had always been my champion, my foundation and my touchstone. I often worried about becoming untethered when she slipped out of her mortal coil, because my mother loved me in a way I knew I'd never be loved again. When I was helping her on with her jammies, she stared at her seventy-seven-year-old face in the mirror, shaking her head. "It's always a surprise," she said. "I still feel twenty-one inside."

Five weeks after her diagnosis, Margaret Ruth Hayes-Miller from Buford, Georgia, was gone. She'd been resigned and seemed relieved, insisting that she'd done all she wanted to do in life, including her recent trip to Hawaii with dear Aunt Edna.

The hospice folks told me that often when someone is facing the final curtain, they get a last burst of joyous lucidity. Three days before my mom passed, I pulled out her old jewelry box and she brightened, telling me how she'd acquired each piece, her face full of wonder and delight. It saddens me to say that most of her final movements involved holding an imaginary cigarette and bringing it to her mouth. A godawful addiction. Probably the worst.

I stayed right beside my little mama, but she hadn't moved for several hours, and her breathing had become rattled, so I knew she

was close to leaving. Suddenly she sat up, and with her eyes open
wide, she reached up high, her face awash in stunned ecstasy. Had she
seen my daddy? Her mother? A giant tunnel of welcoming light? I
knew I'd miss her like the earth angel she'd been all my life, but I also
knew she was headed in the right direction, and I'd see her again
when the consummate mystery claimed me.

PAMELA DES BARRES

I was also with my daddy when he died. Here is a passage from *Take Another Little Piece of My Heart*, my second memoir. The subtitle of that book is *A Groupie Grows Up*. I discovered that losing a parent turns you into an instant grown-up, taking away any clinging vestige of childhood, no matter how old you are when it happens. I was thirty-three when O. C. Miller drew his last gasping breath.

We had all gotten into nightgowns and jammies and I wanted to
check on Daddy one more time before heading into a fitful
dreamland. The sight of him took all my air out and made me feel
invisible. He was curled up on his side, eyes rolled back into his head,
bent hands clasped, gasping, wrenching final air into his failed
lungs. The death rattle is real and it stings the ear like a hive full of
defiled bees . . . I had an absurd, agonizing desire to do Daddy's nails
one more time, innocently watching Hoss Cartwright kick the butt
of a bad guy on TV; but, pressing up against the wall, digging way
inside myself, I grabbed ahold of my unbeaten, invincible spirit and
pinched it, hard. Pushing myself to walk over to the bed, I took hold
of his crumpled hand. "Daddy?" No response whatsoever. His lips
were blue, his eyes seeing into another realm, ragged breath rattling
in and out, in and out. With deep dread I had to call my mom in
and I guess the tone of my voice shook her up. She rushed in, con-
fused and fatally frightened, her eyes telling the thirty-seven-year-old

story of courtship, love, marriage, betrayal, pain, heartache, acceptance, more love, understanding, profound compassion and finality. When she saw Daddy, she let out a scream I'll never forget and fell on him. "Oren, Oren, no, don't go yet!" But Daddy never moved, just that loud, ragged breath signaling his imminent exit from the physical plane.

"He can't go yet, Pamela," my mom whimpered in a sore, unfamiliar voice.

"Oh, lordy," Aunt Edna wailed, "he could be like this for a week!"

At that point I came out of my shocked stupor, vowing he would have his release way before the night was over . . . so I took a seat across from Daddy, closed my eyes and started speaking to his spirit.

"It's time to go, Daddy, it's time to set yourself free. Take a deep breath, let go, let go, let go, my darling, sweet Daddy."

It was a precious litany from my soul to his, and after about thirty minutes I realized his breaths were coming slower and slower, and even though I knew it was for his infinite good, when the final breath was pulled in and never let back out, I collapsed onto the bed, curled into him and felt the living warmth drain away. I stroked the back of his neck where soft gray hairs grew, and I inhaled his Daddy scent over and over, until my face was soaked with tears.

PAMELA DES BARRES

WHO IS SOMEONE YOU DIDN'T APPRECIATE UNTIL THEY WERE GONE?

My mother and I walked in the same shoes of doubt and uncertainty. We were so much alike that it worked as identical magnetic poles, pushing us as far apart as could be. Anytime this similarity raised its ugly head, I kicked it in the teeth and ran the opposite direction. I didn't like myself much, so how could I like the one who made me this way? I hated her reticence, stumbling over her own feet trying to be who she thought the room wanted her to be. I hated that this was my role model, leaving me with my own feet of clay, crumbling beneath me.

But she wrapped me up in it from the moment I was born. Love is so easy when you can't talk. The unspoken nature of it reflected everything she ever thought she was or wanted to be. When I found words, she still tried to hold on to me, slippery little fish that I was. When the darkness took hold, she valiantly tried to watercolor it, but I shook it off and retreated into my hole. Love hate love hate. Who do you think you are and why do you think you know me? It was so easy for me because I could not even conceive how she felt. She was a wall. She was a tank and she took every evil thing I threw at her.

As I grew, my anger toward her absorbed into the person I became. I didn't like who I saw in the mirror, especially when those itching thoughts crept up my legs and along my spine: "You're just like her." I wrapped myself in ripped fabrics and metal zippers and black black black. Nothing like her. No, not me.

Until she was gone. I sat in a void for the longest time, and then one exquisitely lonely day I started stripping away the paint that covered us. Under the first layer I found the shy, insecure girl who never thought anyone liked her. Under the next I saw the one who landed on a stage, realizing that was the safest place to be. Beneath that was the girl with a cigarette, head thrown back in abandon, in laughter, never knowing she was going to leave this earth before her daughter realized she was a superstar.

MOLLIE STAFFA, AUSTIN

The extended use of simile and metaphor is so effective in Mollie's writing that each gem seems to slip and sluice through this piece like a ride on a water-park slide. You know from the first line, "My mother and I walked in the same shoes of doubt and uncertainty," that you're in for a literary hurricane.

THE LAST TIME I SAW _____, I HAD NO IDEA IT WOULD BE THE LAST TIME.

Perhaps I chose not to know. My father made a special trip to Houston and we took a drive to Zilker Park, amid the live oak trees, silent observers of that sacred moment. He turned to me, blue eyed and gray haired; a handsome, gentle face.

"The value of life is measured by the people you have loved and are loved by," he said softly. "I've been blessed to have four people whose unconditional love gave my life purpose and meaning. You, my dear daughter, are one of those people."

A heart as huge as his should stay strong and healthy. But life had broken it more times than it could rebuild. It was tired. And soon it would be in the hands of a surgeon.

"If I don't make it home from the hospital, I'm at peace with that."

Denial took over. Bigger than life, my father—a poet, musician, artist—a man who talked to angels, who taught me to dance—small feet on large leather shoes. How can someone so bright move into the shadow of mere memories? Never. As I dance with wild abandon to the music I love so dearly, I dance with you, Daddy.

SAMANTHA VANDERSLICE, AUSTIN

The image of Samantha's small feet on her daddy's large leather shoes is such a touching, personal remembrance. But even the death of someone you don't know very well can rattle you to the core, especially if it's someone famous whose life has been splattered over headlines. As in her earlier piece about the teen murder she witnessed, Linda takes you to a hot-spot memory that still reverberates.

LET IT BLEED

As usual, CBGB was packed and many of the regulars, like Joey Ramone, Dee Dee Ramone and Sid and Nancy—as if they were a single entity rather than two separate people—were hanging out.

Joey Ramone was draped over a pinball machine, rarely looking up, his long, lanky body owning the game.

There was a shroudlike miasma of smoke hanging over everything, the air as humid as a jungle night. The AC had long since lost the battle to the number of bodies crammed inside the small club, and their dripping rancid sweat. It was quite impossible to talk while the bands played, a bit better between the sets as the DJ blasted Dead Boys, Adverts, Dolls and Ramones.

As always, we stayed till they threw us out, and the Bowery was a sight to see, alive with people—some who wouldn't be around much longer and a few who would go down in history as punk rock legends.

It was four a.m., September 8, 1978, among the wasted spillage on the sidewalk outside, when I saw Sid and Nancy for the last time. You could hear her before you saw her, as usual, her loud, strident, grating voice carrying far into the predawn duskiness. A few people covered their ears, but she never noticed. Sid was all but nonambulatory, almost hoisted over Nancy's shoulders. He slurred and stumbled, smiling foolishly . . . Nancy was all too happy to take care of him, as she always did, making sure they got their dope and works to stave off the jonesing. She was almost motherly to him, in a very unmotherly way. Her body language shrieked, "Back off, bitches!" in case another chick got any wrong ideas.

Only a few weeks later she was fatally stabbed to death at the Chelsea Hotel and poor old Sid was accused of murdering her. Ironically enough, they were the second couple I knew in two years where the boyfriend was accused of murdering his girlfriend. I've known some doomed couples in my time.

LINDA LEATHER, NEW YORK

DESCRIBE HOW THE DEATH OF SOMEONE YOU DIDN'T KNOW DEEPLY AFFECTED YOU.

For David Bowie

You were Always, like the cosmos; you were Ever, like a stone
You were All the Time, and Endless; you were velvet, flame,
and bone
You were violet nights of mystery, the electric blue of day
And not once since first I loved you did I think you might
not stay

You were bigger than your body; you were paler than the moon
You were ninety kinds of discord all perfectly in tune
You were psychedelic oceans, spinning whirlpools of pain
You were every color on the wheel inside one
stretching brain

You were sensual like starlight and erotic like an eel
And you slithered like a drop of oil and spoke like
melting steel
You were warm like sex and cold like glass and made of
lucid dreams
As wise as fetus in the womb, as smart as laser beams

You were muscle, blood, and ether; you were Plato's
Forms to me
The zodiac incarnate, you were always going to be
You were wicked, you were holy, you could never be defiled
And the universe was spinning on your perfect
smirking smile

233

You are Always, like this heart-bleed; you are Ever, like
   the scars
You are All the Time, and Endless; you are living in
   the stars
You are crimson nights of longing, the metallic spark of day
There will never be another, and you're never going away

NICHOLE JAYMES, LOS ANGELES

WRITE ABOUT A FUNERAL.

HAVE YOU EVER BEEN CLOSE TO DYING?

*I was swimming with my friends and family at Tappan Lake, and
we were playing a game to see who could stay under the water longest.
I won because I didn't come back up.*

*There are pictures of me in all the local papers that week—lying
on the ground with a teenage lifeguard giving me CPR, a relatively
new procedure. They gave up on me and pronounced me dead until
a doctor vacationing on the other side of the lake arrived and
worked to get a heartbeat. Apparently, my heart stopped a few more
times on the way to the hospital some forty minutes away; the ambulance was so seldom used that they had to stop for gas. I include
these details because there are so many places where I could have just
slipped away.*

*I didn't know about all of that; I woke up five days later bruised
all over, very sore and hungry. But I do remember dying very clearly.
And what I remember hasn't changed since I told my mother in 1965
when she cautioned me not to tell anyone in our small town lest they
think me cuckoo.*

*I remember struggling to get up, to no avail, then surrendering to
the force pushing me down. As I finally sank back into the sand at the*

lake's bottom, I rose up out of the water and into a very bright light.
There was a faint glimmer/glimpse of an angelic being and I felt
something lift me into that light. Then there was a swooshy feeling
like I was zapped into a higher place —high above the water. I have
a strong memory of coming out of darkness into a very bright light; I
also feel like I was transported from the bottom of the lake to looking
down at the gurney in the hospital where I landed—and landed *is*
actually the word I thought of then.

My next memories are of being above the gurney looking down at
my mother and then being in my body again. And I remember
talking to the people who came to visit me, but they acted like I wasn't
even there.

TERRY MORELAND HENDERSON, LOS ANGELES

So many people have described that same bright light that Terry remembers so clearly all these years later. I can almost hear the merciful thwump when her spirit landed back into her body.

IF YOU COULD PLAN YOUR DEATH, WHAT WOULD BE THE BEST SCENARIO?

When my most beloved friend and mentor, Gail Zappa, passed on last year, I spoke at her funeral and sobbed like a little girl, weighed down and overcome by the loss of such a hugely vital lifelong soul mate. It was a chilly day in L.A. and the air was somber with sorrow. As Gail was being lowered into the ground above her husband, her youngest son, Ahmet, spoke these words: "Well, Gail is finally back where she's always wanted to be—on top of Frank!" The mood rose up like an angel food cake, and her friends and family started smiling, happy to have known such a whopper of a lady.

Gail definitely wound up where she belonged that day, but with so much humanity inhabiting the planet and dropping like gnats, I've decided not to clog up Mother Earth with another giant chrome casket, or

235

LET IT BLEED

even to mess up the air with my scattered ashes. I've been poking around and found a perfect solution, created by a couple of forward-thinking Italians: organic burial pods! While still alive, you can choose your very own tree to be planted under and wind up as nourishment for your favorite oak or elm! Doesn't that sound like a perfect solution for this overloaded planet?

DO YOU WANT A FUNERAL? DO YOU PLAN TO BE BURIED OR CREMATED OR WOULD YOU DONATE YOUR BODY TO SCIENCE?

DO YOU FEAR DEATH? WHAT DO YOU IMAGINE HAPPENS AT THE MOMENT OF DEATH?

DO YOU BELIEVE IN AN AFTERLIFE? REINCARNATION?

WHAT WOULD IT SAY ON YOUR HEADSTONE? WHY?

DOES THE SPIRIT CONTINUE OR IS THIS IT?

HOW WOULD YOUR OBITUARY READ?

WHAT WILL YOU MISS ABOUT EARTH/LIFE WHEN YOU DIE?

I will miss marveling at things on earth. There are so many fascinating, wonderful things to explore before I die. I want to see a lava lake full of hot lava even though that sounds like something I need to die and go to hell to see. But that lava lake is somewhere here on earth and I want to see it while I'm still alive.

I need to see the Great Barrier Reef; I need to jump into the water and snorkel there. I need to see the northern lights. I need to sleep in an igloo. I need to see more tropical islands.

I will miss the mornings that are practically silent except for birds singing outside, until my dog comes scratching on my door to feed her, and I will miss her too. I will miss sleeping and dreaming alive even though I will be resting in peace eternally.

I will miss my friends and family; I will even miss being annoyed or stressed out by them. I will miss my three black cats purring and biting and scratching me. I will miss being surrounded by hungry animals who get extremely excited when I am about to feed them.

I will miss procrastinating and wasting time on my computer. I will miss playing Candy Crush, watching Saturday Night Live *and watching videos of kittens and hamsters on YouTube.*

I will miss sushi and Girl Scout cookies and pasta and eggs. I will miss going to my office and complaining about work. I will miss Los Angeles traffic and the shortcuts I am forced to take to get anywhere. I will miss washing the dishes in the kitchen with the back door open while hearing the opera singers rehearse at the house behind me.

I can't think of anything I will not miss. It's a good thing I'll be dead because I'll miss everything.

BAMBI CONWAY, LOS ANGELES

LET IT BLEED

CHAPTER THIRTEEN

I

Ticket to Ride

After that fatal dose of reality, why don't we lighten things up a tad? Besides delving deep into our lives in my workshops, I also give my students an array of fictional assignments, and their relief is palpable when they escape their own stories, conjuring up captivating people, places and circumstances. But writing these descriptive fanciful tales has also helped them to dig into their real lives in a more provocative way. Letting your imagination take flight by making something up will help pinpoint what you find fascinating, what interests you; this will enrich your ability to write an irresistible yet completely factual memoir. These prompts can actually liberate you to look even deeper into your own quixotic experiences and see them a bit more objectively, which allows more freedom of expression. And of course, in all our writing, fact or fiction, we bring ourselves into it, so a true tidbit often comes to light and is revealed. It's also a blast! So let's begin with a little imaginary musical dream!

YOU HAVE BEEN ASKED TO BOOK FOUR ACTS OF YOUR CHOICE INTO CARNEGIE HALL FOR A CONCERT. DESCRIBE THE EVENING.

PUT YOURSELF IN THE MIDDLE OF A HISTORIC MUSICAL MOMENT. WHERE ARE YOU? WHO ARE YOU WITH? WHAT YEAR IS IT? ARE

YOU ONSTAGE AT THE HOLLYWOOD BOWL WITH THE BEATLES IN '64? ADJUSTING MOZART'S WIG BEFORE HE PERFORMS FOR THE KING? DANCING ON A PEDESTAL IN JIMI HENDRIX'S "FOXY LADY" VIDEO (LIKE I DID)?

YOU'RE BACKSTAGE AT A LED ZEPPELIN CONCERT REUNION. USE THESE WORDS IN YOUR STORY: GRANDIOSE, CANTANKEROUS, CREAMY, ELEVATED, GRENADE AND OPPORTUNISTIC.

The two following prompts inspired my writers—art worshippers after my own heart—to channel their inner Van Gogh. Stardust writes in the voice of the master himself, and Trellawny is his muse.

WRITE IN THE VOICE OF A HERO OR HEROINE.

Today I drew the irises. I went to the field where they grow and stood among them. They swayed so innocently that I was caught in sudden rapture. How could I capture such beauty?

I attempted such an action by staring at a white flower amid the sea of blue, capturing its radiating agelessness in a single stroke of my pencil. So fragile, so pure, so indefinite. I was ensnared in their yellow innards as they called my name. I heard only the rustle of the breeze through nature. I felt the grass underfoot. I couldn't break my stare, those daring irises.

I returned to the village I call home. The rustic purity of the fields eludes me there, replaced by man and his denial of what is right and beautiful. I was pushed aside by passersby who didn't so much as look at me. But 'twas not their fault; they cannot see what dances around them. I see what they cannot. I see the blue, the stillness in the fields where these flowers grow season after season.

As I sit at my easel, charcoal stick ready to repeat those lines, I think of her. Like the people who wander the streets below, she rejected the heart I placed around her. But who am I to cut and stem this flower? I do love her. Should love not be cherished?

And my irises, I drew them so desperately—I wanted her to see them. I could still recall the rustle of stalks like the rustle of her long blue skirts through parlor doors . . . I could hear the sounds of the breeze form a voice on the wind, melting from the trees, from the sky, from the irises. Those blue flowers as blue as her eyes.

While I drew the flowers for hours this day, all I could hear were the laughs and power of her uttered hms and ahs. As the sea of irises formed to paint her face, I noticed the open window and the sounds pouring in through that portal. I jumped and in three strides the panes were closed. With the sound silenced I looked to the mirror, saw my own eyes and fell deeply into them. I came to rest on a bed of irises and you were beside me. I touched your face but it fell into thousands of blue petals.

All I heard then was your laugh, so I put my hand to my ear and my fingers curled around it. When my hand came away all was quiet. And what did I see in the mirror? Myself, holding a knife in one hand, and my ear resting in my lap.

Now I am in the local hospital, where the kindly doctors have attended to me as best they can, but I fear my ear is now detached from my head forever. What shall I do now? Why, send it to you, of course, my beloved and most enduring mistress. She who whispers endlessly in my ear shall now have my ear. That is what happened today, my love. And my gift is wrapped in a gold gilt box, coming to you. After all, what use have I for my own misbegotten ear? I need only these hands to draw—to draw the irises.

SARA STARDUST, LOS ANGELES

At only twenty-two, Stardust has the free-falling ability to give in to her whimsical imagination and gets lost in prompts such as this one. She's almost completed a book she calls a medieval rock-and-roll fantasy, titled *The Holy Wood Chronicles*. It stars Bon Scott and Ozzy Osbourne.

IF YOU COULD SPEND AN EVENING WITH ANYONE, ALIVE OR DEAD, WHO WOULD IT BE AND WHAT WOULD YOU DO?

I would ask him to paint me. If it were today, he would probably cut off both ears out of pure fear of the world that spins in harsh contrast to what he knew—or the world he tried to know. From the age of twelve, I have loved the works of Van Gogh. I've adored him longer than the musicians who make the sweet sounds I need to hear and dance to. There is something about the way he saw the world—or how I think he saw the world, based on his stirring paintings. Some so vibrant, others so dark, just like music. The paint lifts out of the canvas like a lyric speaks to me in a song.

Some might agree that some of Van Gogh's self-portraits could be likened to today's "selfies" on social media. But they were, of course, so much more introspective than the drunken "don't I look hot?" mirror gaze that has leaked into today's version of self-portrayal via "art."

Vincent Van Gogh: I would ask him to paint me. I want to see myself the way he might have seen me. I want to tell him that that bitchy whore he sent his ear to wasn't worth his blood. That I feel a strange connection to him because he shot himself in the stomach eighty-nine years to the day before my birthday (poor sot, I always think of him, especially, on that day). That the way he saw the world is still unique and magnificent, all these years later. He did it. He stood the test of time.

I would liken him to great composers, like Beethoven and Led Zeppelin. I'd tell him that sunflowers have always held a special place in my heart, that they're tattooed on my back. I would ask Van Gogh to paint me, and my sunflowers, in his way. And we would have

LET IT BLEED

wine. And we would talk about everything and nothing. And we
would listen to music. And dance.

And I would never see him again.

TRELLAWNY GRAHAM, TORONTO

Like Trellawny I am transfixed when I stand in front of a Van Gogh painting. His pulsing swirls swim out of the canvas and anoint me like droplets of holy oil. My heart throbs along with his brushstrokes like a drumbeat that comes in colors. It's a kaleidoscopic happening!

For this same assignment, Margaret imagined meeting the devil at the crossroads with a certain musical pioneer, bringing the myth to life, and almost succumbed to Beelzebub's tempting offer in the process. Her visceral descriptions, such as "molten dust," and "inky miasma," add to the trancelike atmosphere.

I had, it seemed, arrived just in time. The road was steamy and red in the setting sun, and dust rose like smoke from hot coals. A figure appeared to me out of the fiery haze and walked toward me. He drew closer and I saw that he wore a dingy jacket and a droopy hat and carried a worn guitar under one arm.

As he approached, he took a nearly empty bottle of whiskey out of his jacket pocket, unscrewed it with one hand and took a swig. Seeing me, he held it out and invited me to join him. I almost refused because I knew who we'd meet if I walked with him, but this was the reason I had come and this was the walk I had to take if I were to know the truth.

So we went on together, moving further and further into the now enveloping shroud of molten dust until we heard the shrill whinny of a horse and stopped stock-still. I felt the vibration of its hooves as it thundered toward us and I wanted to run, but my companion had taken my hand and held me still.

242   PAMELA DES BARRES

"Girl, you don't want to get in his way!" he warned me in a gruff whisper, pulling me from the middle of the road.

He asked me, plaintively then, to give a message to his friend Willie Brown. Of course I agreed and we walked on. As the sun sank into sudden darkness, we arrived at that lonely crossroads.

The horse's pounding hooves came closer and closer and then it was upon us. It was huge and black and the figure astride its broad back was clothed in the deepest black of all. Its rider's voice was terrible, yet seductive as he spoke to my companion.

"I hear you're a pretty good guitar player, boy," he drawled, "but I understand you'd like to be a whole lot better . . ."

My companion, now visibly trembling, only nodded. I stepped back, suddenly chilled through.

"Hello, uh, hello, Satan. I believe it's time to go."

In an instant they were swallowed by an inky miasma. A gust of malodorous wind swept past me and carried upon it the banshee wail of a tortured guitar string that underscored his fading words: "Got to keep movin', got to keep movin' . . . There's a hellhound on my trail . . . hellhound on my trail."

I fervently wished to escape the source of the desperate dread I felt, but found myself hesitating, my icy fear flaming in sudden, stunning desire. A desperate longing caught me up and in an instant I saw that it was I who played those haunting cries on my guitar, I whose song was the howl of the hounds of hell . . . I who also yearned to make that mad music . . . but know I never, ever will. Still, why not? Why shouldn't I follow that same hellish trail?

But I know how this tale ends. Robert Johnson, albeit immortal, will shortly die and walk side by side with Satan into infernal eternity.

I force myself to turn away from the tempter's false promises, and the shimmering notes I heard myself play turn discordant and shrill, then fade away as I find myself emerging from the sulfuric haze,

243

LET IT BLEED

already many long miles from that wicked crossroads, knowing that
I too have to keep moving . . .

MARGARET FARRELL, LOS ANGELES

I hope you recall my little tirade about the wickedness of clichés! I gave this assignment in my L.A. class, and here's what Ms. Farrell came up with. Try changing a few common clichés into more original prose yourself!

CHANGE THESE CLICHÉS INTO MORE ORIGINAL PHRASES, AND WRITE ABOUT A BUS TRIP.

Don't beat around the bush

Always look on the bright side

Heart of stone

Come hell or high water

Easy as pie

Speak of the devil

I had made up my mind. I would go, I would accomplish my goal, and I would return. "Okay," *I told myself.* "You've decided; now stop flapping your wings and fly!"

And, yes, there are dangers to be faced and overcome, but when you're chilly, find a warm spot!

I set out for the bus stop, only to have the bus splash me as it passed me by. "That driver must have a mechanical pump *in his chest," I muttered, but vowed to press on, whether met by a* three-alarm fire or a flooded intersection.

I had known this journey would be challenging; nothing so facile as me effortlessly stumbling over carpet lint *this time.*

"I'm going to get there," I told myself, "and you can take that to the bank."

And then, there it was, I'd made it! Think of the financial institution and it shall appear!

MARGARET FARRELL, LOS ANGELES

TWENTY YEARS FROM NOW YOU ARE RECEIVING A LIFETIME ACHIEVEMENT AWARD. WHAT IS IT FOR?

It's always stunning to me how much brilliance is lodged in our brains, ready to dash out of the starting gate like a high-strung greyhound (simile). The imagination is our own personal playground (metaphor), crammed with possibility. When I give these assignments and start the countdown, my writers are cut loose to snatch the ideas from the air; and when they read them aloud afterward, they shake their heads in wonder. Where does this stuff come from? It's just a matter of trust. Remember what the Buddha said: "Jump! You cannot fall."

Here's another prize from Kris. She's a lactation specialist in Austin, one of my fave dancing partners, a music-loving wise-doll and a unique thinker, always with a snappy retort. It's a trip how far my students go with these fictional assignments. Kris has no clue how this tale tumbled out of her:

A WOMAN COMES HOME AND FINDS SOMETHING ON HER KITCHEN TABLE THAT DOESN'T BELONG THERE.

Irene opened the door and stopped cold when she saw it there.

It was a lamb in a box.

A live baby lamb.

Cute little thing, but she felt the anger rising up.

Shawn knew better than to bring his projects into the house, let alone the kitchen, let alone on the goddamn table. Where did this kid come from? When she picked him up at school, the teachers and the 4-H leader spoke to her about him as if she had any idea who he was. Nope. She had seen the ropy, rubbery cord being cut as he exited her body fourteen years ago, but at this point she believed it had been an elaborate magic trick, an optical illusion.

He was completely formed and self-styled from the start. Shawn knew livestock and had dedicated an amazing number of years to those creatures to get recognition. Irene was merely his staff. She cooked meals, paid the bills and always smiled politely at the rodeos and the feed store. She felt like an immigrant in her own country.

The baby lamb smelled oily and felt warm as she slid it from the box into her arms and sank slowly onto the floor. It was an incredibly cute thing and she knew just enough to be concerned for its welfare. This little mammal was young and dumb. Shawn had never been, and only lately she'd realized in complete shock that these animals and their many shitty, cloven-hooved brethren could mean thousands—maybe tens or hundreds of thousands—of dollars toward Shawn's future. Toward college. A whole lifestyle, full of crew-cut Christian grandkids and expensive mud-covered pickups and a daughter-in-law named Haley that would always be a mystery to her.

Easing the lamb out of her arms, she remembered the little plastic guitar and glitter cape she'd given Shawn at eighteen months old and how they'd both been unused, never played, not flown.

"Face it!" she told the bleating lamb, now settling down on one of her good towels folded neatly inside the box, "there will be no record contract for this boy."

KRIS KOVACH, AUSTIN

YOU'RE STUCK IN AN ELEVATOR WITH A PRIEST, A PROSTITUTE AND OPRAH WINFREY. WRITE ABOUT THE CONVERSATION.

WHAT IF JESUS CAME BACK TODAY AS PROMISED IN THE BIBLE? WHO WOULD HE BE?

Don't act surprised. He's been telling you all along he's Jesus, shouting it from the rooftops and sharing it in his version of updated hymns for all the kids who attend his mass hysteria—induced concerts.

He didn't realize it would be this *hard to convince people that he was God's son. He was able to do it the first time and that was waaaaay before social media and his own personal hashtags. The only problem was that when he and the Holy Father sat down to sign up for Twitter and Instagram, both the Jesus and God screen names were taken. And as we all know, it's impossible to get a customer service representative from either company. Being the creator of the universe doesn't mean shit to the CEO of the twittersphere, who is probably Lucifer himself.*

So the Holy Son had to come up with another moniker.

He did nearly all the same things, but with a little more artistic flair so it would sound familiar to his followers. He turned water into Cristal at all the famous clubs, he named his baby after the direction of Polaris, he married a prostitute (there's a rumor that her next sex tape will be called "The Second Coming"), but he discovered that they're not called prostitutes anymore, they're called Kardashians, and his wife brought along twelve disciples: Kris, Kourtney, Khloé, Kylie, Kendall, Scott, Lamar, Rob, Pitbull, Brody, Bruce & Caitlin.

So next time you see Jesus interrupting Taylor Swift to tell you the actual word of God, give him the respect he deserves, even if nowadays he has to go by Yeezus.

Now if someone could just hurry up and nail him to a cross.

BELL POP, LOS ANGELES

247

LET IT BLEED

Yikes! Did this hilarious prompt cause a commotion when Bell read it aloud! It freaks me out imagining that the Lord's muse, Mary Magdalene, might be Kim Kardashian this time around!

GO TO A COFFEE SHOP AND OBSERVE A STRANGER. MAKE UP A TALE ABOUT WHO THAT PERSON IS.

His cap said "Sad Boys"; his shirt said otherwise. The Hawaiian pineapples danced across his chest in a jovial manner, just as they had done since the print was produced in 1979. Those pineapples mocked him. He was the shirt's third wearer. It had been an impulse buy at a thrift store. She told him to buy it and, in a bid to become the man she wanted him to be, he handed over twenty dollars and then worried about washing all the years of ingrained dirt away. Every time he wore it, he thought of her.

He thought of her now as he stared down at his phone, willing her to call, text, post something on social media. Anything that would show him she still existed. His hand hovered over the keypad. But there was nothing left to say. She had made it clear. It was over. He put the phone down and turned it over. He fiddled with the arm of his black Buddy Holly glasses and stared out the windows, watching the world walk past. He wondered if he would ever be able to walk down a street without wishing she was by his side.

He told himself to focus, think of something else, and called the waitress over to order a cup of coffee. Iced coffee. It was hot outside, after all. The winter had fled and let summer take over, heaping generous helpings of sunshine on us all. The waitress nodded and disappeared to fetch his order. He stared after her. She was attractive. Dark haired, petite, round of mouth. It was a nice mouth. A mouth to kiss. Would he ever kiss again? If he was like the man his girl left him for, he'd ask the waitress for her number. Pick her up at the end of her shift

and whisk her off to a bar and charm her with champagne. But he
was never going to be that guy. He couldn't even tie a tie. He sighed.
He needed to find a job that paid better. Nobody needed journalists
anymore. Not unless they wanted to work for free. The novel wasn't
happening. He couldn't write since she'd left. But the sun was shining.
At least the sun was shining.

ERIKA THOMAS, NEW YORK

Such an elegant depiction of dejection, right? The image of pineapples mocking him from the thrift store shirt delighted me no end. This is an assignment you can give yourself on a daily basis and you'll never lack for human specimens to fulfill your fantasies. Is she a fallen nun? Has he just escaped from a turbulent marriage? By tromping around in someone's imagined existence, you're free to create.

Just for kicks, try using someone else's words as a jumping-off point for your own imaginative foray. Scan a news site for an intriguing headline and write your own story. Or . . .

OPEN ANY BOOK TO ANY PAGE AND READ THE FIRST SENTENCE OF THE SECOND PARAGRAPH. THEN JUST RIFF ON WHAT MIGHT COME NEXT. LET YOUR IMAGINATION OFF ITS LEASH!

You can also use this fictional device to tell on yourself. Call yourself "she" and "her," or give yourself a new name, and dare to face down your darkest day as this daredevil dame. You can also change history in this same way. Write a different outcome to a difficult situation. Win instead of lose. Dance instead of sitting it out. Say yes instead of no, or no instead of yes. Use the prompt below.

IF YOU COULD GO BACK AND CHANGE AN EXPERIENCE IN YOUR LIFE, WRITE A FICTIONAL VERSION OF HOW IT WOULD HAVE PLAYED OUT DIFFERENTLY.

WHAT WRITER HAS SPOKEN TO THE REAL YOU?

**WRITE A SHORT STORY BASED ON A FAVORITE SONG, USING
THE TITLE OF THE SONG AND SOME OR ALL OF THE LYRICS AS
YOUR PLOT.**

I hope you feel stretched out and exhilarated from your excursions
into the fictional realm. Just to show how the same muscle can be flexed
when examining your own life, here is a similar prompt—but one that
asks you to look at a true occurrence. These two very different memories
were conjured up by contemplating the same song title by an old pal
of mine.

**WRITE A REAL-LIFE PIECE USING ALICE COOPER'S TITLE "ONLY
WOMEN BLEED"**

> He punched her hard in a discreet place
> In her side but never her face
> She heard the ribs crack as the blow met its mark
> Next the back of her ears, ringing, then dark
> Women may bleed but men can bleed too
> She heard the same thought "What would Lizzie do?"
> She gave herself in to the madness of love
> Blows rained on him from below and above
> Crimson spots upon her breast
> Blood red ribbons on his chest
> Only women bleed?
> A myth indeed!
>
> DIANNE SCOTT, AUSTIN

*I remember watching some puberty movie in fifth grade, and the gist
was that when Orphan Annie got as tall as her basement ceiling, she*

got her period and became a woman. So for my whole life I thought, Okay, when I get tall enough to touch my basement ceiling, then it'll be "period time." But here's how it really went:

I was swimming around in my parents' sweet above-ground pool, wearing my black one-piece bathing suit with this totally hot, dreamy blue-eyed baseball player who was working on my parents' house with his dad. But mainly he was waiting till I got home from driver's ed so we could get in the pool and have lessons. My first lesson was How to Make Out 101. I aced that. Then it progressed to Boobie Touching 105. Passed that with sizzling colors. Then finally it was Blow Job Time. So he got his thing out and it reminded me of the time my friend Aaron showed me his wiener and it looked just like a floating hot dog from 7-Eleven. But I quickly blocked that image and went for the gold. Which is kind of hard to do when you're underwater, holding your breath and trying to focus. So when I got out of the pool to go to the bathroom, lo and behold, what did I discover but a crimson tide. No surprise, really, because I was already way tall and hitting that basement ceiling, no problem.

I knew dreamy baseball dude was waiting for me in the pool so we could finish our escapades, but I didn't know how to put in a tampon, which looked like a miniature baseball bat with a string. And the darn thing just wouldn't go in, even though I put my leg all up on the sink like a ballet dancer. It was like a cotton swab to nowhere.

I sure wanted to get back to the pool and make out some more, get my boobies touched and all that fun stuff, but I was worried there'd be a crimson lake around us. I did the only thing I could think of. I lay down in the bathtub and tried to push all the blood out. I thought maybe it was like giving birth and if I pushed hard enough, it would all come out like the Alice Cooper song, "Only Women Bleed." So I pushed for, like, five minutes and felt satisfied that enough had come

251

LET IT BLEED

out. I ran the shower and giggled at the fact that my brothers would
be stepping in my period blood remnants later, and voyaged out for
more good times on the make-out train.

Thankfully it worked out, because we made out for, like, two more
hours without incident.

BRANDY BATZ, LOS ANGELES

CHAPTER FOURTEEN

I

Bringing It All Back Home

This chapter is about living in the Right Now, and how you became who you are this very day. Let's ponder how all the sacred joy, heart scarring, soaring, rocking, reeling, tumbling, bleeding, dancing, traveling, worrying, lovemaking, sorrow, loss and healing created who you are at this very moment. Ask yourself if your priorities have changed since you began careening down the Route 66 of your life. Who and what inspires you right now? I'll bet you've discovered parts of yourself that had been hidden; maybe even the reason you had to go through certain trials and tribs has become more clear. My hope is that you've realized it's all been worth it!

A huge reason why memoirs and autobiographies continue to intrigue, confound, delight and sell in massive numbers is the life lessons hidden within the confessional tales that the author has been audacious enough to share. I have been so moved by a startling admission, or a hard-won acceptance, that I was changed somehow and I'm sure it's happened to you too. And happily, my tales have helped other women to appreciate their own music-loving souls. Let's plumb your new depths to discover your truest self and who you are right now.

DESCRIBE THE PERSON YOU ARE TODAY.

DESCRIBE A TYPICAL DAY IN YOUR LIFE.

So the other day it was so hot outside I felt like I was swimming in Kenny G's pubic hairs after an especially hot soprano sax smooth jazz solo, so it goes without saying that I was in no mood to teach the children any type of anything, so I busted out the clay.

"Okay, kids, I want you to make two clay versions of yourself: the first one representing your physical self and the second representing how you mentally see yourself." I rattled off that the physical self was easy—just how you looked: hair color, eye color, build, etc. The mental self was how you saw yourself on the inside—the inner you. I told them I would be a unicorn who uses her horn to spear people and sprinkle purple dust and fireballs. I also added that my horn would not kill, of course, but just make people disappear into a box of cereal for a while. I then told them they would then compose speeches about the project and present them to the class, because I had to make it educational.

They started and were just loving it. Some of the highlights were a physical "me" that looked much like Penny from Pee-wee's Playhouse, *several dinosaurs, a monkey swinging from a tree with a bunch of bananas, Indiana Clay—a take on Indiana Jones—a cannibal bunny, a cat that turned into Satan and much more. What can I say? I teach at a hippie school and these kids are dark and special.*

Then Lukas walked up with his clay dude and it had a long, dangling male protuberance. Very thin and dark, like a black whisper of a ween. Of course, anytime a kid sculpts a ween, the rest of them can sense it and come running to gasp and laugh. Then everyone started making clay weens, telling me they were poles or hammers or trees. It was a clay penis epidemic! And I couldn't help but wonder if my fifth grade notebook with drawings of my classmates in erotic positions had some type of magical powers and was now seeping into my current classroom as a demented payback.

After about seven oh-so-cleverly-disguised peni, I had to give a lecture about appropriateness in school. Which I was not so good at and they knew it, and we all cracked up. But out of respect, they did stop making the peni, which was good. Little do they know, but they will find out someday, that a clay penis is not really any good anyway. Too soft and malleable. But that's a life lesson for a different day. And maybe, just maybe, we have some future dildo sculptors in our midst.

BRANDY BATZ, LOS ANGELES

WHAT IS YOUR MORNING RITUAL? YOUR NIGHTTIME RITUAL?

GO THROUGH YOUR CLOSET AND WRITE ABOUT A SPECIAL PIECE OF CLOTHING THAT HOLDS MEMORIES.

The furry vest? Incredible, right? This wild and silky silver pelt sensually imitates the creamy vest the vampire seductress wears in the movie The Doors as she latches on to her prey. She's not really a vampire, merely a tall glam model. But she sends out an unmistakable untamed manner with that soft vest that screams, "Touch me, baby!" and Morrison can't help but betray true love once again.

The vest captures the spirit of a precious few bold women from a certain era. While I'm eternally grateful for the space in time I occupy, that era fuels my imagination like no other. A palpable ache surfaces when I imagine what that time must have been like. When mystical women charmed young beautiful musicians, and the energy

*transferred between them birthed a revolution in music that paved
the way for an evolution . . . in thinking and behavior. For countless
souls. Did they know they were generating waves of alchemy in the
pursuit of their particular passions? What spirit possessed them? From
where did their audaciousness come?*

*What I'd give to go back and be one of those women for just a day.
As it is, I'll wear this vest from time to time and remember that we're
all connected. And I'll take comfort in the simple joy of one spirit rec-
ognizing and appreciating another. Because what they did mattered.
So I'll try to be grateful . . . not jealous.*

TAMMY MOORE, AUSTIN

DUMP OUT YOUR PURSE. BESIDES THE OBVIOUS CONTENTS, LIKE
YOUR WALLET AND PHONE, WHAT ELSE IS IN THERE?

HOW HAS YOUR COMPUTER OR CELL PHONE CHANGED
YOUR LIFE?

HOW DO YOU FEEL ABOUT SOCIAL MEDIA—FACEBOOK,
TWITTER, INSTAGRAM, ETC.? HAVE YOU RECONNECTED WITH
SOMEONE THROUGH SOCIAL MEDIA?

HOW DID YOU MEET YOUR CLOSEST CURRENT FRIENDS?

ARE YOU STILL CLOSE WITH ANY OF YOUR CHILDHOOD OR
TEENAGE FRIENDS?

DESCRIBE SOMEONE WHO HAS ENHANCED YOUR LIFE BUT
YOU'VE NEVER MET.

I admire the women who sing songs that manage to get on the radio despite patriarchy's constant cock-blocking: En Vogue freeing me, so the rest would follow; Courtney Love any day on my tape deck, taking everything and I wanted her to; Stevie Nicks and her voice in my ear like a cat in the dark. The people I admire are those riot grrrls who sent me their zines, that first one in the mail like a message of rescue post–suicide attempt.

I'm on my way to the Alien She *art exhibition Friday night, two hours of Los Angeles rush-hour traffic, the sun shining down, radio music turned up all the way. My zines are at the show and I'm honored. My trajectory in Los Angeles post-NYU has been such a long and painful struggle, often fraught with despair, rejection, self-condemnation. Zines are my way of cutting up what I don't like. An art historical tradition that may have begun with the Cubists and their collages, the German Expressionists or the Dadaists and their critique of a cruel culture, or Hannah Höch and her cutting deconstructions. Zines are my way of dealing with emotions and thoughts. Instead of cutting up my body, I cut up pictures, pasting my words and art with the words and art of others as transformative art-making. Zines I created all by myself, alone in my room: first at NYU, for a group I cofounded that hardly anyone joined, Support against Sexism. Again later in L.A., newly sober and finished with bulimia, a sharp self-mutilation emerging. And again, as a way to transcend suicidal depressions and jobs that oppressed me. Then once more with riot grrrl, salvation in shared zines like notes in a classroom or messages on the wall.*

People I admire are the women who write; some right here in this room, and the many women who've written and continue to write ourselves into history so it is herstory *too. Our story. And that's all she wrote! But that's not* all *she wrote.*

LUCRETIA TYE JASMINE, LOS ANGELES

LET IT BLEED

IS THERE ANYTHING IN YOUR DAY-TO-DAY LIFE THAT WASTES YOUR TIME, MONEY OR ENERGY?

WHAT IS A HABIT (OR TWO) YOU'D LIKE TO BREAK?

ARE YOU ON TIME OR DO YOU OFTEN RUN LATE?

DO YOU PROCRASTINATE? IF SO, HOW DOES IT AFFECT YOUR LIFE? IF NOT, WHAT IS YOUR SECRET?

DESCRIBE THREE THINGS YOU ARE PUTTING OFF.

I'm a procrastinating perfectionist and a perfect procrastinator. The only thing I'm consistent with is inconsistency. Yep. I'm a creative. I start a lot of things. I finish very few. When I was thirty-nine years old, I started a list of forty things I'd do by the age of forty, "40 by 40," I called it. Now it's "40 at 40." I suppose I should finish that damn list by my forty-first birthday lest it become "40 by the year 2040"!

One item on the list is to complete my Georgia Music Map. I'm a Georgia girl, born and raised, and I'm proud of my Georgia roots. Granted, I have no desire to ever live there again, but damn it, I'm a Georgia Bulldog, I drink Coca-Cola like it's coffee and I like my chicken fried. I also like Georgia music. So I started this artistic map that names all the significant Georgia musicians and where they're from in Georgia. My hometown of Macon boasts Otis Redding, Little Richard and the Allman Brothers (I grew up thinking they were actually Georgia boys and since one is buried there, they made it onto the map!). The thing about me is that I get so close to finishing projects and then I just quit. Poof! Up in smoke. Yeah, it's psychological and a psychiatrist would be happy to take my money to diagnose this dilemma, but I already know the reason—it's fear based, because, quite frankly, all our psychoses are rooted in one fear or another.

Fear of failure.

Fear of success.

Fear. Fear. Fear.

Well, I just saved twenty thousand dollars with that self-diagnosis, but that won't get that damned map completed. And no matter how many closet organizers I buy or issues of Real Simple *magazine I read, it won't get my closet organized. (The beef I have with* Real Simple *is if I only owned five blouses, three sweaters and five pants/skirts I wouldn't need organizational help.)*

The third thing I've been putting off is publishing my novel. I don't even want to admit how many presidential elections have transpired since I started writing that novel. Oh yes, of course it's "almost" finished—everything but the final edit.

Okay, I'll share one bonus entry from my 40 at 40 list. I want to have sex in a pool. Is that too much to ask?

ANGELA SPENCER, NASHVILLE

It's excellent that Angela realizes by the close of her piece that her procrastination is fear based, but she is still able to keep it light and engaging by sprinkling in astute dollops of humor.

IF I ONLY KNEW THEN WHAT I KNOW NOW . . .

HOW DID YOU GET THROUGH YOUR MOST RECENT HEARTBREAK, BE IT A LOVER, FRIEND OR ANOTHER KIND OF LOSS? WAS IT EASIER OR HARDER THAN WHEN YOU WERE YOUNGER?

HAVE YOU BEEN ABLE TO LET GO OF LONG-HELD GUILT TRIPS? DESCRIBE THE PROCESS.

259

LET IT BLEED

DO YOU STILL HOLD ON TO ANY STIFLING REGRETS? IF SO, REWRITE THE EVENTS WITH THE ENDING YOU WANT.

DESCRIBE A TIME YOU HAD TO DO SOMETHING YOU DIDN'T WANT TO DO.

WHAT ARE YOUR FIRST THOUGHTS WHEN YOU WAKE UP IN THE MORNING? LAST THOUGHTS WHEN YOU SLIDE UNDER THE COVERS AT NIGHT?

HOW WELL DO YOU SLEEP AT NIGHT? IF YOU WAKE UP, WHAT KIND OF THOUGHTS KEEP YOU AWAKE?

DESCRIBE YOUR NATURE. GLASS HALF-EMPTY OR HALF-FULL? OPTIMISTIC OR PESSIMISTIC? HAVE YOU ALWAYS BEEN THIS WAY?

DO YOU STAY CALM IN TIMES OF CRISIS? WHAT DO YOU DO TO CALM YOURSELF DURING AN EMERGENCY?

ARE YOU ALTRUISTIC?

DO YOU FEEL YOU HAVE MADE A POSITIVE DIFFERENCE IN SOMEONE'S LIFE?

You can know someone the entire span of your life, and yet discover that you don't really know them at all. You know the sound of their voice, a particular way their brow furrows with concern or anger. The way they carry themselves with a certain confidence. But there are so many facets a child overlooks. It's not until one is an adult that the events of life can bring a new understanding, a new introduction of sorts, to someone you've known since the day you entered the world.

It started with an eight-second message from the parent who doesn't usually do the calling, and in those eight seconds, I knew that life was about to take a dramatic turn. Probably not a good one.

"Valerie, it's your pa. Could you call me back at home as soon as you can, please? Thanks . . ." There was an uncomfortable urgency coupled with an eerie calm in his voice.

I picked up the phone and dialed with a fear in my gut, the kind that causes your fingers to misdial the numbers you've punched for more than twenty years. There was also the fearful knowledge that my mom wouldn't be answering the phone as usual.

The words came at me like the punch of a skilled boxer: you know you're about to get hit, but it still stuns and surprises you. "Your ma is in the hospital. She's okay. We're okay. She had a heart attack this morning and she's in surgery. I need you to come down here if you can."

My big strong dad. The fixer. This man who has cut a larger-than-life shadow over my entire existence. He needs me? Why? He's bulletproof. He's the guy that Batman would call to take care of business!

Mom was okay. But the days and weeks that followed brought more devastating news. A stunning diagnosis of breast cancer. My only motivation was to somehow "rally the troops," keep my brother and his daughters from falling apart, get Mom on the path to wellness and do whatever I could to help my dad keep the house running and not neglect his own needs.

I ran on autopilot. The events and conversations are vague. Like a glass that hasn't been rinsed, filmy, with unidentifiable remnants floating on the surface. Those days are still a blur, but my relationship with my dad has changed in a wonderful, frightening, profound way. And I am grateful for those days with him.

LET IT BLEED

I am stirred by the ding of my phone with a Facebook alert. I read it through tears of joy and gratitude.

"Valerie . . . Your ma is posting this because I am computer illiterate. Some say I just don't compute. During the lowest ebb of my near seventy-three years, you kept me fed, kept me company, kept me sane, kept me going. You pulled me through the only crisis that has ever brought me to my knees. There are no words in any language to describe the pride I feel for my daughter. I am a lucky and pride-filled father . . ."

VKJ, LAS VEGAS

HOW DO YOU REACT WHEN YOU SEE A PERSON ON THE SIDE OF THE ROAD WITH A SIGN READING "HOMELESS—PLEASE HELP"?

DO YOU DO ANY KIND OF VOLUNTEER WORK? IF SO, WHAT KIND AND WHY? IF NOT, WHAT STOPS YOU?

DO YOU HAVE CONCERNS ABOUT THE ENVIRONMENT? GLOBAL WARMING? RACIAL OR SEXUAL INTOLERANCE?

ARE YOU A FEMINIST? WHAT DOES THAT MEAN TO YOU?

Guilty as charged, if we're talking strictly about gender equality. It seems pretty simple . . . Men wouldn't be here if not for our ability to carry life. That alone justifies our "equality."

But then every brave sister, post–draft era America and elsewhere, who rocked a military uniform, deserves equality. Even if she just dared to show up for the battleground of life and got back up every time existence forced her to the ground.

So does every mother raising children alone, giving of herself at the cellular level until there's nothing left. Or so it seems, until she looks into the eyes of her child and finds the strength to do it all over again.

So does the female artist who keeps bringing her talents fearlessly forward until she generates her own star amid a male-dominated industry.

These are the women I relate to. The warrior souls. The sacrificial lionesses.

But am I a card-carrying member of the ongoing resistance to the male domination movement? Here's where we enter the gray area, because the alpha in me steering me toward survival is the same force that wants to be completely dominated by the alpha in him.

In the bedroom.

Where I'm tired and want to give in.

Where I want him to take control and prove he's worthy of my gifts when I allow this holy surrender. I want to get lost with him, proving that there is something bigger than me, more powerful than me . . . It's symbolic of the ultimate desire, don't you see?

That we are here by the resolve and desire of the Infinite . . .

That we are safe in Its fiery embrace.

That we can merge ourselves into a complete Power we do not possess on our own, and in return, be transformed into more than we were before we submitted.

Yes, I want that. I need that. And I don't apologize for that.

TAMMY MOORE, AUSTIN

ARE YOU EVER FACED WITH ANY FORM OF JUDGMENT OR INTOLERANCE? IF SO, HOW DO YOU HANDLE IT?

DO YOU HOLD ANY JUDGMENTS AGAINST ANYONE?

LET IT BLEED

WHAT'S YOUR FAVORITE THING ABOUT YOURSELF?

WHAT STILL MAKES YOU FEEL OVERWHELMED?

ARE YOU HARD ON YOURSELF?

DO YOU EXPECT TOO MUCH FROM OTHERS?

ARE YOU GENEROUS?

ARE YOU LOYAL?

WHAT DO YOU NOW CONSIDER TO BE A GREAT
ACCOMPLISHMENT?

HAVE YOU GOTTEN WHAT YOU WANTED IN LIFE (SO FAR) OR
HAVE YOUR YOUTHFUL DREAMS ESCAPED YOU?

WHAT IS SOMETHING YOU'VE ALWAYS WANTED TO DO BUT
HAVEN'T MADE THE TIME FOR?

ARE YOU HARBORING ANY SECRETS THAT ARE HOLDING
YOU DOWN?

WHAT IS YOUR PET PEEVE?

WHAT IS YOUR DEEPEST DESIRE?

WHAT GIVES YOU THE MOST SATISFACTION?

IS IT EASY FOR YOU TO FORGIVE?

There are some things you don't even want to think about, so you stuff the signs and hints way, way down—like hiding valuables in the bottom back of your underwear drawer . . . only you believe these valuables are cursed. You pretend that if you can't see them, they aren't really there, and when you tell yourself these same things over and over, you start believing it's not a skip in the record, it's just the way the song goes.

Forgiveness is not an easy thing to do. When bad things happen, the usual reaction is hate, disgust and punishment. Somehow these are the cursed gems in my underwear drawer. Lately I've chosen to try something different. Instead of hate, I've chosen love. I've heard that you need to separate the crime from the criminal. I've loved many bad things in my past, and I still love most of them.

But instead of disgust and punishment, I try to help and to heal. It's not so easy, this road less traveled off the beaten path, but I do think it's better. I honestly believe that if we at least try to understand, then maybe something good can blossom and curses can be cured. At least, I want to believe this is true, because forgiveness creates a better world, or even a better relationship compared to the alternative that seems unbearable.

MYSTIE CHAMERLIN, NEW YORK

Whoa! What an insightful comparison Mystie made, linking the belief in negative back talk to a skip in a record! She wasn't letting nasty thoughts inhibit her writing that night, and it just popped into her head during those magical twelve minutes!

DO YOU HAVE ANY ENEMIES? IF SO, HAVE YOU FORGIVEN THEM?

DO YOU FORGIVE YOURSELF EASILY?

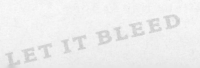

WHAT IS THE MAIN THING THAT BOOSTS YOUR SELF-CONFIDENCE?

WHAT EXCITES YOU? MOVES YOU? DELIGHTS YOU? INSPIRES YOU? TWELVE MINUTES ON EACH.

WRITE ABOUT A FAMOUS QUOTE THAT IS MEANINGFUL TO YOU NOW AND WHY.

"Marriage is a great institution—but I'm not ready for an institution yet." (Mae West)

There are layers to this quote. I am forty, going on sixteen. I've just discovered how to live in playfulness and other nonserious, nonintense states. I can't fathom the idea of marriage. I want to climb into an old beat-up car with a hot mess of a man who smells like cigarettes and whiskey, kick up dust on long-forgotten country roads, with irreverent rock and roll as the sky in the background. I want to hang out the window while he's got his foot on the gas pedal, going eighty, laugh and scream as we fly past the town church. This is what happens to pastors' daughters, I was always told, because I am one, but I never believed it.

I am begging the universe to turn me loose. I don't want the guy with the job and the house. I don't want the nice guy with the suit. Give me the guy with the old cowboy boots, the half-eaten Converse sneakers and the worn hat. He's got rope bracelets and a non-haircut. He's got a bed, a dog, a guitar and a paintbrush. I'd rather live that crazy five minutes with the wind whipping through my hair and a cowboy smacking me on the ass than a lifetime as Mrs. I'm So Bored.

BOBBIE BEEMAN, LOS ANGELES

WHAT OBSTACLE HAVE YOU BEEN STOPPED BY?

WHAT OBSTACLE HAVE YOU OVERCOME?

HAVE THERE BEEN ANY DIFFICULT INCIDENTS IN YOUR LIFE THAT YOU STILL FEEL BITTER ABOUT?

WRITE ABOUT SOMETHING YOU THOUGHT YOU'D NEVER "GET OVER," BUT SOMEHOW DID. WHERE DID THAT STRENGTH OR UNDERSTANDING COME FROM?

WHEN WAS THE LAST TIME YOU HAD A GOOD (OR BAD) CRY?

WRITE A SENTENCE EACH ABOUT TEN THINGS YOU ARE GRATEFUL FOR.

I AM MOST MYSELF WHEN I AM DOING . . .

I am most myself when I am doing what I love—seeing live music. Oh, it's a passion, a love, a need. Lately, I've been going to concerts by myself. I don't want to be distracted or talked to or concerned that the other person is having a good time. I want to find my spot on the floor, defend it tooth and nail. I want the excitement to sit and roll in my belly then explode out of me when the first note hits. I am un-encumbered for two hours, singing, dancing, feeling, carefree and happy. The memories of the song and my teenage years combine with me now, in the moment, creating a new sensation—the euphoric, pure joy that music selflessly gives. And the band—they gel and look knowingly at one another when the chord is right or they've found a groove—the groove—and the band knows it's good. So good. And I

267

*see these glances and I catch the feeling and it's like I've been let into
their club, I'm a new member and all the secrets are being shared.
And I stand and stare and sing and sway. I feel it! I'm part of it and
I'm in on it and I am it. For those two hours I am perfect, I am my
favorite songs, I am my favorite bands, I lose myself but I am myself
and it's awesome and I am me.*

RISSA DODSON, LOS ANGELES

DESCRIBE THE MOST RECENT LIVE MUSIC EVENT YOU WENT TO.

**WHAT ARE THREE THINGS YOU LIKE ABOUT YOURSELF AND
THREE THINGS YOU'D CHANGE.**

WRITE ABOUT WHAT MAKES YOU FEEL TOTALLY ALIVE.

*I am very lucky, I have had many moments. Being in a room of strong
women, you can hear the air change with the focus of concentration as
we all write. Being in New York City, on this expansive white couch,
right now, 109th and Riverside, with vague traffic noises outside. The
air was thick and humid yesterday, but autumn is relentlessly blowing
in over my shoulder. Long day of work, good moments and frustrations,
and a good long nap on the train. I was bantering with the boy I love.
I told him he was a genius; he said he was inspired by my beautiful face.
His face was beautiful as he said it, wide smile and beaming eyes.*

*We joked further. "Can you read my mind?" I taunted. "What am
I thinking now?" He shrugged. Of course the answer was "Let's fuck,
let's fuck!" He thought a moment and said, "You want more coffee?"*

*And we are here, still at the beginning of the night, with each
other's stories to look forward to. The connections and the moments of
learning. Everyone else's beautiful moments of life.*

TAMMY ROSE, NEW YORK

It's beguiling how Tammy begins by describing the room she's in, backtracks to a recent titillating moment with her lover, then winds back up in writing workshop, excitedly awaiting the words from her kindred comrades.

And here *you* are, dear reader, dear writer, down to your final prompt.

WHAT ARE YOU LOOKING FORWARD TO THE MOST RIGHT NOW?

Hopefully completing your memoir!

CHAPTER FIFTEEN

I

Ta-da!!! We have reached your femoir finale chapter! Let's pop open a bottle of champagne (or sparkling apple cider) and turn the music up loud! You've worked your way through the prompts, plunging fearlessly into your one-of-a-kind sprawling life. You've explored yourself from your origins to your Now to your dreams for the future. You've questioned the whys and wherefores and plumbed the depths of your beingness.

For some of you, this collection of writings is enough—you wanted to express yourself and capture your essence so your words will live on for loved ones to ponder, learn from and rejoice in. The rest of you still have some decisions to make. If you're planning to turn your life story into a completed book, get ready to pore through your tales, compile all those exercises and figure out what's going to make the cut.

Consult Your List

Go back to the list you made at the very beginning. Do you have writings on each of the key episodes, events, people, places and ideas you wanted to include? If not, ask yourself some probing questions that will fire up your writing sessions and keep going. Be sure to stick to the twelve minutes for now.

The Order of Things

The order in which you choose to reveal your life will divulge a lot about you as a creative artist. Do you want to propel us forward chronologically, in traditional storyteller mode? Most memoirs and autobiographies are told in chronological order, which makes the narrative easier to follow and get caught up in—but you do not have to begin at the beginning. I'm sure you recall that many of these memoirs begin with a pivotal, scorching opener, which should entice us to jump on our boards and ride the wave until the last page reaches the shore. Now that you've done all this writing, are you sticking with your original first paragraph, or have you decided on a different opening scene?

Storyboarding

If you can imagine your life as a movie, scene by scene, this technique, used by most filmmakers, is a worthwhile tool for laying out the order. While they use sketches of scenes that will appear on the screen, we can use our words. Find an empty wall space or get a big piece of cardboard. Then grab a bunch of Post-it Notes and start jotting titles for each life event you plan to use in the book. Visualize the scenes in your own life movie and fiddle about with them, moving and substituting Post-its until you feel it flows. When I'm writing screenplays, this method helps me see what events and situations should be kept in or left out in order to keep the narrative chugging along. When it's all laid out, you may decide that not every event has to be included to get across what you need to say.

What to Keep

When you've gotten your assignments the way you want to present them and visualized them with storyboarding, you should be getting the gist of what you want to get across with your memoir. You'll find that many of the pieces that helped you discover surprising things about yourself, or led to memories you'll want to include, won't necessarily make it into the memoir. Even though an event may be hugely significant to you personally, it may not carry the same resonance for a stranger. Does it further your story? Make a vital point? What's at stake? Your readers need to root for you, so keep them guessing a little bit so those pages keep turning.

How Much to Tell

Instead of taking the reader through the entirety of your existence, you may want to focus on just a particular part of your life, as Mary Karr did with her memoir *Lit*, about her alcoholism and recovery, and Alice Sebold did with her decision to share the story of neglect by her father and rape by a stranger, and the effect it had on her life, in *Lucky*. Patti Smith, in *Just Kids*, chose to write about her relationship with the controversial artist Robert Mapplethorpe. As I mentioned at the beginning, Bob Dylan wrote a massive best-selling memoir by expressing only exactly what he wanted to share, keeping his romantic and family life to himself, focusing mainly on his mind-boggling musical history. Many recent memoirs are genre based, such as Elizabeth Gilbert's soul-searching in *Eat, Pray, Love*, or focus on the author's career path, like *Kitchen Confidential* by Anthony Bourdain and ballerina Misty Copeland's *Life in Motion*. You may take a tip from these writers and focus on your relationship with a special someone or on your experiences as a teacher, lawyer or chief of staff!

What to Leave Out

How will your memoir make others feel? While you are actively making the decision to tell your story, others who appear on the pages may not feel comfortable with what's revealed about *them*. My nearest and dearest got to take a peek inside my books before I sent them to the publisher. Even though there were some scandalous passages, my ex, Michael, insisted I tell *my* truth and didn't ask me to delete a single word.

The only thing I decided to alter in my second book, *Take Another Little Piece of My Heart*, was to disguise a certain massive celebrity per his request. It wasn't a legal matter, since he had a bigger-than-life public persona, but he had asked me kindly not to write about him, so I figured out a way to tell on us both by calling the Household Name "Him."

As I suggested earlier, don't try to get back at anybody or get *even* with your memoir. Don't be cruel; it will haunt you later. After letting friends and family read it, pay attention to those who bristle. Perhaps you can find a gentler way to say what needs saying. Not everyone applauded my efforts either, so be sure to smear on a couple layers of skin-thickening cream. For instance, Miss Sparky said, "I don't remember it happening that way . . ." and I responded, "That's the way it happened to me. If you remember it differently, why don't you write your own memoir?"

How Will It Make You Feel?

How much are you willing to reveal about your inner workings? Will you bare all? When my first book came out I got a whole lot of flak for daring to invite my readers under the covers with me and my musical beaus. I was careful not to be too graphic, and have zero regrets, but I remember asking, "Did I live it up just to have to live it down?" You'll have to live with yourself and a lot of the people you write about, so before you blab about someone's foray into the dark side, put yourself in his or her boots. You don't want to feel like people have just picked through your trash, but if you don't bare enough it may not be enticing enough to beguile your readers.

A two-word sentence from one of my diary entries became the fodder of much media hoopla: "Huge cock." Was Don Johnson ticked off? Did he make a fuss? What do you think?

Connective Tissue

Let's have a little fun with this analogy. Pretend you're Dr. Frankenstein (Mary Shelley penned *Frankenstein* at age twenty-one!) and you are building a femoir as exceptional as you are. What you have with your twelve-minute writings is the skeleton, or the "bones," of your history. In order to make these incidents stitch together in a seamless story, you will need to add transitions that fill in the blanks and link your prompts. These transitional sentences and paragraphs are the "connective tissue"—the ligaments, tendons and muscles that unite the skeleton into a whole. You want to make sure one section easily leads to another without jarring the reader.

Often time will have passed between the two stories, so you'll need to summarize what happened between one scene and the next. You can make days, weeks or years pass with one sentence, if you need to! "The following year I . . ."

In other cases one scene will trigger a relevant insight. To connect them, reflect on what you have revealed in the previous paragraph, how it ties into a realization, or how it could lead into a similar situation, and it will be a smooth transition.

In *Dandelion*, Catherine James manages to create seamless transitions from one narrative to the next:

"Diana was hardly a religious woman, but she used God to disguise her unwavering meanness. Whenever I was sick or got hurt she'd tell me to think about why God was punishing me. I didn't believe God was punishing me; I knew it was her."

From this description of the meanness of her mother, she easily moves into her own spiritual beliefs.

"I'd been blessed with vivid spiritual dreams since I was old enough to remember. I once dreamed I was sitting by a river talking with Jesus. He held my hand and gently placed something in my palm. It was a simple golden key."

While on the subject, here's a passage from *Take Another Little Piece of My Heart*:

"On El Cerrito Place [Michael] still had insane bouts with the relentless monster insomnia, which I tried to tackle with massage, herbs, spiritual advice, and a lot of pleading to Jesus for some blessed zzz's for my man."

This is how I connected it to the first sentence in the next paragraph, to set up a different train of thought.

"Despite my over-devotion to Michael, I stayed close with my parents, being their adored only child, and watching my daddy fall prisoner to his failing lungs was a poison dart in my already lacerated side."

Fleshing It Out

During the original twelve-minute prompts, you were so focused on the heart of the action, you may find that vivid description is missing in some of the pieces you've chosen to use. The details of "what happened" may be there, while the setting and players involved may not yet be described in words. Now it's time to start fleshing it out by recalling the scene and adding more physical description, insight and reflection. In our little Frankenstein analogy, these descriptive details are the "flesh"—skin, eyes, hair and all the other finishing touches that make every human being unlike any other.

You may know exactly what a person or place looks like, but the reader doesn't, so review the exercises in chapter 4 on using all your senses to bring the scenes to life. Remember that people have not only physical aspects, but also emotional and psychological traits that you may want to include. Give yourself some miniprompts just for description. Sometimes just one telling sensory detail or physical trait can be dropped into a sentence here and there throughout the scene, giving the reader a few vivid shorthand cues of what it was like to be there. Take, for example, the single trait that Ernest Hemingway chooses to encapsulate everything we need to know about his fictional character Lewis in *A Moveable Feast*: "I tried to break his face down and describe it but I could only get the eyes. Under the black hat, when I had first seen them, the eyes had been those of an unsuccessful rapist."

II

Where to Call It a Day

When you're finally finished writing your life, the last paragraph will most likely come from appreciation for yourself and all you've been through.

Catherine James closes her memoir with the death of the person who brought her to life, and almost took it away from her.

"My mother's soft touch confused me. Our relationship had been a fine dance between fear and self-preservation. If she had not been melting, would we have had this moment? Her touch felt like sparkling electric shocks with immaculate healing. It wasn't me as the grown woman. In my mind's eye I saw the child. It was like being bathed in the sweetest water, and the warmest light. There was a divine mutual forgiveness, and the past no longer mattered."

I chose to close both of my memoirs in a similar fashion, with some understanding and reflection. I bring my story full circle at the end of *I'm with the Band*. After a lifetime of worshipping Elvis, I turned down a date with him because I had just gotten engaged.

"I said no because I was in love with Michael Des Barres. I heard myself say no and I knew I was totally in love with Michael Des Barres. I could have sat beside the King, but I wanted to sit on the face of my prince. And he *was* COMING!

"He arrived with five dollars in his pocket and his hair dryer in a paper bag. He didn't even bring a toothbrush or a pair of socks, much less a pair of trousers to put on the next day. He left everything behind, including his address book, intending to forget his former life and create a new one with Pamela Miller from Reseda, California."

Here's another dollop of self-reflection in the final paragraph of my epilogue in *Take Another Little Piece of My Heart*:

"Now that I'm finished with this book, I'm sitting here wondering why I felt I had to dip deep down, shred and expose myself, like a gutted doe strapped across somebody's headlights. And I recall that beautiful cosmic movie, *Starman*, the one in which Jeff Bridges . . . plays that sweet, innocent soul from another planet. Remember, when he saw the dead deer strapped to a hunter's car and, with otherworldly compassion, raised it from the dead and watched it trot back into the forest? The reborn doe, recapturing her life. That's sort of the way I feel."

You've done it—you've reached the end! Don't worry about the words being perfect. If told with honesty, passion and spirit, your story will be meaningful and touch the hearts of the right people. Now we breathe *life* into our words. Whooooooosh! The animating life force—the love, intensity and intention that you put into crafting your story—will make it come alive! It's alive! *Alive!*

Keeping It Real

If you plan to publish your memoir, you'll want to make sure things happened as you describe them on the page. That doesn't mean you need to have a photographic memory or reproduce conversations verbatim. As long as the overall gist accurately reflects what happened, as the modern saying goes, no worries. (People now say that instead of "thank you." It's weird how the vernacular changes through the years.)

You may want to go back and fact-check your story, asking (trusted) people who were there what they remember, if you wish to include them in your process. (They may try to give you advice at this point, so listen to what they have to say, but your voice should always be the loudest.)

At the very least, see if you can consult diaries, journals, your calendar or old appointment books to get the dates of incidents as accurate as possible. You may find that flipping through these records will also stir your memory pot and produce more fodder to fill out your memoir.

At this point you may want to put the manuscript away for a couple of weeks, then read it through. Maybe even aloud. Is anything missing, or are any passages repetitive? Is there a scene you'd like to clarify further or an idea you'd like to reinforce? Have you used certain words too often? Perhaps you can conjure up a more descriptive word for "fun" or "sweet."

Legal-Ease

When I turned in the final *Band* manuscript to William Morrow, it had to go through the company's team of attorneys, and when I got it back, there were only two things that had to be excised: events that I wrote about but had not witnessed. The first involved a certain rock god who was triple-jointed and turned himself into a sex pretzel on the Zappa kitchen table one night, pleasuring himself in front of a few GTOs. Unfortunately, I was not in the room for this marvelous display and therefore had to delete the torrid tryst-for-one. The second was actually a well-known fact about a '50s teen idol—that he had been a heavy heroin user in his popdom heyday—but since I hadn't witnessed the needle and spoon action, it had to come out too.

I also learned that if someone you write about is considered a "private person," you have to be careful about maligning or blaspheming them in any way. Luckily, I had no intention of harming my folks or my high school boyfriend, Bobby Martini, or anyone else that flitted through my life. I was just telling the truth, telling on myself.

Now it's up to you. Tell on yourself. For yourself.

Tell it without holding back. Tell it without second thoughts. Tell it without fear, judgment, timidity or trepidation.

Tell it like it is, like it was, like you want it to be. Tell it with panache, bravery, gutsiness, moxie, courage and spunk. Tell it with love.

And why should you write about yourself, you still might ask?

Saint Walt has an answer to that one:

> That you are here—that life exists, and identity;
> That the powerful play goes on, and you will contribute
> a verse.

Here's Susyn's response to the same prompt, which just shows how we all travel to the beat of a different drum, as the divine Linda Ronstadt once crooned.

ACKNOWLEDGMENTS

A great big hugful of thank-yous to all of my adored, generous and gifted writing students! And to my lovely Penguin compatriots, Sara Carder, my editor, and Joanna Ng, along with Gabrielle Moss, who gave me the idea for *Let it Bleed*. My agent, Peter McGuigan at Foundry, is still the best agent on this spinning globe and I adore him for all kinds of reasons. Thanks ever so to Eric Gleiser for his artistic input, and to the diligent Claire Harris at Foundry, who helped me corral the plethora of release forms. And I couldn't have made it through without the savvy suggestions from my dear Diana Faust.

From Walt Whitman to Anaïs Nin, from William Blake to Jack Kerouac, from our last American Nobel Prize winner, Toni Morrison, to the most recent American Nobel laureate, Bob Dylan, for creating "new poetic expressions," I thank you from the center of my heart for your groundbreaking, soul-expanding inspiration.

I am exquisitely grateful to all my girlfriends and boyfriends around the globe forevermore, my spiritual teacher, Light, for keeping me sane, my ex-hub, Michael, and our son, Nick, both of whom sharpen my brain, hone my wit and fill my heart.

Thankyouthankyouthankyou . . .